"As a long time evolutionary co-creator for the conscious evolution of culture, I resonate with the worldview, assumptions and wisdom Harry offers toward the evolution of a new culture. Harry Bury's unique perspective from within all sectors of society allow us to experience the cultural patterns and assumptions that bring the current reality and the obvious need for a culture shift in patterns and assumptions. His dialectic learning model of experience and cognition leading to reflection and action is the evolutionary education needed for integral learning and living in this millennium. This book is essential reading for the conscious evolution of society."

Barbara Marx Hubbard, Founder of the Foundation for Conscious Evolution and Author of "Conscious Evolution: Awakening the Power of Our Social Potential"

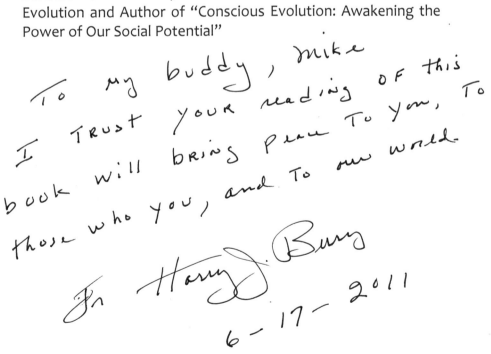

To my buddy, Mike
I Trust your reading of this
book will bring peace To you, To
those who you, and To our world.

In Harry J. Bury
6 - 17 - 2011

An Invitation to Think and Feel Differently in the New Millennium

An Invitation to
Think and Feel Differently
in the New Millennium

by

Harry J. Bury, Ph.D.

Professor Emeritus
Division of Business Administration
Baldwin Wallace College

Trafford Publishing
Bloomington, Indiana

Order this book online at www.trafford.com
or email orders@trafford.com

Most Trafford titles are also available at major online book retailers.

Printed in the United States of America.

ISBN: 978-1-4269-4265-5 (sc)
ISBN: 978-1-4269-4266-2 (hc)
ISBN: 978-1-4269-5242-5 (e)

Library of Congress Control Number: 2010918806

Trafford rev. 02/21/2011

Trafford PUBLISHING®   www.trafford.com

North America & International
toll-free: 1 888 232 4444 (USA & Canada)
phone: 250 383 6864 ✦ fax: 812 355 4082

This book is dedicated to all of the students with whom I have had the privilege of sharing knowledge, and from whom I have received far more than I've given, at the Graduate School of Commerce GSC, Burapha University, Thailand; Southern California University for Professional Studies SCUPS; North Central University, Ho Chi Minh City, Vietnam; and Baldwin-Wallace College, Berea, Ohio, USA.

FOREWORD

I have witnessed the Reverend Harry Bury's work for several decades, marveling at the many creative ways in which he has led a truly extraordinary life, integrating spirituality, political activism, scholarly research, and pedagogical inventiveness. It is especially meaningful to me to be invited by him to write the Foreword to this book—a book that is designed to ignite and inspire new ways of viewing the world-as-it-is and the world-as-it-can-be. This book is the culmination of Harry Bury's many pilgrimages—which have been not merely of a geographical nature, into distant lands, but also of an epistemological nature, into a variety of worldviews and paradigms. In so many ways, this book is the culmination of insights systematically gleaned from a life richly lived. Harry Bury's commitment to global well-being has inspired him to travel widely and to serve in a variety of international contexts, including Vietnam, Thailand, and China. As an educator with a deep commitment to social and political justice, Harry Bury has abandoned the comfort of the proverbial ivory tower of academia to literally throw himself into turbulent social and political situations as a political activist and to experience firsthand the volatile events and situations that bring out the best and worst in human nature. It is important to remember that his perspectives are well grounded in a number of extraordinary real-world experiences. His book, full of optimism and hope, is therefore born not out of naïveté, but out of a deep encounter with life in the real world, seeing human nature in its many dimensions, its peaks, its plains, and its valleys.

This book is an extremely rich integration of several modes of discourse and intellectual dimensions that often exist in splendid isolation. It leverages the powerful synergy of theory with practice, scholarship with experience, spirituality with science, and thought with emotion in illuminating new possibilities for human emancipation in varied domains of human endeavor including work, wellness, intimacy, education, justice, environment, politics, and spirituality. All of these are areas of human life in dire need of fundamental transformation, and Harry Bury does a remarkable job of stretching the imaginative capacities of the reader to help him or her to envision valuable breakthroughs in human functioning in each of these areas.

Many of the books that address these domains of wellness, justice, environment, and politics pay attention only to the realm of action; Harry Bury takes an incisive look at ways of altering the fundamental assumptions that have created a corrosive world and replacing these constraining assumptions with newer, liberating ones that will free the human spirit and produce very different social, political, economic, and spiritual realities. In doing so, he goes beyond the symptomatic treatment of societal aberrations and focuses, instead, on the underlying systemic issues, the hidden mechanisms, and the dynamic interplay of human nature, institutional structures, and societal consciousness. The fundamental premises that Harry Bury describes at the core of the emergent worldview are ones that go, indeed, to the very source of humanity's distress in a world unfortunately divided against itself.

An effort to rethink our fundamental assumptions along the lines advocated in this book can play a major role in the rejuvenation of humankind. What lends special credibility to Bury's analysis and to the emancipatory possibilities that he envisions is the fact that he supports his vision with powerful examples drawn from the real world. As we read through this book, we begin to appreciate how the individual chapters encourage us to envision new possibilities, while at the same time feeding our practical imagination with real-world examples of extraordinary breakthroughs already achieved. It is a tragedy that in the climate of cynicism that prevails so widely, so many of the remarkable examples that Harry Bury cites—based on his extensive research and global experience—are not discussed more often or reported more widely in the public media. This book is a necessary antidote to the negativity that is so widespread among us, and it will go a long way in helping professionals in public policy, business, nonprofit organizations, and government to be more creative and innovative in their responses to the challenges of today.

Social, political, and economic realities do not exist in a vacuum, amenable to "objective," dispassionate analysis in a laboratory, because their interpretation involves human subjectivity, and with that subjectivity come a variety of considerations that imply value judgments, power relations, the paradigms of institutions, and the agendas of actors that occupy important positions within these structures. This book is yet another significant contribution to the major paradigm shift that we are witnessing in a number of the policy disciplines, in the direction of a postpositivist trend that recognizes the power of human subjectivity in constructing positively valued futures. More and more scholars are beginning to wake up to the recognition that the model of an "objective" reality, riddled with problems that can be remedied in very practical ways by the systematic application of "problem-solving" methods, is an anachronism. There is growing awareness that what comes to be defined as a problem is not just an objective fact, but a decision that is laden with judgments, a priori justifications, and unstated assumptions. Thus, while economists study "poverty alleviation" as one of the key problems of the times, others are asking whether the real problem *is* poverty—or whether it is greed. In other words, problems acquire their character and reality based on the legitimacy of the vantage point from which they come to be defined. Since the world's rich people get to decide what the key problems are, they think of "poverty" as the problem. If the world's poor people had the power to name the problem, they might just say "greed!" In other words, what comes to be defined as a problem itself involves a set of value-laden judgments, power relations, and the presumed legitimacy of discourse embedded within a status structure that privileges some views and marginalizes others. Harry Bury's contribution lies in showing us a way out of this quagmire by highlighting our capacity for transcending this simplistic, duality-based consciousness that polarizes and permeates much of our discourse. In our everyday consciousness, we live in a polarized world of problems versus solutions (the author invites us to explore, discover, and visualize a world based on what gives life and vitality), truth versus falsehoods (the author invites us to consider the simultaneous validity of multiple narratives and to explore bold possibilities even in the absence of absolute certainty), and good versus evil (the author implores us to recognize the redeeming attributes and honorable intentions of most, if not all, of humanity). Harry Bury also presents the possibility of a unified consciousness that can be achieved if we picture ourselves as one, instead of being resigned to the fragmented condition of seeing the world as constituted of multiple groups with competing interests and narrow identities.

Whether you are a student, educator, activist, or professional, this book will inspire you to rethink the fundamental assumptions that may have governed your consciousness. It will, moreover, inspire you, with the help of elegantly articulated examples of real-world excellence, to expand the breadth and variety of your own practical imagination, to create and invent innovative solutions to the dilemmas that you face on a daily basis. In today's information society, it is possible to find many books that give you access to large amounts of information. It is much harder to find books that actually provide you with the impetus to think and to feel differently, and to free yourself from entrenchment in obsolete templates of analysis. Harry Bury's work is a rare example of a book that effortlessly helps you scale new heights of creativity in designing a society that represents the best in breakthrough thinking. I hope you will enjoy reading it as much as I did!

Suresh Srivastva
Professor Emeritus, Organizational Behavior
Weatherhead School of Management
Case Western Reserve University

PROLOGUE

PEACEMAKER
RISK TAKER
VISIONARY

Harry Bury, a priest activist from the Archdiocese of Minneapolis-St. Paul, could be retired and fly fishing on one of the thousands of islands in Minnesota. That might have been his goal over fifty years ago when he was ordained a priest, but something called "Peace" interfered with that dream.

Early in his priesthood, Harry was a Newman Club chaplain at the University of Minnesota ministering to university students. The Vietnam War was in progress and Harry believed that young lives were being wasted on an insane war and that he had an obligation to speak out against the war. He joined the group of like-minded clergy including a Jewish layman, who responded to an invitation to fly to Saigon and protest to U.S. authorities our involvement in Vietnam. They chained themselves to the gates of the U.S. Embassy in Saigon, but not before alerting the media. As they predicted, they were arrested and taken off to the local jail. Their action, of course, did not end the war in Vietnam, but television news stations and media from all parts of the world covered the event.

Back in Minneapolis, Harry's diocese was in the midst of a fund raising campaign. Because most of the big corporate donors supported the War, the action of Harry and his companions greatly disturbed the archbishop. Harry was called in for a chat, and the archbishop suggested that he continue his education at Case Western Reserve University in Cleveland.

After Harry earned a doctorate in Organizational Behavior, he joined the faculty at Baldwin-Wallace College in the Division of Business Administration, where he has taught undergraduate and graduate students for over 31 years. Harry has also facilitated management programs in Thailand, Vietnam, China and South America.

Just when I thought Harry was ready for retirement at one of those lakes in Minnesota, a peace group from Michigan prevailed upon him to join them for a month in Gaza in an effort to create a peaceful environment so that the Israelis could leave their homes in Gaza and the Palestinians could move in without violence.

While he was there, four armed men broke into the room where Harry and three other priests were staying and kidnapped Harry. They put a hood over his head, took him by car to another location, and interrogated him. Holding a camera phone before his face, he was ordered to say that he was a CIA agent. Harry said he could not do that because it was not true.

One of the men put a gun to Harry's head and said he would shoot him if he did not comply. So Harry complied. The abductors put the hood back on his head, took him some distance from the house and released him. Harry was able to contact his team, who notified the police. Realizing that the level of violence in Gaza was escalating, Michigan headquarters ordered the team to leave Gaza. Congressman Dennis Kucinich of Ohio and his staff assisted Harry in his safe departure from Gaza.

Someone asked why Harry would place himself in such danger. I think the answer might be found in the movie Zorba the Greek.

After the failure of a logging venture that Alexis Zorba (played superbly by Anthony Quinn) believed would bring wealth to him and an English entrepreneur (played by Alan Bates), Zorba tells the Englishman that although he has wealth and good looks, there is something lacking in Bates' life. Naturally, Bates wants to know what that is.

"Madness," Zorba replies.

The movie ends with Zorba and the Englishman with arms linked dancing madly in the sand instead of grieving that their costly enterprise collapsed.

There's something of the madness of Zorba in Harry Bury. His madness is creative imagination. He imagines leaders of nations engaging in the arduous process of negotiation rather than military might. He imagines our nation leading the way to peace, not war. He imagines a peaceful resolution between the Palestinians and the Israelis. He imagines both sides realizing that their children are the innocent victims of their violence.

Harry believes in dialogue, compromise and discussion. He is mad enough to believe that even amid disaster and devastation, it is possible for people of good will – Palestinians, Israelis, Iraqis, Americans –- to lock their arms and dance, thanking God for the gifts of life.

Maybe if more of us had Harry's kind of madness, our world would be a much safer and saner place to live.

George Eppley
Emeritus Professor of English
Cuyahoga Community College, Cleveland, Ohio

ACKNOWLEDGMENTS

I am most grateful to the following people who so generously gave me their time and energy, enabling me to interview them, some for hours, in preparation for the writing of this book. Titles listed represent their position at the time of the interview.

Thomas Aldworth, Author, Chicago, Illinois

Billie Baker, Principal, William E. Keplea School, Huntington Beach, California

Helen Caldicott, Physician and Co-founder of Physicians for Social Responsibility

Darrell Fasching, Author, Professor of Theology, University of South Florida

Dr. Kathryn Fioravanti, Professor, International Health Department, Georgetown University, Washington, D.C.

Thomas Fox, Editor, *The National Catholic Reporter*, Kansas City, Kansas

Lewis and Ann Frees, Organizational Behavior Consultants, Bethesda, Maryland

James Gill, Roman Catholic Priest and Psychologist, St. Luke's Hospital, Silver Spring, Maryland

Steven Hammond, Director of Information Services, Phillips, Inc., Salisbury, Maryland

Jennifer Holmes, Webmasters Institute of Noetic Sciences, Petaluma, California

Riki Intner, Author, Family Counselor, Santa Rosa, California

Donald Kommers, Professor of Law and Political Science, University of Notre Dame, South Bend, Indiana

Max Lafser, Unity Minister, West Sound Unity, Bremerton, Washington

Nance Lukas, Professor of Leadership, University of Maryland, College Park, Maryland

Carolyn J. Lukensmeyer, Founder and President, AmericaSpeaks, Washington, D.C.

Ernan McMullin, Professor of Philosophy, University of Notre Dame, South Bend, Indiana

Terry McGuire, Physician, Davidsonville, Maryland

Amy Nord, Student at Concordia St. Paul University

Marvin O'Connell, Professor of History, University of Notre Dame, South Bend, Indiana

Christian De Quincy, Professor of Philosophy, John F. Kennedy University, and Managing Editor, Institute of Noetic Sciences

Marshall B. Rosenberg, Author and Psychologist

Michael and Justina Toms, Hosts, *New Dimensions Radio*, PBS

Lois T. Vietri, Professor, Department of Government and Politics and Academy of Leadership, University of Maryland

Jeffrey Voorhees, Organizational Development Consultant, San Francisco, California

Marisha Zeffer, Institute of Noetic Sciences, Sausalito, California

Friends and colleagues who have, through their skills, ideas, and encouragement, made this book possible: I shall always be most grateful to these wonderful people.

Susanne Alexandra, Freelance Writer and Author, Cleveland, Ohio

Shirley Beaver, Author, St. Paul, Minnesota

Charles Bisanz, Attorney, Organizational Development Consultant, and Professor, University of St. Thomas, St. Paul, Minnesota

Judie Boland, Spiritual Seeker, Cleveland, Ohio

Fred J. Bury, Hospital President, West Bend, Wisconsin

Leo Cachet, Monk, Detroit, Michigan

Nancy Nelson, Entrepreneur Extraordinaire, Minneapolis, Minnesota

Rebecca Cawrse, Student Assistant, Baldwin-Wallace College, Berea, Ohio

Judy Cowley, Assistant Superintendent of Education, Archdiocese of Chicago, Illinois

Joe and Mary Chadbourne, Environmentalists, Cleveland, Ohio

Donald Conroy, Psychologist, Minneapolis, Minnesota

Barrett L. Cupp, The Sherwin-Williams Company, Cleveland, Ohio

Donald Daher, Free Thinker, Aikin, Minnesota

Thierry D'Argoeves, Professor of Business, Assumption University, Bangkok, Thailand

Tina Diliberto, Student Assistant, Baldwin-Wallace College, Berea, Ohio

Suthira Duangsamosorn, Ph.D., Assistant Professor and former Head, Department of Business English, Assumption University, Bangkok, Thailand

Anita and George Eppley, Authors and Professors Emeritus, Cleveland State University and Cuyahoga Community College, Cleveland, Ohio

Edward Ehlinger, Physician, Minneapolis, Minnesota

Herbert Fasth, Businessman, Chicago, Illinois

George Garrelts, Professor of Theology, Mercyhurst College, Erie, Pennsylvania

Dale Hammerschmidt, Physician, Pathologist, Minneapolis, Minnesota

Kathy Hayden, Division Secretary, Baldwin-Wallace College, Berea, Ohio

Linda Heen, Freelance Writer, Minneapolis, Minnesota

Karen Hoovler, School Psychologist, Cleveland, Ohio

Marissa Jordan, Author and Student Assistant, Baldwin-Wallace College, Berea, Ohio

Patti Kleve, Accountant, Cleveland, Ohio

Frank Kroncke, Author and Political Activist, St. Paul, Minnesota

Warren Kump, Physician, Radiologist, North Memorial Hospital, Minneapolis, Minnesota

Bill Laufer, Film Producer, Director, and Actor, Cleveland, Ohio

Tiffany Laufer, Author of Children's Stories, Designer of this book's cover, Cleveland, Ohio

Diana Lehotsky, Student Assistant, Baldwin-Wallace College, Berea, Ohio

Katherine Lewis, Student Assistant, Baldwin-Wallace College, Berea Ohio

David Majd, Professor of Mathematics, North Central University, Vietnam

Sarah Myers, Massage Therapist, Cleveland, Ohio

Tarita Mosley, Editor and Student Assistant, Baldwin-Wallace College, Berea, Ohio

Joseph Neumeir, Attorney, Minneapolis Minnesota

Lee Orcutt, Poet, Afton, Minnesota

Diane Rehor, Speech Consultant, Cleveland, Ohio

John Riley, Professor of Theology Emeritus, University of St. Thomas, St. Paul, Minnesota

Rosemary Ruffenbach, Artist, St. Paul, Minnesota

Walter Schaffer, Humanitarian Exceptional, Cleveland, Ohio

Param Srikantia, Professor of Organizational Behavior, Baldwin-Wallace College

Gwen Siefert, Student Assistant, Baldwin-Wallace College, Berea, Ohio

John Marc Taylor, Justice Consultant, Cameron, Missouri

Doan Van Toai, Dean, North Central University, Ho Chi Minh City, Vietnam

Edward Vargo, Author, Bangkok, Thailand

Stephanie Williams, Nurse and IT Consultant, Cleveland, Ohio

TO THE READER

Each chapter of this book begins with a number of quotations suggesting that we are not alone in our thinking and feeling differently in the New Millennium. Take a few minutes to reflect on the implications of each quotation; these implications set the tone for each chapter.

After reading the first six chapters, you can read the remaining eight in any order; each stands separately.

Thank you for coming along on this journey. Enjoy this story, the story of our lives and our future.

CONTENTS

CHAPTER ONE

Emerging Worldview

We are living through one of the most fundamental shifts in history—a change in the actual belief structure of Western society. No economic, political or military power can compare with the power of a change of mind. By deliberately changing the images of reality, people are changing the world.
Willis Harman
President of the Institute of Noetic Sciences in California
Co-founder of the World Business Academy

Most of us, and especially our large social institutions, subscribe to the concepts of an outdated worldview, a perception of reality inadequate for dealing with an overpopulated, globally-interconnected world.
Fritjof Capra
Physicist

The world we have made as a result of the level of thinking we have done thus far creates problems we cannot solve at the same level of thinking at which we created them.
Albert Einstein
Renowned Physicist

If we continue in the same direction, we will end up exactly where we are headed.
Ancient Chinese Proverb

Dream power

Like Martin Luther King, I have a dream. I have a vision of how the world can be immensely better than it is. Not perfect, mind you, but much more meaningful and fulfilling for the majority of humans on earth. I have great confidence that, together, we human beings can create an environment wherein virtually everyone can experience a large degree of happiness in their personal lives. I believe our very purpose is to bring joy and happiness into our own lives and into the lives of others.

My purpose is threefold:

1. To describe an Emerging Worldview, a new story which changes the way we view life and the way we feel about it;

2. To illustrate this Emerging Worldview, through stories, telling how significant areas of our lives change when the Emerging Worldview becomes our common view in the New Millennium;

3. To invite you, the reader, to contribute to this evolving vision in the New Millennium.

I believe, along with a host of others, that "If you envision it, you can become it!" Our lives are self-fulfilling prophecies. That is, the expectation of an event tends to cause it to happen. So, if we strongly believe that something will occur in our lives, our belief will happen for good or for ill.

This book is my opportunity to present an Emerging Vision, my hope for the world. I share it with you so that you might have an opportunity to expand *your* way of thinking, fill your heart with the promise of positive change, and add to this vision.

Too often, when you and I look at what is going on in the world, we see devastating wars, shrinking environmental resources, extreme poverty, oil spills, as in the Gulf of Mexico, and more signs of potential catastrophe. We are in danger, not only of becoming discouraged, but of unintentionally creating the very things we fear—by concentrating on the negative. This book is intended not only to encourage us, but to actually *be a means* to bring about the positive, to bring about what we value and desire, both for ourselves and for everyone else in the world.

It has always saddened me when I have seen people—any of us—hurting each other. So I asked myself, "Why do we hurt each other, instead of creating an environment which enables people to enjoy the wonders of existence?" It then became obvious to me: If we change the way we think and feel about significant fundamental issues, we can change our behavior. For instance, if I stop unconsciously thinking I'm right all the time, and instead actively listen to others and truly consider their ideas, this will have a huge positive influence on all my relationships. To wit, in improving my relationships, I will enhance my own life and the lives of others who know me. This way of thinking and feeling has led to my discovery of the following transformative assumptions.

Four Conscious, Fundamental Assumptions

If a critical mass of people in the various nations on our planet were, together, to adopt the following Four Conscious, Fundamental Assumptions, we would transform the world for the better. These assumptions are:

1. We consciously assume that we are forever in the process of discovering what is true. We never arrive. Hence, we do not have absolute certainty about anything. It follows, then, that nobody is right and nobody is wrong.
2. We consciously assume that no problems exist. We visualize and create what we want. Nobody wants problems. Hence, we responsibly create our own world free from problems and full of meaning.
3. We consciously assume we are all one *if* we picture ourselves as one. Separation from each other is also simply an assumption.
4. We consciously assume that we all are good. We intend always to do what we believe is good. Hence, there are no bad-intentioned people in this world.

ASSUMPTION I. We Are Forever In The Process of Discovering.

The first assumption acknowledges: We never actually discover the total truth. Being finite creatures, we can see only a part of the truth. We cannot see the whole picture, with all its variables and complexities of relationship.

What we do perceive is influenced by our specific upbringing; our heredity, biology, history, and culture; and our beliefs, values, and feelings in the moment. We are never totally objective and able to see complete truth. What we do see is *our* story.

In consciously assuming that we don't have complete answers, we become open to new ideas and different points of view. When we think we know the whole truth and therefore know what is right, we close our minds and lose our motivation to examine other ideas. When we recognize, however, that what we perceive is not reality, but our bias based on our upbringing, we open our minds and investigate, study, and actively listen to others. We then are surprised by what we learn. Feelings of excitement and joy are the result. Learning more and more is its own reward, and it never ends.

In the Emerging Worldview, which I believe is evolving, people assume that we are in the process of discovering. We do not know "the truth." We are not inclined, therefore, to fight over who's right and who's wrong. We enjoy one another's company because we can accept another's point of view without agreeing with it. We can empathize with another without completely sharing the other's values.

ASSUMPTION II. We Visualize & Create What We Want.

Since everything in the world has its pros and cons, we assume that it's dysfunctional to focus on the negative. If we appreciate what is *positive*, with the intention to make it even better, our behavior moves us in the appropriate direction. We move away from a "fix-it" mentality and come to appreciate what appears good in our lives. We create stories about what we want for our future. Over time, when we continue to focus, these stories become our reality.

If, however, we think *negatively* or *cynically* about a situation or event, we then act in such a way that our thought pattern becomes self-fulfilling. Believing we are going to fail the test, we often do fail. Feelings of dissatisfaction and discouragement result.

When we think positively about our lives, when we visualize ourselves as successful individuals, happy with our success, we indeed act to make our belief an actual reality.

Rather than believe that the ten-hour flight from Tokyo, Japan, to Minneapolis, USA, will be an exhausting and dreadful experience because others have told us so, we instead tell ourselves that we look forward to the flight, expecting it to be a joyful and refreshing experience. We see it as an opportunity to work without interruption, to relax, watch a movie, sleep, be served—and indeed, so it is! Hence, we create our own happiness. We appreciate that reality is mostly what is in our heads and in our attitudes. Only secondarily is reality what happens in the world around us.

Thus, in the New Millennium Worldview, we have changed the way we think and feel about what is happening in the world. We have learned to think appreciatively in order to create positive, constructive stories. As a result, we are complaining less and enjoying our lives far more.

In the New Millennium Worldview, we perceive the world through the lens of strengths and potentials, not through the lens of deficiency. We focus on what we find attractive in another person, in a situation, or in an organization. We assume that the glass of life is half-full rather than half-empty. As a result, people feel more hopeful and cheerful.[1]

ASSUMPTION III. We Are All One.

Just as the human physical body has many different parts with diverse functions and yet remains one person, so the

New Millennium Worldview assumes that human beings and their environment are essentially one. What is good for you is necessarily good for all; otherwise, it isn't actually healthy and beneficial. Thus, the outcome is that we become personally responsible and accountable for achieving the *common* good.

We consciously assume that we humans, and indeed the entire universe, are all essentially of one fabric. We have different functions and roles, but we have one essence and purpose. We are connected to everything in existence in a manner that goes beyond interdependence and results in unity or oneness.

In the New Millennium Worldview we assume our survival and our development are based on discovering that we are all different in function, but one in purpose and design. We seek to survive and develop through a pragmatic and consistent effort to be functional. Oneness with the totality is becoming the experience of many human beings. We conclude that what is good for one must also be good for all others and for the planet. As this significant change in assumption occurs, we experience a change in the attitude toward all that exists. Everything appears to be good.

ASSUMPTION IV. We Intend To Do What Is Best.

In the first assumption, we do not deny that there is objective truth, but rather we assume that we cannot know it. Similarly, although we have *free will*, I suggest that people are coming to realize we rarely use it. Rather, we consciously assume that we always do what seems best and assume we are not free to do otherwise.

At every moment we encounter numerous alternatives regarding how we want to live our lives or what we want to do in the next few hours. We automatically sort through the alternatives and select what seems best to us; at that point we cannot do anything else. For instance, if a friend and I determine that the best way to spend the next few hours is to play tennis, we are not free to choose anything else. Only if we receive new information can we change our mind. If my friend received a call saying her husband was in the emergency room, she would contact me at once and say, "I cannot play tennis with you as planned." Notice the words! She did not say "I choose," she said "I cannot." She must be at her husband's side. She is not *free* to choose anything else. We always do what seems best to us based on our values. Our intentions are to do what appears good at any moment in our lives. We are only *free* to do what is deemed best.

In the New Millennium Worldview, we consciously assume that we are all automatically moving toward what we believe to be good for us. We seek to do what we perceive is to our benefit and cannot do otherwise. Hence, no bad-intentioned people exist. No one is evil. Well-intentioned people, however, make mistakes recognized by their negative consequences. When this occurs, we don't look for others to blame or condemn. We seek to learn from our mistakes and the mistakes of others, so as to avoid these damaging behaviors in the future.

THE BOOK'S APPROACH

Storytelling has been found to be a powerful method for creating transformation. Hence, I first use stories to tell about the ways people's assumptions are transforming. Then, the final eight chapters of the book offer stories depicting, in practical terms, significant areas of life in which the New Millennium Worldview Story influences the thinking, feeling, and behavior of people and organizations, and in turn has positive consequences for our planet.

In Chapters Seven through Fourteen, using visualization, I tell stories in the *present tense* as if they were already a common occurrence. This book is **not** a prediction of the future. Rather, the stories are instruments for creating the future. Each story tells of what life is like:

- When people believe we do not know **the** *whole truth* and, therefore, are open to others' points of view;
- When we see the cup of life half-full rather than half-empty;

- When we go beyond a "fix-it" mentality and appreciate "what is" and see everyone's potential;
- When we realize we are one *with each other,* so that what is good for one is good for others;
- When people believe everyone is acting in their perceived best self-interest (and also in the best interest of all, since we are all one), and thus no one intentionally sets out to do evil.

It is a powerful vision on the road to becoming the dominant and believable story!

THE BOOK'S INTENTION

My hope for you is that you will move out of your comfort zone, to think and feel differently about significant issues in your life—intimacy, healthcare, work, education, justice, the environment, politics, and spirituality. Together, we can then co-create a new story that makes life wonderful for ourselves and for those who come after us.

My wish for you is that you will walk away with the Four Assumptions clearly in your mind. Envision these assumptions in the minds of thousands of other people. Imagine a worldwide change in people's behavior. See them living together in peace, protecting the environment, learning and sharing information, living healthy lives, and much more that you yourself create. Imagine the benefits of these fundamental assumptions, standing together, interconnected and interdependent, complementing and reaffirming each other.

This book is not intended to present evidence as proof that the Four Assumptions driving the New Millennium Worldview are correct. This book assumes that we cannot prove anything beyond the slightest doubt. The best we can do is to adopt a point of view on the basis of the most logical evidence we can find, try it out, experience how it feels to do it, and examine the consequences of our actions. If the results are good, we proceed with our original assumptions, until occurrences suggest a change in those assumptions.

In addition, the intention of this book is not to make predictions or prophecies, nor to demonstrate that the New Millennium Worldview is actually emerging. Rather, it intends to tell a story and paint a picture of what life will be like when the New Millennium Worldview becomes the common story.

Because the New Millennium Worldview Story is told in the present tense as though it has already fully emerged, we therefore—in subscribing to the Four Fundamental Assumptions upon which the New Millennium Worldview is based, and visualizing the results—are already contributing to the realization of this new way of thinking and feeling.

I believe you will find that the unfolding New Millennium Worldview presented in this book is hopeful and appealing. However, it is certainly not the last word. My invitation is for you the reader, from personal experiences and dialogue with others, to come up with many powerful additions to this story, far beyond what I have suggested. Your vision, together with those of other readers, will develop the New Millennium Worldview Story into still more new and meaningful stories.

CHAPTER TWO

Shifting Worldviews

The world hates change, yet it is the only thing that has brought progress.
Leo Tolstoy
Russian Novelist

We perceive and are affected by changes too subtle to be described.
Henry David Thoreau
American Transcendentalist Author and Naturalist

Nothing is permanent but change.
Heraclitus
Greek Philosopher

What are World Views?

Worldviews, from my perspective, are mostly unconscious stories human beings accept as the way things are: what we call reality. They are extremely important because they determine how we live our lives. Willis Harman points out: "[E]very society ever known rests on some set of largely tacit, basic assumptions about who we are, what kind of universe we are in, and what is ultimately important to us."[1]

Although we are largely unaware of the assumptions upon which it is based, a worldview gives meaning to our present circumstances. Our personal worldview influences our expectations of the future and is a product of our society, our culture, and the people who play a significant role in our upbringing. Because our view of the world is not consciously acquired, we take little notice; it usually operates below our level of consciousness.

In the midst of our own worldview, it's difficult to imagine any other way of thinking and feeling. People who thought the world was flat and the center of the universe had difficulty conceiving of it in any other way. They felt angry at the suggestion that our planet could be round—becoming upset at the thought of planet Earth as no longer the center of the universe. It did not fit their programmed theology or geography.

Our view of the world works for us to some extent, or else it would not have come into being. However, as we experience changes in our lives and the world around us, we tend to discover that our view is not as effective and meaningful as it once was. We become aware of our need and our power to change. We begin to question our fundamental assumptions. This questioning often produces a new way of thinking and feeling, a new story about what is "real" or "true."

LUYCKX'S WORLDVIEWS

Dr. Marc Luyckx, a consultant to the European Commission, suggests that we examine three worldview stories.[2] According to his research, people's view of the world changes as their world of work changes. Luyckx describes three stories arising from evolving working conditions. The first two stories dominated thinking and feeling during the past two millennia. The third story is emerging and may be the dominant view in the New Millennium. Luyckx refers to the three different worldview stories as:

- Pre-Modern: The Age of Enchantment
- Modern: The Age of Disenchantment
- Transmodern: The Age of Re-enchantment

THE PRE-MODERN WORLDVIEW STORY: ENCHANTMENT

The Pre-Modern Worldview apparently dominated thinking and believing for about 10,000 years. During this period, most work activity was centered on agriculture. The agrarian-based religions of the Middle East, such as Christianity, Judaism, Islam, and Animism, believed the earth was flat and the center of the universe. Their sacred scriptures, or God's revelation, were couched in this Pre-Modern Worldview. A significant belief was that God acted directly in the world through what we call miracles.

Luyckx's model uses the metaphor of the pyramid, with "our God" or plural gods at the apex of a hierarchy revealing "absolute truth." A male God reveals what to believe and how to behave to the male clerics. They in turn interpret "the truth" for the King and his court. The male politicians tell the men what to believe and do. The men, in this patriarchal schema, proceed to inform and control the behavior of women and children as well as aliens or strangers. See Figure 2.1.[3]

GOD AS <u>ONE</u>, ABOVE CREATION

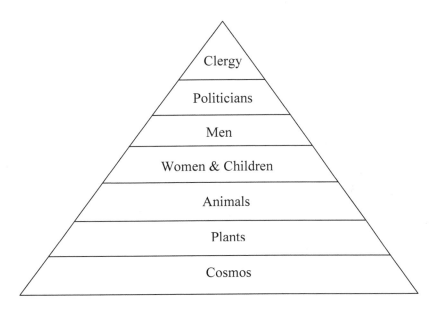

Figure 2.1

What is good and bad is defined by God and delivered by "His" representatives, with emphasis on obedience and respect for authority. They paternalistically maintain control over others, "for their own good," through a system of rewards and punishments. People at the lower levels are carefully trained to be dependent upon those in power. It is assumed that society functions best when citizens are conforming, docile, obedient, and subservient.

In this Pre-Modern Story, life has meaning assigned to it by God. It is an *enchanting* time, for everything physical is judged to be good and sacred, created by God out of His goodness and love. When humans refuse to believe and act in accordance with God's authority, negative consequences follow. Upon repentance, however, God forgives such sinful behavior, and humans eventually receive their reward in Heaven, a place of everlasting happiness. Those who do not repent go after death to a place of everlasting punishment called Hell. People who believe in this story view our present experience as mostly a painful one. For them, it is a life that they must endure, until they die and experience unimagined joy in life after death. Their only other hope is for God to perform a miracle, making life more tolerable—which people believe happens from time to time, especially if one is good and prayerful.

It appears to me that a similarity exists between Luyckx's worldview of the Pre-Modernists and the attitudes of the *Traditionals* described in the research of sociologist Paul H. Ray and psychologist Sherry Ruth Anderson, who list some of the values and beliefs of the Pre-Moderns in their book, *The Cultural Creatives:*

- Patriarchs should again dominate family life.
- *Feminism* is a swearword.
- Men need to keep their traditional roles and women need to keep theirs.
- Family, church, and community are where you belong.
- The conservative version of their own particular religious traditions must be upheld.
- Customary and familiar ways of life should be maintained.
- It's important to regulate sex—pornography, teen sex, extramarital sex—and abortion.
- Men should be proud to serve their country in the military.
- All the guidance you need for your life can be found in the Bible.
- Country and small-town life is more virtuous than big-city or suburban life.
- Our country needs to do more to support virtuous behavior.
- Preserving civil liberties is less important than restricting immoral behavior.
- Freedom to carry arms is essential.
- Foreigners are not welcome.[4]

According to these attitudes, much of life in the Pre-Modern Worldview Story is composed of "shoulds," "have-to's," and "musts." I would add the following additional Pre-Modern values to the list:

- Clear, black-and-white categories resulting in a feeling of certainty should be taught in our schools.
- It is a must to follow conservative religious teachings to the letter.

THE MODERN WORLDVIEW STORY: DISENCHANTMENT

The second of Luyckx's Worldviews is the Modern Story. The Age of Reason and Enlightenment swept through much of the Western world in the sixteenth and seventeenth centuries. In the mid- to late nineteenth century, people left the countryside for the city in search of work. Moving off the land meant leaving the sacred and the enchanted behind. As human beings gradually moved into the cities where jobs were available, they became ever more separated from nature. The wisdom and autonomy of the farmer were replaced by the monotony and compliance behavior of the factory. Modern society became *disenchanted*.

Miracles were dismissed as superstition or deception. For the Modernist, authority resides in science and reason rather than in what God says. Modernists view the world as a machine that can be taken apart, analyzed, and put back together again. Interaction among the parts can mostly be reduced to one simple relationship: cause and effect.

In Figure 2.2 below,[5] the Modern Story has "Reason" displacing God as the ultimate authority. Expert scientists replace religious men and guide the politicians. The politicians instruct men, who in turn direct women, children, and strangers. Everyone beneath the politicians needs to be controlled "for their own good." People receive rewards or punishment as they respond to the commands from above.

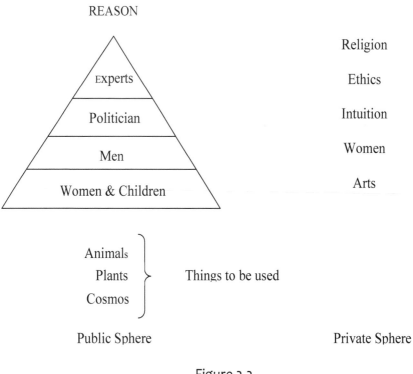

REASON

Religion

Ethics

Intuition

Women

Arts

Experts

Politician

Men

Women & Children

Animals
Plants
Cosmos

Things to be used

Public Sphere

Private Sphere

Figure 2.2

Some of the values that Ray and Anderson believe describe their second group, called the *Moderns*, appear to me to be quite similar to the group of people Luyckx describes as having a Modern worldview:

- Making or having a lot of money
- Climbing the ladder of success with measurable steps toward one's goals
- "Looking good" or being stylish
- "When the going gets tough, the tough go shopping"
- Having lots of choices (as a consumer, as a voter, or on the job)
- Supporting economic and technological progress at the national level
- Rejecting the values and concerns of native peoples, rural people, Traditionals, New Agers, religious mystics[6]

Ray and Anderson found in their research that "Many Moderns also share unspoken assumptions about 'what works' that the other subcultures [worldviews] may not share." They list the following:

- It's flaky to be concerned about your inner or spiritual life.
- You have a right to be entertained by the media.
- Your body is pretty much like a machine.
- Most organizations lend themselves to machine analogies.
- Either business knows best, or big government knows best.
- Bigger is better.
- Time is money.
- What gets measured gets done.
- Setting goals is very important and effective, and so are measures of goal attainment.
- Analyzing things into their parts is the best way to solve problems.
- Science and engineering are the models for truth.
- Being "in control" is a top priority at work.
- Efficiency and speed are top priorities.
- The mainstream media's awe for and sense of importance of the very rich is about right.
- It makes sense to compartmentalize our life into very discrete and separate spheres: work, family, socializing, making love, education, politics, religion. It's a very complete kind of compartmentalization, covering what you do and believe, and what you value.[7]

"Why be concerned?" Modernists ask. Despite some negatives, the Modern Worldview has provided many household and work conveniences, giving us more free time. It has also brought us biomedical technologies effective in dealing with medical emergencies and alleviating pain and suffering. Our world is not standing still; it continues to change. "Trust the Scientific Process," say the Modernists. Science and technology will solve all our problems, be they dangers to the environment, wars, or poverty. Doing science has replaced prayer.

THE TRANS-MODERN STORY: RE-ENCHANTMENT

The third worldview is Luyckx's Transmodern Story. As knowledge-related tools began to take precedence over industrial tools around 1950, a fundamental shift began within society. We passed from the Industrial Age through the Information Age into the Knowledge Age. In this new story, people view and experience the world quite differently. Many enthusiastically embrace new information technologies, diversity, and a sustainable environment. Many are also open to spirituality, both publicly and privately.

God is "reappearing." A *re-enchantment* with the world is taking place. All of creation is becoming sacred, and "Planet Earth" is alive in the minds and hearts of many.

Science is no longer the absolute and incontestable yardstick. It now interacts with other values such as spirituality, ethics, and cultural diversity in an emerging, inclusive vision. The Transmodern Worldview Story is not yet dominant, according to Luyckx. However, it continues to evolve and grow. The worldview of material progress through science and business, while still valuable, is losing its top billing and dissolving into the background.

Experts and specialists are also losing their power as computer technology levels the playing field. Computers now enable many people to have wide access to information formerly controlled and doled out on a perceived "need-to-know basis" by the ruling elite, the scientists, and the corporate aristocracy.

People in the Transmodern Story are taking control of and becoming responsible for their own lives. A sense of empowerment results, as people experience genuine democracy and a sharing of decision-making power among employees in the workplace. Employees are now referred to as "knowledge workers" and are no longer treated as irresponsible children. Self-managed teams are replacing supervisors and replacing the "command and control" mentality. (See Chapter Nine on The World of Work.)

Scientists are becoming aware of the negative effects of the industrial society and see themselves as socially responsible for the destruction of nature due to scientific and technological activity. Science and technology, in turn, have lost their innocence in the eyes of the general public. People now believe profit and techno-scientific logic cannot take precedence over human values, spirituality, and creating a world that works for all.[8]

Politicians are struggling to regain lost trust by reuniting politics with ethics. The Women's Movement has made significant strides, resulting in more equality for women. Diversity is valued, enabling everyone to discover purpose and personal meaning in their life. The hierarchical structure is breaking down, and equality is taking precedence. Consequently, the Modern Story is being replaced by an inclusive, participative, and diverse idea of leadership. In Figure 2.3, a round dinner table with an opening in the center represents the Transmodern Worldview, replacing the pyramid of the last two millennia as previously illustrated in Figures 2.1 and 2.2.

The empty space in the center of the dinner table represents God: "The Unknown," "The Truth," "Eternal Oneness," "The Holy." Although every name and metaphor limps when attempting to represent God, still, the figure is helpful in picturing God as the center of everything, thus including all of creation in the Transmodern Worldview Story.

An equal place at the dinner table is set for each of the various groups. No one is excluded. All are welcomed, accepted, equal, and unique. No one makes comparisons of "better" or "worse."

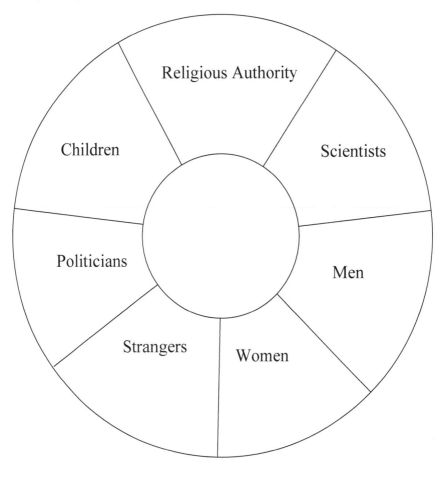

Figure 2.3

As I considered Luyckx's description of the worldview of those he terms the Trans-Moderns, it appeared, again, that they were quite similar to the values and attitudes that Ray and Anderson attribute to those whom they designate *Cultural Creatives*.

Following the preface of their book, Ray and Anderson present a series of eighteen statements; they say that if the reader agrees with at least ten of these statements, he or she is likely to be a Cultural Creative. I would say that the more one identifies with these statements, the stronger one resonates with what I am calling New Millennium Thinking and Feeling.

You are likely to be a Cultural Creative if you . . .

1. love nature and are deeply concerned about its destruction
2. are strongly aware of the problems of the whole planet (global warming, destruction of rain forests, overpopulation, lack of ecological sustainability, exploitation of people in poorer countries) and want to see more action on them, such as limiting economic growth
3. would pay more taxes or pay more for consumer goods if you knew the money would go to clear up the environment and to stop global warming
4. give a lot of importance to developing and maintaining your relationships
5. give a lot of importance to helping other people and bringing out their unique gifts
6. volunteer for one or more good causes
7. care intensely about both psychological and spiritual development
8. see spirituality or religion as important in your life but are also concerned about the role of the Religious Right in politics
9. want more equality for women at work, and more women leaders in business and politics
10. are concerned about violence and the abuse of women and children around the world
11. want our politics and government spending to put more emphasis on children's education and well-being, on rebuilding our neighborhoods and communities, and on creating an ecologically sustainable future
12. are unhappy with both the left and the right in politics and want to find a new way that is not in the mushy middle
13. tend to be rather optimistic about our future and distrust the cynical and pessimistic view that is given by the media
14. want to be involved in creating a new and better way of life in our country

15. are concerned about what the big corporations are doing in the name of making more profits: downsizing, creating environmental problems, and exploiting poorer countries
16. have your finances and spending under control and are not concerned about overspending
17. dislike all the emphasis in modern culture on success and "making it," on getting and spending, on wealth and luxury goods
18. like people and places that are exotic and foreign, and like experiencing and learning about other ways of life[9]

This New Millennium Story of reality shifts the ways we feel and think, what we value, and how we act. According to Ray and Anderson,

> Most of us change our worldview only once in our lifetime, if we do it at all, because it changes virtually everything in our consciousness. When you make this shift, you change your sense of who you are and who you are related to, what you are willing to see and how you interpret it, your priorities for action and for the way you want to live.[10]

It's a matter of consciousness: a conscious change of mind and heart, a shift in our understanding. This mind shift is happening slowly, but perceptibly. Similar shifting is occurring in Europe.

I have taken the time to describe Mark Luyckx's three theories because the New Millennium Worldview described in this book integrates Luyckx's Transmodern Worldview, and it manifests many of the cultural changes discovered by Paul Ray and Sherry Ruth Anderson.

SHIFTING OUR WORLDVIEW

Worldviews have shifted throughout time and continue to shift. The question is how best to achieve a shift in worldview.

In a newspaper article, "A Shift in Worldview," community writer Sandra Duffy says:

Can a change in one person change the world? The theory of quantum physics postulates, based on experiments with split electrons, that the natural world is an interdependent symphony of living energy—the knowledge of one part is the knowledge of all.

An example is found in birds in England in the 1930s that learned to open the tops of milk bottles on porches. Soon, birds all over the world were doing it. [Even though] the Blue Tit birds were **not** migratory. Rupert Sheldrake, a British scientist and author, called it *morphic resonance*. If a few English birds can impart survival skills worldwide, a sufficient number of merciful [people] should be able to shift the worldview of [others] into awestruck observers of the natural world, bridging their differences and working in warm and supportive community to fit in, not to dominate and exploit.[11]

The moment we question our worldview—the fundamental assumptions of our upbringing—our personal views shift. And as the new worldview shift spreads, the world community enters a time of transition. During the transition period, the community is not without a view of reality, but is between and among current worldviews—seeking to understand the New Millennium Worldview.

Change is the very essence of a worldview shift. Those who initiate change are often labeled dreamers, thinkers, radicals, deviants, revolutionaries, heroes, visionaries, or other such terms—take your pick!

Individuals whose new thinking and feeling inspire them to challenge assumptions—confront the conventional and go contrary to or beyond the current worldview—are often moved by a vision. This vision enables them to see how their change in thinking and feeling affects many aspects of life in a positive way; not least among these is a better and better understanding of their world.

While human beings need and desire stability, we are, at the same time, moved to seek significant change. As American writer Leo Buscaglia says, "Change. It has the power to uplift, to heal, to stimulate, to surprise, open new doors, bring fresh experience, and create excitement in life. Certainly it is worth the risk."

When a large number of people accept change in thinking and feeling, a new story occurs.

People who push for change are usually met with strong resistance because others hate to abandon their status-quo worldview. A struggle ensues. Religious institutions, governments, politicians, scientists, and communities—i.e., the typical person on the street—get involved to the degree that each has a stake in the new or the old model. However, once the worldview of the majority shifts, it is as though we've put on a new pair of glasses, seeing through new lenses. The world looks different. And, as always, most of us assume that everyone else sees the world the same way we do.

Thinking Differently

When the Four Fundamental Assumptions become conscious and begin to make sense to others and become widely spoken of publicly, many people simply begin to think differently without being consciously aware of the change. Eventually, this alternate way of thinking becomes the norm—until yet another "worldview-shifter" appears on the scene.

Yet a minority continue to see reality through the lens of the old worldview. Filled with regrets, they remember the "good old days," and actively seek to recreate them. Pre-Moderns today criticize Modern Worldview thinking and feeling. As the New Millennium Worldview becomes conventional, the Moderns who don't come along will join the ranks of the Pre-Moderns and find little that's appropriate about the emerging, evolving world.

In the mid-sixteenth century, when Copernicus contradicted Ptolemy and Aristotle, stating that the sun did not revolve around the Earth, but rather the Earth revolved around the sun, the few people who knew about Copernicus's new theory did not resist it intensely—because his idea did not influence the daily lives of most people.

Galileo popularized Copernicus's model, explaining that the Earth was round rather than flat, and similar to the other planets—not the center of the universe. The idea caught on, but many, including the authorities in the Vatican, condemned him.[12] Only a forced recantation saved Galileo's life.

Once the implications of unconventional thinking impact people's daily lives, the worldview shifter is often mocked, threatened, even punished as a heretic, an unrelenting deviant. It is a rare occurrence when a worldview shifter is honored in her/his own lifetime, especially when that person has worked to popularize an unconventional point of view whose benefits are not immediately obvious.

Only after Martin Luther King's death did the United States name a day in his honor. Like many others, he had to die a martyr's death for the country to express gratitude for his efforts to make his dream of racial equality a reality. In the face of segregation, he pictured little black children and little white children walking hand-in-hand to school. Today, his dream is happening, and his vision of a black President of the United States has become a reality.

Fear of Change

To most of us, the idea of bringing about a change in worldview, even within a small group of people, is nothing short of daunting, seemingly impossible—at least at first glance.

Common reactions to unanticipated change in our lives are fear, denial, or even rejection of the very existence of change. This occurs when we fail to perceive the important benefits that can result from change. If the change truly seems to be necessary, and we are given time to adjust to it, we come to accept it.

Proactive Rather Than Reactive

What seems obvious bears repeating: The world is always changing; it never stays the same. One approach to world changes is to recognize them, accept them, and be determined to go along with them; that is, to change oneself. It is far more effective to take responsibility for our actions (changing them when we see the need)—to be "proactive" rather than to be a "reactive" complainer and/or blamer, which accomplishes little. When this change happens to a critical mass of people, a *new story* comes into being.

Imaging

As stated in Assumption II, change also happens when people proactively initiate it. We change our assumptions, which influence our attitudes and beliefs, leading to a change in behavior. When many others join in and act upon the vision, each individual's change has significant impact on the evolving world.

In the United States, when we were able to envision smoke-free airplanes, and then smoke-free buildings, both phenomena actually happened quite quickly. Fifty years ago, only a few people could have predicted such an occurrence. The same is true of seatbelts, nonexistent thirty years ago. Today, people all over the world voluntarily snap on seatbelts upon getting into their car—acting in their perceived self-interest.

Before Gandhi, the people of India had little hope of being free of British rule, and therefore gave little thought to it. But Gandhi's vision gave them hope. Together—with Gandhi's inspiration, direction, and determination—people sprang into action, becoming proactive, until India was no longer a colony of Great Britain.

These changes happened because people became convinced of the benefits of wearing seatbelts, of the absence of secondary smoke, and of India's being free. Many people made the change, and then laws followed, enforcing such behavior.

A major shift in worldview is happening at this very moment. This New Millennium Worldview involves numerous social and personal changes; it is changing the way we think and feel about our behavior, our interactions with other people, and the inter-relatedness of the whole of creation. And it is profoundly impacting significant aspects of our lives, such as the environment, education, healthcare, politics, criminal justice, spirituality, our intimate relationships, and the way we do business. It is based on the premises I have previously described as the Four Fundamental Assumptions.

CHAPTER THREE

We Are Forever in the Process of Discovering

There are no truths, there are only stories.
Jewish Proverb

Reality is nothing more than a collective hunch.
Lily Tomlin
American Comedienne

We can know about some things; we never know something.
Albert Einstein
Renowned Physicist

All models are wrong—some models are useful.
W. Edward Deming
Management Consultant

Absolute Truth is unknowable

We have defined worldviews and examined how they are in the process of changing. Next, we explore the first of the Four Fundamental Assumptions on which rests the New Millennium Worldview.

As stated in the first chapter, the First Assumption tells us that "the truth" is far too vast to be fully known by any of us humans. As the New Millennium Worldview is developing, neither absolute objective truth nor relativism is an issue. People simply believe that the whole truth is, to finite minds, beyond comprehension.

Absolute and complete truth may well exist, but we do not and cannot know it in this life. Far from feeling discouraged by this, people are excited to find out that this lack of perfect knowledge is a wonderful opportunity to engage in learning. We feel the joy of discovering and learning something we hadn't known before. Former United States Secretary of Defense Donald Rumsfeld's statement about what we know [regarding intelligence and defense policy], uttered on more than one occasion, is at once funny, contorted—and close to the mark:

As we know, there are known knowns. There are things we know we know.

We also know there are known unknowns. That is to say we know there are some things we do not know. But there are also unknown unknowns, the ones we don't know we don't know.[1]

Systems Thinking

In the New Millennium Worldview Story, we recognize that what we appear to know is only a small portion of what we could know *if* we understood the total system.

Imagine that everything knowable (the total system) lies within the boundaries of Figure 3.1.[2]

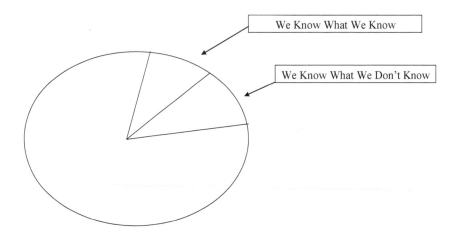

Fig. 3.1

For example, we know we can read and write French, and we're aware we don't know how to read and write Chinese, Vietnamese, or many other languages. What we do know is minuscule compared with all of what could be known. The unknown is a complete mystery. We don't even know what we don't know and what could possibly be known. All the concepts and possibilities have not yet even occurred to us.

We Know Only Parts

Consequently, individuals, as well as society as a whole, are unable to comprehend total reality, even though we are continuously striving to better understand it. The best we can do is to "know" *partial* reality. Parts, however, can only be understood in the context of the whole. For instance, we can understand the function of the fuel pump if we understand how it contributes to the functioning of the automobile. Automobiles, however, can only be completely understood if we understand highway systems, the people who drive cars, and other aspects such as air pollution and aesthetics. We need to understand the whole system before we can perfectly understand the parts. Understanding the total system, however, is humanly impossible.

Assuming that we do not know absolute truth, we are motivated to be open to other points of view. We ask more questions. Our imagination and intuition are awakened. Greater openness to and acceptance of other perspectives emerges. The possibility of our becoming creative and innovative increases. We tend to be open-minded. On the other hand, when any of us are certain about anything, we tend not to think about it and not to seek further information except that which reinforces our beliefs and enables us to persuade others that we are right. Thus, believing that we know something is certainly true results in our being closed-minded!

In the New Millennium Emerging Worldview, people are moving away from a closed, dogmatic, and static story of life. We no longer believe in a "clockwork" universe with but one explanation or description of the world; Pre-Modern and Modern Worldviewers, satisfied with their story, demand just such a single answer. Instead, a more open, questioning, and creative story is emerging.

Perceptions

Things only *seem* to be a certain way. They *seem* to be this certain way because we were told by our parents, school, culture, and friends that things are such and such a way. Had we grown up with different parents, attended other schools, lived in Sweden instead of Thailand, had other friends—then things wouldn't *seem* the way they do now.

New Millennium Thinkers and Feelers have come to realize that things *seem* the way they are, not because they *are* the way they are, but rather because *we* are the way we are. Hence, if we change the way we are, and the way we assume things are, maybe, just maybe, things will become what we imagine them to be. People who have accepted the New Millennium Worldview assumptions believe this. We believe we can create a new reality through the way we perceive life. We believe perceptions are the personal views of an individual. They are formed from a person's assumptions, which, in turn, evolve from that person's upbringing and life experiences.

Perception involves a threefold process, in which we observe, interpret, and judge events, things, and people, based on our fundamental assumptions. See Figure 3.2.[3]

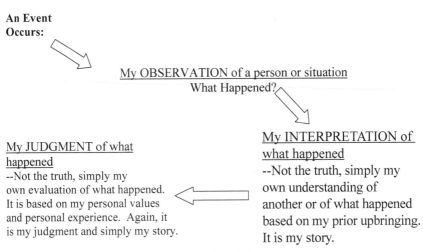

**An Event
Occurs:**

My OBSERVATION of a person or situation
What Happened?

My JUDGMENT of what happened
--Not the truth, simply my own evaluation of what happened. It is based on my personal values and personal experience. Again, it is my judgment and simply my story.

My INTERPRETATION of what happened
--Not the truth, simply my own understanding of another or of what happened based on my prior upbringing. It is my story.

Fig. 3.2

Our observations are simply whatever we "sense" (see, hear, feel, touch, taste, and smell) as we experience a person or a situation. They are, so to speak, the existing raw material. Even here, two people can look at the same person, thing, or event and actually see it differently.

Our interpretation of what we observe is our story about what is happening, based on our previous experiences, beliefs, and values. It is valuable, even important; nonetheless, it is *our* story and not "the" absolute, objective truth.

Our judgments of events or persons are another part of perception. Judgments are simply our conclusions of whether what we observed and interpreted is beneficial or not. These judgments are not "the truth," but simply our story, our reality.

John Godfrey Saxe's "The Blind Men and the Elephant," based on an ancient Indian legend, provides a perspective on this search for "the truth":

It was six men of Indostan
To learning much inclined,
Who went to see the Elephant
(Though all of them were blind),
That each by observation
Might satisfy his mind.

The first approached the Elephant,
And happening to fall
Against his broad and sturdy side,
At once began to bawl:
"God bless me! But the Elephant
Is very like a WALL!"

The second, feeling of the tusk,
Cried, "Ho! What have we here
So very round and smooth and sharp?
To me it's very clear
This wonder of an Elephant
Is very like a SPEAR!"

The third approached the animal,
And happening to take
The squirming trunk within his hands,
Thus boldly up and spake:
"I see," quoth he, "the Elephant
Is very like a SNAKE!"

The fourth reached out an eager hand,
And felt about the knee.
"What most this wondrous beast is like
Is mighty plain," quoth he:
"'Tis clear enough the Elephant
Is very like a TREE!"

The fifth, who chanced to touch the ear,
Said, "E'en the blindest man
Can tell what this resembles most;
Deny the fact who can.

This marvel of an Elephant
Is very like a FAN!"

The sixth no sooner had begun
About the beast to grope,
Than seizing on the swinging tail
That fell within his scope,
"I see," quoth he, "the Elephant
Is very like a ROPE!"

And so these men of Indostan
Disputed loud and long,
Each in his own opinion
Exceeding stiff and strong,
Though each was partly in the right,
All were in the wrong![4]

Though each man was partly in the right, none of them was able to mentally grasp the whole reality of the elephant. Our human understandings have been formed in similar ways, resulting in our individual, narrow viewpoints. These interpretations and judgments are all we have at any particular moment in human history. Like the blind men, we each have only a piece of reality. No one is capable of seeing the whole picture or knowing the whole story.

Our intellectual blindness, however, is not the permanent condition that physical blindness often is. We can learn and, consequently, see more clearly, although we never see and understand our elephants completely.

Implications

From our life's beginning we are taught how to see the world and what to do to survive. Our desire for survival motivates us to conform to social norms. We are brought up by family, teachers, friends—who are our very culture—to believe in the way things are (truths) and the way things should be (values). Many, if not most, of us fail to question the "reality" of this story. The result is unconscious fundamental assumptions about life. And these unconscious fundamental assumptions shape our present perceptions, attitudes, beliefs, expectations, and feelings.

We are influenced by our parents, teachers, friends, and the media, as well as the situations within which we live and act such as our workplace. These influences are not necessarily consistent within a person or within society. This inconsistency explains why even twins, not to mention the rest of us, disagree on fundamentals. For instance, coming from the same culture, even the same family, we may disagree about what is true (such as: God exists; humans are basically good). We may also disagree about our values (e.g., everyone has the right to life, liberty, and the pursuit of happiness, a meaningful job, health care, sufficient food, to be considered innocent until proven guilty).

Our fundamental assumptions form the basis for our beliefs and values, which in turn influence how we perceive people and events. For instance, some of us may believe violence is good and is necessary sometimes in order to bring about peace. Others may believe violence is never beneficial because it creates more violence. Emerging Worldview Thinkers and Feelers conclude, when such disagreements occur: One person is not correct and the other wrong. People and events are perceived in different ways based on different upbringings or past socialization.

Our perceptions and attitudes further determine our expectations and dreams, which lead to the goals we set, our plans to achieve the goals, and finally our actions to implement our plans. If our expectations are met, we believe our perceptions are "the truth" and "good." We then often seek to persuade others that we are right and they are wrong. If our expectations are *not* met, we may be more open to changing our minds.

For instance, if we believe violence is a legitimate last resort for achieving peace, we set a goal to create an invincible military. We then implement plans to raise money to develop a well-equipped and highly-trained fighting force. We have high expectations that we'll prevail in a possible war. If it works, and we defeat our enemies and this results in at least temporary perceived peace, our belief is reinforced, as was the case for America and its allies in the First and Second World Wars. Since then, America has encouraged other nations to arm themselves against their enemies, often described as terrorists.

If, however, our violent acts are not successful, then we may desist from spending tax money on building up a military. We may use such money for other strategies, such as research and development and building strong industries, as has happened in Japan since World War II and in Costa Rica.

In the New Millennium Story, when our expectations are met, we do not conclude that our understanding of the situation is the truth. We never believe, for example, that a theory is true just because it works. Newton's Three Laws of Motion are not natural laws just because they appear consistent with our experience. They are assumptions which were creatively projected onto nature.

With new information, we can change our assumptions, even our assumptions about Newton's laws. We don't seek, however, to persuade others that we are right. At most, we offer our ideas to others as possibilities, in much the same manner that I am doing with this book.

As this new thinking emerges, it's not uncommon to hear a person exclaim, "I have come to realize, perhaps too late in life, that what I see is not the way it is, but simply the way I think it is." Maybe, if we all assumed this, there would be less need to fight against others, and a greater need to seek to understand one another.

Labeling and Perception

We assume that people are not actually what we **judge** them to be, perhaps lazy, selfish, and incompetent, or, for that matter, intelligent, outgoing, and inspiring. Whatever labels we assign to them are not the truth, but simply our story about them from our point of view.

Thus, the labels we give people reveal more about us than about them. Our interpretations and judgments of others, even when based on observations of their behavior, are projections of our own values and attitudes, because we don't have full knowledge of how and why the person came to deserve, in our eyes, the said label. However, we can decide to change our perceptions for the good of all. If we perceive other people as friendly, more than likely we perceive ourselves as friendly; we act friendly towards another and friendliness is returned, confirming "the truth," in our minds, of our judgment and label. Similarly, if we label another as hostile, we tend to treat him with hostility and, sure enough, he becomes hostile toward us.

Emotions and Perception

Our senses grasp an infinitesimally small portion of reality, we assume. Further, our brain organizes the available sensory information or environmental stimuli in order to make sense out of millions of bits and pieces of data. In other words, we perceive what we think we need to perceive and miss the rest of what is occurring. What we do observe becomes the material for our interpretation and judgment, both of which are affected by our emotional state. We ignore what we don't want or enjoy, unless ignoring is impossible because of the strength of the stimulus. If a beggar's pleading becomes so distracting and disturbing that we cannot ignore him, we may give him some money just to be free of him. Otherwise, if not seeing a beggar satisfies our desires, we ignore him, as though we didn't see him. Later, we easily forget him, as though he never existed.

We tend to distort the world and narrow it down to fit our values and emotions, while preserving the illusion of understanding it. Our perceptions, our understanding, our conclusions of what we call "reality," tend to be skewed and limited. That is, our worldview is our "story," *not* objective truth. If most others share it, this view becomes the dominant story at a particular time in history. Other stories can also exist with many benefits as well. Our knowledge of a part of reality is "a perceived truth," "a belief," or "an opinion." We realize that these perceived truths, beliefs, and opinions are based on our experience. When they don't align with other people's beliefs and opinions, perceived truths are called "biases." If they do align with the majority's beliefs and opinions, they are perceived, in the New Millennium Worldview, as "agreements." From the Pre-Modern and Modernist perspective these agreements are called "facts."

Thus, in the New Millennium Story, what we formerly referred to as "facts," we now understand as "agreements" we share with others. Such agreements offer us only a faint hint of the fullness of reality. In our culture, we may believe in these agreements, such as the meaning of democracy, but this doesn't mean our understanding is "the truth," or that people in every culture must agree with us. Other people could very well understand the term quite differently.

Those espousing the New Millennium Story have come to realize that just because Mom and Dad believe something, or because our politicians or church leaders make a pronouncement, or because some concept is found in a book or in the newspapers, or because we hear about an occurrence on the radio or TV, it does not mean it is the whole, absolute truth. At best, it captures a piece of reality, similar to the experience of the six blind men of Indostan. Emerging Worldview Thinkers and Feelers see it as simply other people's interpretations and judgments, "their stories" about what might have occurred or is occurring.

Science and Perception

Most nonscientists, thinking in terms of the Modern Worldview, assume that all questions which scientists address have, or will have, a definitive answer. These nonscientists do not recognize that the absolute true answer to a scientific question is found only after all evidence has been assembled—which is not possible, as we have seen above.

Genuine scientists, even those who believe in the Modern Worldview, are at ease admitting they don't "know" everything there is to know about a topic, although they've studied it all their lives. They further believe they can improve their scientific understanding by trying to prove their best hypothesis to be incorrect, instead of trying to confirm what they already believe is true. This enables them to be open-minded and **not** dogmatic about what they know. It also gives them the right, even the obligation, to question every "truth" put before them.

Because the scientific method does not claim absolute truth, scientists are ecstatic if and when they attain a specific result ninety-nine percent of the time. Even if an experiment results in a perfect score, (or one hundred percent), genuine scientists realize they could not possibly have tested every variable. Somewhere at least one exception could occur, nullifying the conclusion. Science is a medium which simply delivers probable progressive approximations to absolute truth, not absolute truth. Hence, in the New Millennium the average person thinks like a scientist when it comes to claiming to know or understand reality.

Other Disciplines

The elusiveness of "truth" occurs not only in science, but in other disciplines as well. Historians, for example, do not exist in a vacuum of absolute objectivity. Their interpretations and judgments are based on prior assumptions, beliefs, and values. Two historians could view the war on terrorism quite differently, based on the values they bring to their study. A Jewish historian might see an issue as Muslim fanaticism. A Palestinian historian could perceive the issue as Palestine's struggle for peace and freedom. Yet, from the Modern Worldview perspective, each believes their perception of reality is "the truth" and the other is wrong. Vietnamese and American historians may similarly differ on the history of the Vietnam War, each believing their own version is the truth in terms of what actually occurred.

Similarly, classroom professors (particularly in business) who believe the Modern Worldview Story often profess the opinions and perceptions of scholars and textbook authors, as well as their own beliefs, as though such proclamations are absolutely true. Yet their statements are their own studied opinions, not truth and not objective reality. In an effort to provide clear explanations so that students will understand the theories, they make statements in class that often come across as the "truth" or the *only* way to achieve a certain objective. Even when they themselves realize that they are not professing absolute truth, but simply expressing their opinion, they rarely remind students that this is the case. This tendency appears to be based on fear, fear that the students might take the information less seriously or not see the benefits of conforming to conventional practices.

By contrast, in the New Millennium Worldview, students are aware of, and agree with or reject, the personal biases of the teacher. Sorting through the information received, students are encouraged to compare information and theories with their previous upbringing, life experiences, and other theories which are contrary to the ones being presented. Because their teachers expect them to play the devil's advocate, students question information, theories, and conventional practices. They are constantly invited to come up with their own ideas, to arrive at "their inner, personal truth."

In so doing, students perceive their conclusions as personal, without seeking to force their beliefs on others as though what they believe is absolutely right. They share their ideas with the intention that others will agree with them or, hopefully, build upon these offered ideas, or point out some insufficiency in them. Students appreciate that others may arrive at different conclusions from the *same* information. Conformity to accepted practices is not the highest priority. (See Chapter Ten, The Story of Education.)

Implications

The assumption that we are always in the process of discovering the truth has significant implications for our lives in the New Millennium. Dogmatism is no longer credible. Openness, flexibility, questions, and exploration are valued. Proposed solutions and answers, which may be useful, are tentative. No one fights over who is right and who is wrong. No one is branded as "evil" simply because they do not believe and act the way we do.

To believe we know or possess "absolute truth," the whole truth, and nothing but *absolute truth*, is an assumption leading to arguments, rage, and even wars with those who disagree with us, as is evident in the Palestinian-Israeli conflict.

Believing that we are right and everyone else is wrong is one of the greatest obstacles toward peace and peacefulness.

As this first fundamental assumption is internalized, people find that being open to discovery and being open-minded is a more functional way to live in the New Millennium. The beginning of wisdom is: *Admitting we don't know something*. And, although we question and do not expect to find "the answers," we often do experience a better understanding, which motivates us to keep searching.

Dialogue

In the New Millennium Worldview, dialogue is a social process for resolving opposing views. It encourages respectful communication and creates an environment of trust. In dialogue, participants actively listen to one another. They refrain from evaluating the speaker or his/her ideas or feelings.

Unlike a debate, which is basically a competition, in dialogue nobody tries to win. There is no attempt to gain points or even to make one's particular view prevail. Rather, we listen to one another with an open mind and heart. Listeners accept the speaker for who he/she is and carefully consider what he/she says without making judgments of right or wrong, good or bad. The overall objective is understanding.

Assuming that no one is absolutely right or completely wrong enables parties to enter into dialogue to find mutual understanding with regard to an apparent difficulty. This enables both parties to be flexible, to share information, and to be open and honest about their feelings and concerns. These behaviors further lead to being empathic, with the result that both parties become sensitive to one another's desires. Deep trust ensues.

The more emotionally mature the individual and society, the more likely individuals and society are able to reach agreement through dialogue, because they begin to see the benefit of different perspectives. If the situation requires it, the agreement becomes law. The law itself, however, is not chiseled in stone. Like members of society themselves, it is open to change. In the New Millennium Worldview, the law is meant to be a catalyst for change, rather than the ultimate arbiter of "the truth." In Chapter Eleven, we discuss how Emerging Thinking and Feeling deals with lawbreakers.

Commitment and Perseverance

Even without knowing anything absolutely, we seek and determine the best approach in any given situation. Through commitment to our determined approach, we avoid wishy-washy instability or half-hearted behavior. Based on our values, we act on what we know and feel while being open to changing our position.

Moreover, rather than complaining and giving up in a certain situation, we realize that "what is" in the moment does not "have to be." What appears to be reality is one way of looking at an event or behavior. Changing the lens through which we see often results in a different picture of reality. The old view could be painful. A new picture can provide hope. With hope come energy, effort, and action for improvement. Feelings of depression, disdain, and criticism give way to feelings of confidence, peace, and understanding.

Changing Our Minds

We persevere because we care deeply. However, caring is not closed-minded. Precisely because we care, we leave the door open for changing our minds. Changing our minds is perceived as a strength, not a weakness.

New Millennium Thinkers and Feelers are quite comfortable in admitting their ignorance and their willingness to learn; it is not only okay, it's a *sign of intelligence* to say, "I don't know." It's even okay to admit, "I made a mistake. I was wrong." Consider the beautiful, intricate beadwork of the Anishinaabeg (or Ojibwe-Chippewa) people, which always contains at least one deliberate mistake, a mismatch, because "no human is perfect."

New Millennium Thinkers and Feelers further realize that it can even be advantageous to social relationships to *make* mistakes. Psychological research shows that people who make mistakes are more likable than those who seem perfect. People who make mistakes are seen as more approachable and less judgmental than perfect people.[5]

Under Pre-Modern and Modern assumptions, it's difficult to admit we don't know something or admit we've made a mistake. In February of 2007, when asked if she had made a mistake regarding Iraq, U.S. Secretary of State Condoleezza Rice was adamant in stating that she had not made a mistake in supporting the invasion of Iraq! Similarly, Senator Hillary Clinton insisted she had not been wrong in voting for the invasion of Iraq.

Since the general assumption is that there is a "right," as well as a "wrong," *we* want to be right. We dislike being wrong because we may lose face or feel guilty. If we lack confidence or have low self-esteem, we try to compensate by being absolute in our arguments. We insist we are right while unconsciously fearing we are wrong.

From the Modern Worldview perspective, unfortunately, the need to believe we are, or were, "right" does not decrease with time. Rather, we strongly resist recognizing that what we believed for eighty years might not be "right." After all those years, we don't want to admit our behavior may have been unhealthy, or perhaps immoral. What would such an admission say about our lives? We are therefore determined not to change our mind or admit we are wrong. We find solace in our unbending resoluteness.

New Millennium Thinking and Feeling, however, suggests that our awakening is like putting on a new pair of eyeglasses. The world looks different. "Oh, now I see!" We don't belabor the past or feel guilty about it, because we recognize we are all in the process of discovering. We rejoice in and celebrate our new insights and eagerly consider other possibilities. We look backward to learn from past experiences, take in new information, and look forward to a more meaningful future, while rejoicing in the present. We are also receptive to the views of those who are farther along the path than we are. And, grateful for what we've learned, we can see that our previous experience, even when we were mistaken, was not a waste. We have no feelings of guilt, we're at peace regarding the past, and we're happy because of our new understanding.

We might, for example, deny the existence of God during our lifetime. Then, as our human support system falls away in death, we might turn to God for meaning, without guilt or remorse. We simply see and understand things differently now. It's okay to change our minds.

Awakening to past "errors" can still bring regrets. It's natural to wish we had discovered certain information earlier or taken it seriously sooner. If we had done so, perhaps we wouldn't have brought so much pain and anguish to others or to ourselves. However, we recognize our regrettable mistakes as powerful learning experiences. We can do better. We can improve. We can change not only our minds, but our behaviors. Rather than wallowing in guilt, we rejoice that there is still time to make amends and live more meaningfully—enhancing both others' lives and our own.

CONCLUSION

According to the New Millennium Story, no matter how objective we strive to be, our conclusions are biased and subjective. Total objectivity is impossible. What we observe depends on how we look at it—which, in turn, depends on what is going on inside *us*.

Seeking the whole truth is a journey, not an outcome. We never actually arrive at the whole truth on this earth; that would be the end of our journey. Each person holds a piece of the truth. Not one person or society has the whole truth. We are all in the process of understanding reality. We never understand reality in its entirety.

For most of us, the search and exploration for truth is never-ending. Ending means we've found the answers. Within the New Millennium Worldview, it is okay not to have "the answer." It's not only healthy, but it's exciting, to be searching.

Knowledge and understanding are, by definition, never perfect. There are no absolute answers. There is no one right answer.

The New Millennium Worldview assumes that no view is absolutely right or absolutely wrong, including the ideas presented in this book. When there is disagreement, people realize that others simply hold different beliefs and values, based on different upbringing and experience. Facing and working with disagreement through dialogue holds the potential for personal and societal peace, learning, and growth.

New Millennium Thinkers and Feelers believe that to think we know the whole truth is a dysfunctional assumption. A major task and purpose in our lives is to keep searching and discovering. As we search and discover, we understand more fully and often function more effectively. Yet we never arrive at complete understanding. We can always learn more. Marvelous things happen, as we discover when we're open to other ways of thinking and feeling about what is occurring outside of us and within us.

In making an effort to function more effectively within the New Millennium Worldview, we seek to agree with one another. To understand each other, we begin by defining and agreeing on terms.

For the sake of functionality, we assume that the definition we agree upon is the best we can do, until we find more workable definitions. The best we can achieve is our present common interpretation of "reality." It's our "story"; we agree to tell it and live it until another storyteller comes along with even more-meaningful insights.

The Pre-Modern and Modern Worldview stories suggest a black-versus-white world, where everything is clear (or could be, if we research it enough). To the contrary, in the New Millennium Worldview, theoretical applications all depend on the situation. In any given situation, the best we can do is find what is pragmatic in the "now" and what will work better until, with more information, insight, and intuition, we find something more effective. Our decisions on "what works better" are determined by our values— which also tend to change over time. In the New Millennium Emerging Worldview, we just keep on discovering and delighting in the process. Please join us!

CHAPTER FOUR

We Continually Create Our Own Reality

By focusing on what is beautiful, and good, and true, I not only change the way I see the world, I actually change the world.
Willis Harman
President of the Institute of Noetic Sciences in California
Co-founder of the World Business Academy

We are continually faced with great opportunities which are brilliantly disguised as unsolvable problems.
Margaret Mead
American Anthropologist

Happiness does not depend on outward things, but the way we see them.
Leo Tolstoy
Russian Novelist

A rock pile ceases to be a rock pile the moment a single man contemplates it, bearing within him the image of a cathedral.
Antoine de Saint-Exupéry
French Author

I had always thought that we used language to describe the world—now I am seeing that this was not the case. To the contrary, it is through language that we create the world, because it is nothing until we describe it. And when we describe it, we

create distinctions that govern our actions. To put it another way, we do not describe the world we see, but we see the world we describe.[1]
Joseph Jaworski
Co-founder, Global leadership Initiative

We Assume We Create our Own Reality

The belief that we are not victims of fate—rather, that we have the power to create our own reality—is the Second Assumption on which rests the New Millennium Emerging Worldview Story.

We create stories in our minds about what we believe will happen or the way we think things are, and these stories become our reality. Our thoughts and feelings, our values, and how deeply we care about a political event or an issue—such as the invasion of Iraq by the United States, or the question of abortion—determine how we each perceive these issues and events. Our point of view, as we observed in the last chapter, colors how we see things. In the New Millennium, we believe we have the power to effectively transform our lives. We are convinced we can create our own story for our life.

The first step in this process is to "wake up," open our eyes, and truly pay attention to our inner power and to what is happening in our environment.

Tony de Mello, a Jesuit priest, psychotherapist, and author born in India, tells a wonderful tale (from Spanish television) of a father knocking on his son's door and demanding that his son wake up, get out of bed, and go to school. The son responds with the complaint that he does not want to go to school, for three reasons:

> "First, because it's so dull; second, the kids tease me; and third, I hate school." And the father says, "Well, I am going to give you three reasons why you *must* go to school. First, because it is your duty; second, because you are forty-five years old, and third, because you are the headmaster." Wake up,

wake up! You've grown up. You're too big to be asleep. Wake up! Stop playing with your toys[,] de Mello urges.[2]

Signs of Waking Up!

A sign of our waking up can be found in the way we have changed our language. "It is through language that we create the world," American author Joseph Jaworski says, "because it is nothing until we describe it." Emerging Thinking and Feeling assumes all of us can create our own reality by the way we speak, think, and feel about ourselves, about events, or about other people.[3] Understanding this in the New Millennium, we focus on the positive. We no longer say we "have to" do a certain thing. Rather, we "get to" do it. The "have-to's," the "musts," and the "shoulds" have disappeared from our vocabulary. They are replaced by "get-to's" and "want-to's."

We no longer *have to* study, instead we *get to* study. We realize that many people in poor countries would see it as a privilege to be able to attend school or have a job. Therefore, we no longer *must* go to school. Instead, we actually feel pleasure and say, "I get to go to school today!" "I get to go to work today!"

We have come to realize no one "makes us angry." When a person does something we perceive to be a malicious act, such as tell negative lies about us, then, aware of this behavior, we may determine to be angry because we believe anger is the appropriate and justified response. But that person does not "make" us angry; rather, we want to be angry. In this situation, Emerging Worldviewers use anger to confront the lying, to prevent similar lies about us in the future.

In this same way, no one "makes" us love one another. We are aware that we love others because we are full of love and we value being lovable. Hence, we love one another because we want to love. We do not fall helplessly in love. The same is true of loving-kindness. We are lovingly kind to people because we want to be, not because of pressure from others to "do our duty."

New Millennium Thinkers and Feelers assume that kindness is our genetically coded response to the world.

To overcome fear, we now speak differently to ourselves. We tell ourselves, "I *can* do it." "I *can* exhibit loving-kindness to the whole world!" "I *can* love those who hurt me." Our attitude, which we can control, now determines our reality.

Pre-Modern and Modern Worldview Thinkers often assume themselves to be victims of their own weakness and their environment. Fate, luck, or God's actions determine what life is like, giving us excuses for being dependent and passive. "Have a nice day!" is a familiar expression when we leave another person, suggesting a "nice day" is a matter of chance.

Emerging Worldview Thinkers and Feelers have awakened and realize how powerful we are. We realize our happiness is *not* left to chance. We do *not* blame the weather, or our mother, spouse, friends, or managers at work, when we are having a difficult day. We seek and take responsibility for our own happiness.

Therefore, taking responsibility for *causing* a "nice day" represents the Emerging Worldview. In loving-kindness, we send people off with this expression: "Make it a nice day!" People are grateful for the reminder, taking pleasure in the power of creating their own reality, their own "story." And we do this with a smile.

New Millennium Thinkers and Feelers also recognize our own contribution when we are enjoying a great day. We ask ourselves what we are doing to create a happy day for ourselves. If we have an unhappy day, in loving-kindness we look inside ourselves for the same reason, to ask what we are doing to create that unhappy day.

Problems

Jim Lord and Pam McAllister, in their insightful book *What Kind of World Do You Want?*, find it self-defeating that people who believe in Pre-Modern and Modern Worldview assumptions are so mesmerized by "problems." They point out that this focus begins early in life:

Researchers put small tape recorders on the backs of five-year-olds. They found that children are growing up in homes where as much as 90% of the conversation is about how bad things are, what was done wrong, who is to blame, and what not to do.[4]

On the other hand, in appreciating what is right with the world, New Millennium Thinkers and Feelers find the energy to manage what is wrong. The secret is to refuse to dwell on the negative. Seeing and appreciating the good in everything enables us to envision the positive in even the worst of conditions. Convinced that it behooves us to always look for something good, we expect the best, even when things appear bad.

It becomes a self-fulfilling prophecy. When we envision good happening, good happens! It's a dream becoming our actual reality.

We Can Change

We humans are the way we are because we are programmed by our upbringing—the way we were socialized, as discussed in Chapter Three. Influences of family, culture, friends, and our experiences have formed our personalities, which in turn determine what we assume, how we think, how we behave. Emerging Worldview Thinkers and Feelers believe we don't "have to" remain the way we were brought up. We can change—if we wake up and become aware of our feelings, thoughts, and behavior. Having determined to change, we concentrate on what we believe is in our long-term self-interest.

Visualization

Once aware of our own power to change ourselves and our circumstances, we imagine what we want to have happen. We visualize our "dream." Through self-talk we claim what we want. "I'm an excellent skier." Then we do what excellent skiers do: We ski. And the more we ski—many times a day, over many weeks, even months—the sooner our dream becomes actual reality. If we want to move up in the company from secretary to office manager, we see ourselves as an office manager, act like an efficient office manager, and soon enough are promoted. Through this process we actualize power to create our own "story."

We Take Responsibility for Our Own Behavior

Assuming we create what we want, we no longer blame, or even praise, our parents or anyone else for the way we are. Others, especially our parents, of course influence us enormously. Yet, grateful for the benefits we received from our upbringing, we are not trapped by it. We can change—though it isn't easy—the influence our parents and others had on us. We do not blame our parents or others for what has happened to us in our lives.

We might have been told as children that we would never amount to anything, because we are dumb or irresponsible or undependable. Having awakened in the New Millennium, we realize what nonsense such statements and predictions are. We're aware that we can become whatever we want to be, as long as it is not physically impossible. (Certain constraints make particular results impossible, such as adding two inches to our height at sixty years of age, or becoming twenty years younger!)

We realize that we have far more power over ourselves than do our parents, the government, the media, or any other person or institution. Once awakened, we refuse to swallow whole what we hear from parents or pastor or the media or other institutions. We are responsible for our own beliefs and our own behaviors, and we appreciate it. Our only limitation is being asleep during our waking hours; this results in fears, lack of vision, and lack of perseverance. However, once awake, we refuse to dwell on our limitations. Instead we focus on our strengths and potential. Marianne Williamson, in her book *A Return to Love*, captures this spirit when she writes:

> [O]ur deepest fear is not that we are inadequate.
> Our deepest fear is that we are powerful beyond
> measure. It is our light, not our darkness, that
> most frightens us. We ask ourselves, Who am I to

be brilliant, gorgeous, talented, fabulous? Actually, who are you not to be? You are a child of God. Your playing small doesn't serve the world. There's nothing enlightened about shrinking so that other people won't feel insecure around you. We are all meant to shine, as children do. We were born to make manifest the glory of God that is within us. It's not just in some of us; it's in everyone. And as we let our own light shine, we unconsciously give other people permission to do the same. As we're liberated from our own fear, our presence automatically liberates others.[5]

We continually and positively express our preferred visions in the present tense (self-affirmations), as if they already exist. This may appear to be a lie to others, and even to ourselves. For example, I say to myself, "I am free from alcohol," as I take a sip of scotch. Our imagination, however, does not know the difference. The imagination assumes I am abstaining from alcohol. The contradiction between my current reality of drinking scotch and the imagined end-state of abstinence dissolves in the face of continual persistence in our affirmations and visualization. We either stop affirming our freedom from alcohol, or we stop drinking! And the more specific, detailed, and concrete our vision and our self-talk, the more successful we are in creating the change we want to see in our life.

When Roger Bannister, a 25–year-old medical student at Oxford University in England, pictured himself running a mile in under four minutes, a feat which had never been achieved before, he was told what most people believed: The human body is incapable of running so fast. In previous Worldviews, many people would accept this statement as the truth. Roger didn't believe it. Rather, his belief in himself and his vision, combined with ability and practice, with perseverance, made it happen on May 6, 1954. Seeing Roger run a mile in 3 minutes and 59.4 seconds, several other athletes then imagined and dreamed of doing the same thing. Shortly afterward, they, too, broke the four-minute-mile record. Fifty years later, more than 2,000 runners around the world had run a mile in less than four minutes; and the world record is now 16 seconds faster.

These incidents reflect British author Frances Hodgson Burnett's outlook when she wrote:

At first people refuse to believe that a strange new thing can be done, then they begin to hope it can be done, then they see it can be done—then it is done and all the world wonders why it was not done centuries ago.[6]

Artists and composers use mental imagery as a part of the creative process. They see, touch, or hear in their imagination what they intend to create. Both Beethoven and Mozart were able to hear complete musical compositions in their mind. They then put the music on paper just as they had heard it in their imagination.

In the medical profession, visualization has long been an effective technique. Experienced, effective surgeons testify that they never go into the operating room, even for the simplest of procedures, without carefully picturing in their mind's eye, usually consciously but often unconsciously, exactly *what* they will do and *how* they will operate on the patient. They clear their mind to mentally picture performing a successful operation, picturing down to the tiniest detail the process of removing the cancer, and picturing the person being healthy again; and then they perform the operation. Mental rehearsal by previously visualizing success enables them to perform the operation successfully exactly as they pictured it.

Visualization is also used in many business organizations as an essential element in the planning process. With the guidance of consultants, employees imagine the kind of organization they want. Once they have a vision of a preferred future, their dream, they collect data to measure current performance. The gap between "what is" and "what could be" creates tension between the vision (the way the employees want it to be) and the way things are or the current perceived reality. Instead of focusing on what is wrong and trying to fix it, members of the organization picture the preferred future every day and in their minds visually appreciate what the company is doing right. This mental activity leads them to seek and find activities which enable them to achieve their dream. If organization members don't lose heart and give up, but continue to persevere in their vision, remarkably, the preferred vision becomes the reality. (See Chapter Nine, The Story of Work.)

Dutch sociologist and futurist Frederick Polak, after spending his life studying the rise and fall of cultures, concluded that "Every single cultural advance was preceded by a utopian image." The image itself was manifest in the language-tone in the people's culture. If people were overly critical of their nation, the country failed to grow and develop. When people spoke optimistically and positively about their nation, the country became strong and productive. When they spoke negatively, the culture began to disintegrate. Hence, how citizens perceive and speak about their country is of vital importance to a culture. Shared perceptions influence language, and the inner dialogue of a community determines the future behavior of the populace for good or ill. If a community imagines a positive future, it develops and thrives. If it visualizes and expresses negativity, Polak found, the community actually declines and fades into oblivion.

When New Millennium Thinkers and Feelers assume that we have the power to transform both our society and ourselves, this realization, together with the expectation that the transformation can happen, gives us hope. It enables us to go beyond blaming parents, politicians, or the enemy for present conditions. We know we can change if we wake up to our potential and are not afraid to dream, or to be laughed at for our utopian ideals. If we persevere in our dream, we will see the benefits of joining with other people's dreams in actively working toward our shared vision.

It all begins when we wake up to thinking and feeling differently.

Awareness

And how do we wake up? Waking up is a process. This is an event which normally doesn't happen in a single moment. Waking up grows on us, sometimes imperceptibly at first. At other times, a significant emotional event or new information, like an alarm clock, shakes us to our foundations, inviting us to wake up and look at life differently. This could be something positive or tragic; it could be election to political office and being faced with new responsibilities. It could be the struggle to cope with the death of a loved one, or a school experience (positive or negative), or a book which throws new light on how to think about the world. For many of us, awakening comes from the experience of living in another country or coming into contact with tragic human suffering.

In waking up, we look at things differently. We step away from the routines in our lives and question the assumptions we've taken for granted. Once awake, as Marianne Williamson suggests, we appreciate ourselves and become aware of the competence and commitment of others. We become personally involved. Seeing the challenges facing us in our current situation, we imagine and dream of what *could be*. We create a new story, our story, which becomes the ideal we work to attain. This story provides a framework to guide our priorities and day-to-day actions. And, joining with others, we build a *shared* dream and, consciously and collectively, create a new and desired state of affairs. We are driven to make our world a different place.

Read again the resounding words of Dr. Martin Luther King, Jr., speaking at the Capitol in Washington, DC, on August 28, 1963:

> I say to you today, my friends, that in spite of the difficulties of the moment I still have a dream. It is a dream deeply rooted in the American dream.
>
> I have a dream that one day this nation will rise up and live out the true meaning of its creed: "We hold these truths to be self-evident; that all men are created equal."

I have a dream that one day on the red hills of Georgia the sons of former slaves and the sons of former slave owners will be able to sit down together at the table of brotherhood.

I have a dream that one day even the State of Mississippi, a desert state sweltering with the heat of injustice and oppression, will be transformed into an oasis of freedom and justice.

I have a dream that my four little children will one day live in a nation where they will not be judged by the color of their skin, but by the content of their character.

I have a dream today.

I have a dream that one day the State of Alabama, whose governor's lips are presently dripping with the words of interposition and nullification, will be transformed into a situation where little black boys and black girls will be able to join hands with little white boys and little white girls and walk together as sisters and brothers.

I have a dream today.

I have a dream that one day every valley shall be exalted, every hill and mountain shall be made low, the rough places will be made plain, and the crooked places will be made straight, and the glory of the Lord shall be revealed, and all flesh shall see it together.

This is our hope. This is the faith with which I return to the South.

With this faith we will be able to hew out of the mountain of despair a stone of hope. With this faith we will be able to work together, to pray together, to struggle together, to go to jail together, to stand up for freedom together, knowing that we will be free one day.

Martin Luther King, Jr., awakened by the experience of racial injustice, focused on his dream. His dream captivated his life. He thought of almost nothing else. Emerging Thinking and Feeling tells us that, if we share his vision, and picture it clearly and daily in our mind's eye, it will emerge and gradually become a part of our story, too, because: What we consistently think about doing, we invariably do.

The opposite is also possible. If the majority of us are not conscious of his dream, or if we write it off as unrealistic or even unwelcome, or if we deem it unimportant, the dream will not come into being. We have the power to suppress it, or we can make it authentic. It is ours to determine.

In King's last speech, in Memphis, Tennessee, the evening before he was assassinated, he seemed to have a premonition of his impending death. That night, King compared himself to Moses, who, 5,000 years before, had led the Jewish people for forty years through the desert to the edge of the Promised Land. Moses, however, died before he could enter the Promised Land. Moses could only gaze upon it from atop a nearby mountain and imagine it for his Jewish people. And so, the night before Martin Luther King's death, apparently he saw it coming. He ended his address with these words:

> Let us rise up tonight with a greater readiness. Let us stand with a greater determination. And let us move on in these powerful days, these days of challenge, to make America what it ought to be. We have an opportunity to make a better nation. And I want to thank God, once more, for allowing me to be here with you.
>
> . . . I don't know what will happen now. We've got some difficult days ahead. But it really doesn't matter with me now, because I've been to the mountain top. And I don't mind. Like anybody, I would like to live a long life; longevity has its place. But I'm not concerned about that now. I just want to do God's will. And He's allowed me to go up to the mountain. And I've looked over. And

> I've seen the promised land. I may not get there with you. But I want you to know tonight that we as a people will get to the promised land. And I'm happy tonight, I'm not worried about anything. I'm not fearing any man. Mine eyes have seen the glory of the coming of the Lord.

As women and men gathered around him in love and friendship, King found in them a new source of inspiration for his dream. He did not walk alone; he was gifted with friends who shared his vision. They were essential both to the dreaming process itself and to carrying the dream forward.

Martin Luther King, Jr., understood the Brazilian proverb, "When I dream alone, it is just a dream. When we dream together, it is the beginning of reality. When we work together it is the creation of heaven on earth." Martin Luther King, Jr., continues to be an inspiration for those who share his dream.

The New Millennium Emerging Worldview Story is based upon the belief exemplified in King's thinking: It is possible to think, feel, and act differently. We can, and do, change ourselves and our environment.

Implications

We wake up by becoming aware of and taking seriously what occurs in our world. Instead of allowing ourselves, as we see pain and suffering, to become discouraged or cynical, we are motivated to create compelling and positive visions of the future. These events touch our thoughts and feelings, which trigger our imagination.

AWARENESS, IMAGINATION, ACTION

Hunger in the World

<u>Awareness</u>: Watching a special on television, we learn that *eight million* people are dying of starvation and malnutrition each and every day. Our hearts are open to the suffering of these starving innocent people.

Imagination: We picture a world free from hunger; people having enough to eat and able to contribute to the benefit of others. We appreciate what organizations such as Mercy and Sharing[7] are doing in Haiti.

Action: We gather a group of citizens, arrange through our local government to obtain a plot of land, and start a cooperative garden in a poor city neighborhood; or we support other organizations working to feed the hungry. Some of us volunteer at nongovernmental organizations (NGOs). We become aware globally and we act locally.

Education/Justice

Awareness: Far from being depressed by the deterioration of our urban schools and neighborhoods, or by the rise of violent crime, or by the unlawful behavior of some police officers and politicians, we stay positive. Justice is a significant value for us as we awaken.

Imagination: We visualize everyone having a fair and equal opportunity to live meaningful lives through learning in excellent schools. We visualize children graduating and applying their talents in work which is significant, satisfying, and meaningful.

Action: We work together with like-minded persons to improve our schools and neighborhoods. We enable families who have loved ones incarcerated to visit them more easily. We organize groups of citizens to visit people in prison. We also work to change the justice system: from seeking punishment to achieving genuine rehabilitation and reconciliation.

As we have seen throughout this chapter, becoming aware of difficulties and tragedies is not the only way to create change. Without hitting the proverbial bottom (as described in Alcoholics Anonymous meetings: before a person musters the motivation to overcome drinking), many New Millennium Thinkers and Feelers use their imagination and faith in themselves to develop a vision of what could be. Collectively, we then determine to make it happen.

CONCLUSION

We realize that the alternatives we face tomorrow are a consequence of the way we think and act today. People like Martin Luther King , Jr., and Roger Bannister give us hope; they acted in the face of huge challenges, never giving up, but persevering and effectively achieving their dreams. With confidence, we find our own individual way, and collective ways, of making practical and meaningful contributions to the well-being of ourselves and our neighbors worldwide.

We create change, not only for ourselves but for our community and world, by creating a common vision, a common dream. We come together in relationship, and stand together, not necessarily in absolute agreement or unanimity, but with consensus. Together we develop a collective vision of what could be and then we make "our story" a reality.

To arrive at consensus we say: "Our agreement isn't perfect, but it's the best we can do, given our present knowledge and circumstance." Rather than being stuck or held back by constraints, we find ways, through dialogue, to go beyond perceived limits—or we manage to make changes within the limitations.

Sharing a dream in the New Millennium has resulted in new accepted norms and new conventional behaviors. Living a shared dream has become a learned behavior. Agreement follows, which energizes us. A new story unfolds.

Our shared dream is what leads to agreeing on the means of achieving what we want and need. Our shared vision enables us to avoid confusion and co-create with one another, so that, together, in relationship, we accomplish what no single individual could possibly do alone. It is "our story" we agree to tell, and live, until another storyteller comes along with even greater and more effective insights.

CHAPTER FIVE

We Perceive That We Are All One

Once we decide that everything is all us, the rest is detail.
Albert Einstein
Renowned Physicist

Man did not weave the web of life; he is merely a strand in it.
Whatever he does to the web, he does to himself.
Chief Seattle
American Indian, Suquamish Leader

Look upon the whole human race as members of one family,
all children of God; and, in so doing, you will see no difference
between them.
Abdu'l-Baha
Baha'i Leader

Ethics is how we behave when we realize we belong together.
Margaret Wheatley
Chaos Theory and Systems Thinker

No man can sincerely try to help another without helping
himself.
Ralph Waldo Emerson
American Essayist

We Perceive That We Are All One

The belief that one's self-interest and another's are identical, because we are united with one another, is the Third Assumption of the New Millennium Story. Acting in our own perceived self-interest is actually enlightened behavior, given that we have come to appreciate our own self-interest as being the self-interest of everyone else in the world. We are all one and yet wonderfully different.

Perceived Separation

Separation from each other is a perception based on Pre-Modern and Modern assumptions, and our senses confirm this. Perceived separation, however, is essentially a matter of socialization, a result of our upbringing. Separation is not necessarily the way things are. It isn't the only story.

Another way to relate to the world, another possible story, is to assume we are all one; we are all connected and form *one essence*. Hence, it is up to us to determine how we want to perceive our own reality.

Perceived Oneness

Putting on a different pair of eyeglasses, we perceive that the universe does not consist of separate humans or objects, as it might seem. We see integrated relationships based on the roles we each play and the function each provides. We see humans, animals, plants, and inorganic matter all connected in our one world. This results in appreciating everything in our existence. We have a reverence for all of nature and for differences. Therefore, we conclude, since we are not separate from other human beings and nature: We cannot harm nature or other humans without harming ourselves. Whatever is in existence, exists for the purpose of bringing benefits to us all.

Roles and Functions

We differ from one another in terms of role and function. Difference, however, does not mean separation. In an educational organization, some are students while others are facilitators of knowledge. Still others are administrators and staff. Although we each play different roles, we all belong to one organization and are grateful for the contribution each individual makes.

When we enter our homes, we play different roles—mothers, fathers, children, and grandparents—yet we all belong to the same family. When everyone performs their role effectively, the family functions in a healthy manner; this results in feelings of happiness.

Besides difference in our roles, we are different in other ways. Although we have one body, the hand performs differently from the leg. The heart performs differently from the kidney, the eye from the ear.

There is an expression in Thailand: "There must be a little finger and a thumb." Both are needed for the hand to function appropriately. Just as the thumb cannot function effectively without the finger, so we humans cannot function effectively without each other. We are all one, and each is essential and necessary for the well-being of us all. As a consequence, we appreciate and value differences in religious belief and political conviction as well as in sex, color, language, and ethnicity. Following New Millennium assumptions, we see these differences as blessings rather than threats.

Analytical Thinking

At the beginning of the twenty-first century, our world is dominated by Modern Worldview thinking. The Moderns assume that scientific explanations are the only acceptable forms of knowledge. Many believe that these scientific explanations are "the truth." *Analytical* (reductionist) *thinking* is promoted, while *systems thinking* is largely denigrated or ignored.

The analytical worldview model assumes the best way to learn about something is to take it apart and find out how, and of what, it is made. Analytical thinking assumes that a thing is nothing but the sum of its parts. Often ignored are the connection and relationship of the parts.

When we use the analytical model in our everyday life, we tend to focus on isolated parts of a system; then we wonder why our most difficult life challenges are rarely addressed with successful results. We perceive "things" or "events" in isolation since we assume separation, rather than interrelationships and interdependencies. We tend to see static frames rather than patterns of change.

Analytical and purely rational thinking emphasizes the value of our immediate sense perceptions (for example, responding with punishment for misbehavior, rather than educating ourselves to understand what is motivating this misbehavior in order to apply this knowledge to achieve equality and civil peace). In addition, analytical thinking neglects the importance of our feelings/emotional responses. This reductionism and rational thinking further promotes the assumption that we are separate from one another.

Systems Thinking

Systems thinking suggests that everything is part of a larger, interdependent whole. Systems thinking understands we are people together on this planet who are part of a massive web of interrelationships. We're not entirely self-sufficient, and we're not part of a closed system! We are part of an open system, attracted and attached to each other by the merging of *interrelated* thoughts, feelings and actions. The way we pay attention to one another, the way we react, think, and communicate with one another, as well as how we adapt to changes in the lives of each other—all are crucial in determining the health of our relationships.

In systems thinking, our environmental boundaries are arbitrary. We can bind a system as we wish, to fit it to a specific function. The *boundary* of the system depends on its function and how we perceive it; there is no permanent "outside." In terms of function, we might view the system in one way at one moment and another way the next moment. A medical team, for example, may focus solely on the eye when removing a cataract. Later, they may focus on the patient's hand-eye coordination. At another time, the person's body and immediate environment become the focus as examination and intervention view the total body, including its emotions, plus the environmental stresses in the individual's life. Each time, the boundary changes according to our focus. At one moment, the body is the environment; at another time, what is outside the body is the environment, when the focus includes both the eyes *and* how they function—what they are actually able to see.

Our survival and development based on the New Millennium Story depend on our assuming we are all together in one system. To survive and develop depends on our assuming we have different functions, but the same purpose.

We no longer assume that the major challenges of our age can be understood and addressed in isolation. We are not separate from the rest of the world—we are united with it. Our difficulties and challenges are not caused by someone or something on the outside, but primarily by our own actions.

Interdependence

Increasingly, we are living in a globally interconnected world in which all of us are interdependent. Varied cultural perspectives facilitate a synergistic approach in which the whole is greater than the sum of its parts. Through an integration of ideas and actions, a genuine security and a higher quality of life result for everyone. We are all better off because of those who lived in the past and those yet to come, and because all the animals and plants, and the mountains and the streams, are one with us—and we see this when we look beyond ourselves and see the big picture.

Pre-Modern and Modern Thinking often separates and attacks problems in isolation as if they had no relationship to anything else. We try to fix a pounding headache without realizing an infected tooth is involved. We try to address poverty without consideration of education and employment issues. We attack so-called "terrorists" without seeking to understand their motivation in attacking us. We focus on making money without regard to the damage we are doing to the environment.

Transformation

Together, in the Emerging Worldview Story, we have the capacity to view the whole system and experience the possibility of total renewal through transformation. Transformation is not possible, however, through the efforts of individuals thinking and acting on their own, or leaders directing much of the work. We are dependent on one another's heads, hearts, and bodies. We need one another in order to successfully address the major challenges in our society. Because we as a society realize we are interdependent and interconnected, and address the big picture, we discover that we function much more effectively.

Functioning Democratically

As we grow in our discovery of our oneness, we realize it makes sense to act as one. Therefore, approaches agreed upon democratically form the basis of our conventions, norms, and laws, which we monitor constantly. Continual transformation of the system, as a whole, results not only in personal survival, but in a meaningful existence with everyone loving one another through loving ourselves.

No long-term/short-term distinction exists. Actions taken now have effects which will last for years, decades, and lifetimes to come—just as what we experience now are the results of actions taken in the past, even the distant past. Because we recognize that we have been polluting rivers for many years and thus killing the fish, we realize it will take longer to restore life and purify the waters than it did to pollute them.

From Competition to Cooperation

Once we recognize our oneness and our need to act as one, cooperation, rather than competition, follows. Professor Alfie Kohn has suggested that there are three ways of achieving our goal of reaping the greatest benefits with the least cost: 1) competitively, which means working against others; 2) cooperatively, which means working with others; and 3) independently, which means working alone without regard to others. Professor Kohn states:

There is a difference between allowing one person to succeed only if someone else does not, on the one hand, and allowing that person to succeed irrespective of the other's success or failure, on the other. Your success and mine are related in both competition and cooperation (though in opposite ways); they are unrelated if we work independently.[1]

Competition with others, out of a primary concern for our own individual well-being without much consideration for others, can be described as self-centered, self-absorbed, and narrow-minded behavior.

The Pre-Modern and Modern practice of attempting to beat, or defeat, others derives from the assumption that our success and our benefits depend on the failures of others. It is a zero-sum game. If I win, you lose, and vice versa.

In both the short and the long term, this assumption is harmful to the common good and to our personal good as well. When we perceive ourselves as rivals, it becomes difficult to recognize our connectedness and build an overall sense of community. Rivalry leads to envy, jealousy, resentment, distrust, and Prozac. Competition establishes an antagonism which contributes to, rather than diminishes, feelings of bitterness and hostility.

In competition, therefore, we make enemies of our neighbors. Competitive philosophy militates against the experience of community. Lack of community is a central characteristic of the dominant Modern Worldview society. In many places, strangers rarely greet one another unless they need help. Acquaintances barely express pleasantries. A genuine concern for one another is often lacking.

Bertrand Russell has written (bracketed interpolations mine):

There is . . . no way of dealing with envy [and, we would add, with feelings of jealousy, resentment, and distrust as well] except to make the lives of the envious [jealous, resentful, and distrusting] happier and fuller, and to encourage in youth the idea of collective enterprises rather than competition.[2]

Modern Worldview thinking appears to be unconsciously convinced that the results of competition are normal and natural occurrences, even necessary for personal and financial growth and development. We are told that competition is "just human nature." Indeed, such thinking insists competition against others is necessary to improve quality of life for everyone. At the same time, businesses, while exalting capitalism, make every effort to eliminate their competition by forming monopolies in an effort to control the market, thus limiting the "free market."

New Millennium Thinkers and Feelers, on the other hand, are empathetic and reach out to serve others—whether they live next door, are in distant lands, or are generations yet to be born. In so doing, we actually serve ourselves—because we are all one. We believe that when we cooperate, rather than compete, we experience a win-win reality. We consciously assume, therefore: *Cooperative* behavior is human nature; *competitive* behavior is not.

The New Millennium Story suggests that people working cooperatively with each other achieve their goals without the high costs of bitterness and hostility. When a critical mass of people act on this assumption, cooperation rather than competition becomes the norm.

From Exclusive to Inclusive Thinking

To change ourselves and influence the world, we need to begin with the way we *perceive* ourselves. A person who believes: What is beneficial for me alone is beneficial, tends to be self-absorbed and does not engage in systems thinking. Such egocentricity makes it difficult for her/him to truly hear, understand, appreciate, and be grateful to others.

New Millennium Thinkers and Feelers perceive themselves as individually part of the total system. They have an ever-increasing vision of the totality of beneficent life, including everyone and everything. We assume that what is beneficial for others is ultimately beneficial for us. What benefits the rain forests in Brazil also benefits the climates in the rest of the world. In addition, it ultimately facilitates the provision of homeopathic remedies, a gift to all of us found only in Brazil's Amazon forest.

We realize that viewing the common good, together with achieving personal good, is a sign of wisdom. What is good for everyone is good for anyone, and vice versa. What benefits one person is *not* genuinely of benefit unless it is beneficial to everyone.

Inclusive thinking and feeling, therefore, trumps exclusive thinking, when we assume we are all one. Although many of us may have different wants and feelings, the health of our planet depends on our thinking inclusively, not exclusively. By thinking inclusively, we agree to accept responsibility for the well-being of the whole.

We have learned to moderate our personal appetites with the ethic of living in responsible ways, such as sustaining the environment so that others, now and in the future, can not only survive, but thrive. Excluding the interests and well-being of others destroys our ability to cooperate, co-create, and have empathy. It frustrates our ability to integrate our not-so-opposing ideas and values.

In no way does this suggest, however, that we need to stop thinking individually and simply conform to the group. Rather, inclusive thinking calls us to use dialogue to find ways to integrate differing points of view. (See the comments on dialogue in Chapter Three.) When we truly listen to others with empathy, we include them and find ways to include their ideas.

Systems Thinking: Nick's Story

Consider the example of Nick, a virile, self-centered young man whose world is incredibly small because he perceives that only what is good for Nick is good—period. His assumption is based on the belief that he is the center of the universe. He doesn't even realize that his alienation from others is caused by his own egoism—not to mention that his limited concern does absolutely nothing to help sustain the larger cultural systems. But Nick is soon to come to a cultural *systems* consciousness. Oh, yes. Nick wakes up, all right. He's awakened by a significant emotional event. And her name is Kristel.

At first Nick is attracted to Kristel's legs, the way they look when she walks toward him in her Gucci stilettos. But then he begins to love her simply because Kristel is Kristel. For him, it is true love: seeking the good of the beloved—as well as true affection: "I want to spend most of my time with you." (See Chapter Seven on Intimacy.)

As is wont to happen after such an experience, Kristel begins to love Nick, too—and they get married. Marriage is a strategy for spending loads of time together. And, also as is wont to happen, not all is smooth sailing. But perceived weaknesses and limitations do not destroy the respect and love they have for each other. They do *not* try to change each other. Both *accept* their differences, and through talking about them (intimacy through dialogue), they often reach consensus; but if not, they at least laugh about it (intimacy through humor). Cooperation, rather than competition. Love is a catalyst for deep, affectionate involvement, whether it is involvement with a significant other or involvement with the greater world.

In discovering the unique worth in Kristel, Nick has discovered his own value as a person. From this experience of intimacy, and by widening his boundaries, he finds that his world has become twice as large, doubly blessed. In addition, he has the experience of being personally vulnerable. This vulnerability naturally leads to intimacy; and intimacy is the potential for ecstasy.

Through intimate ecstasy, Nick realizes that what is beneficial for Kristel is beneficial for him as well. In truly caring for each other, they find that their respective self-interests are inseparable. When Kristel, recovering from a siege of the flu, feels better, Nick feels better. Or if Kristel suffers from crippling arthritis, Nick suffers, too. His life is less complete, less "good," when Kristel is not well. Our Nick has come a long way by moving beyond his solitary, self-centered, before-Kristel existence. Meaning and worth have been added to his life because of his caring for Kristel, who, in return, cares for him. His narrow world has expanded. And there's more to come.

Nick's world begins to expand even more—exponentially—when along come the twins, Jennifer and Jay. Nick's self-interest has again changed, because what is beneficial for the twins, as well as for Kristel, is in his own self-interest. After all, he loves and cares for his family. They are an interdependent, interconnected family *system* of four. And his family system has now become his own personal dream.

But look what happens next, exponentially speaking.

To the degree that Nick cares for his family, and to the degree that he believes in himself and his own power, he is motivated to act on his environment, to make it good and healthful for his family. This happens when Nick "wakes up" and visualizes his children receiving an excellent education. He pictures their schools as safe and happy places for learning, and eating peanut butter sandwiches, and growing. He concludes that such an educational *system* is beneficial to him and his personal dream, and is worth pursuing.

Similarly, Nick conceives of an effective police force protecting his children from sexual predation or physical assault when they walk to school or to the local playground to play tag with their friends or climb on the jungle-gym. He realizes that a competent, committed, and adequately paid police force is in his self-interest. And he appreciates and values the benefit of other helpers in the community: fire department, garbage removal, street repair, an excellent library, good medical personnel and facilities, as well as parks where one-and-all can commune with nature—all with their own system. However, recognizing that he cannot manage these issues alone, Nick seeks the assistance of others outside his own family. With his personal systems thinking, Nick feels more confident about caring for his family.

The more *confident* Nick feels, and the more he recognizes his ability to make a difference, the more *involved* he becomes.

He's motivated to improve his neighborhood schools, police and fire departments, libraries, garbage removal—because he realizes that what is good for his neighborhood is good for himself and for his family. And he is willing to pay for it—even if this means higher taxes. He stretches his boundaries to include his neighborhood in his family system.

Nick quickly appreciates that working with his neighbors is far more effective than working alone. Just as he needs both himself and Kristel to properly raise Jennifer and Jay in their matching overalls, he needs his neighbors—who drop in at random to tell him kindly how to drive a nail—to create a positive neighborhood environment. As he and his neighbors listen to their collective voices after watching their individual football games, imagination and creativity come alive. Mutual affinity grows. This mutual attraction enables Nick and his neighbors, through dialogue, to visualize a better neighborhood. He and his neighbors then create what they have visualized, as we have seen in Chapter Four. Nick's systems thinking is working for the good of all.

As Nick's involvement increases, it becomes evident that his neighborhood, like Nick himself, is not an island. In order to have excellent schools, appropriate security for his children, well-lighted and properly repaired streets, clean water, and effective garbage disposal, the neighborhood needs the resources of the city's system. He and his neighbors cannot, by themselves, continually improve their neighborhood. The problem of unemployment and the experience of neighbors losing their jobs present too great a challenge for Nick and his neighbors to manage. They need the city's help and realize that what is healthful and beneficial for their city is ultimately healthful for their families, and is consequently in their own self-interest. Nick's systems thinking, each time it expands, adds value to his life and the life of everyone in his ecosystem.

Nick's world has undergone spectacular growth, resulting in his becoming confident and committed through love and affection for his family and neighbors. He now understands that his oneness with others will lead to the successful realization of his personal dream. *His* dream has now become *their* dream. No one is excluded as his boundaries further expand.

And expand they do, yet again, because it naturally follows that active involvement, springing from his love and affection for his family and neighbors, enlightens Nick to further appreciate that the city needs to see the state government prosper. And, as expected, in turn, states or provinces in every nation need *federal* involvement in order to properly serve their people. Big government is no longer the villain!

Unemployment, natural disasters such as the tsunami in Asia (2004), Hurricane Katrina in North America (2005), the oil gushing in the Gulf of Mexico, and worldwide dangers from so-called terrorists all present challenges beyond the scope of cities and provinces. These must be addressed by, or in cooperation with, the federal government. Nick becomes a practical patriot. He and his colleagues assist the federal government rather than criticize it.

Nick realizes that the United States, his home, is interdependent, interconnected, and—yes—one with the rest of the planet. What is happening to the world's forests, oceans, and atmosphere has direct impact on the United States, China, and all other nations on the planet. The needs of all nations of the world, including the United States, can be adequately addressed only when citizens consider the benefits to the *whole* planet through sytems thinking. Hence, Nick realizes that it is in his self-interest to be a citizen of the world. In front of his home he flies the flag of the United Nations. What is good for the planet is good for Nick. What a revelation!

CONCLUSION

The New Millennium Worldview assumes that we as human beings are *part of*, rather than *apart from*, everything else. We are not separate from animals, plants, or any of nature's processes or laws. Our involvement with any aspect of existence ultimately affects all other aspects. We rise and fall as one.

Individuals whose only concern is their own survival, without consideration of others, disregard (and many times even destroy) the environment in which they live, eventually causing their own demise. Persons who actively seek harmony within themselves and with their environment form a cooperative and symbiotic relationship. Both person and environment flourish.

For one person to succeed, others need to succeed as well. Cooperating with one another also has a synergistic effect: the benefits arising from the behaviors of enlightened people working cooperatively are greater than the sum of the good which comes from individuals working separately.

All of us, with our handicaps, challenges, and opportunities, are part of the same system. We come to realize there is no such thing as an adversary. In developing love and empathy, we treat others as they want to be treated. When we are at one with someone, we are at one with ourselves; this brings peace and peacefulness.

Analytical thinking is linear. Perceiving the world from a linear perspective, as do Pre-Modern and Modern Worldviews, leads to comparing ourselves with others. We then convince ourselves we are superior to others, blaming them for our difficulties. Pre-Modern and Modern thinkers spend an immense amount of time and energy in fault-finding and punishing those whom they perceive to be acting irresponsibly. People are separated into the responsible and the irresponsible (good and bad, worthy and unworthy, winners and losers), the former treated with respect and admiration, the latter blamed and even condemned.

When we think systemically, we see everyone, including ourselves, as responsible for challenges (*problems* to the Moderns) generated by the system. This, in turn, leads to new insights into what can be done and how we can act together to improve the system and accomplish our common goals. Time and energy are devoted, not to finding who is at fault and punishing them, but to making the total system better for all of us.

In the New Millennium Story, we shift our thinking from seeing only parts to seeing wholes as well. We move from seeing ourselves and others as helpless spectators to seeing ourselves as responsible participants in shaping our reality. We progress from reacting to the present to being proactive in the present, which is inseparable from the past and the future. Our actions create our own future, as we have seen in Chapter Four.

Assuming we are not alone, we become sensitive to the different values held by others. We begin to imagine new possibilities for ourselves by seeing life at more than just face value. We no longer view life as a zero-sum game of we-win/you-lose, or vice versa. Advancing the interests of others does not create a loss for ourselves. We realize we maximize points in the game of life by taking the interests of others into account. I am you, and you are me; together we stand as one. We appreciate that we, ourselves, have the responsibility and opportunity to self-examine, to bring ourselves to account, to acknowledge our part in failures, and to change our present behavior.

Whenever we do not measure up to our own standards, we invite constructive feedback and are then motivated to improve our performance, becoming ever more responsible for ourselves and others—because we are all one.

CHAPTER SIX

We Always Do What We Perceive Is Best

Whatever someone does, he does for the good.
Thomas Aquinas
Medieval Theologian

Every human act is completely selfish. The only difference between the benefactor and the scoundrel lies in the value systems upon which they base their actions.
Peter P. Dawson
Professor of Organizational Development

There is no such thing on earth as unselfishness . . . There is only good selfishness and bad selfishness. Good selfishness is when I help me and you, and society benefits; bad selfishness is when I help me and you, and society pays the price . . . What we need to do is practice good selfishness.
John Bryant
Operation Hope, Los Angeles, California USA

We Assume We Always Do What We Perceive is Best

In the New Millennium Emerging Worldview Story, the Fourth Assumption states that, when we are mentally healthy, we *always* do what we perceive is best in any given situation and moment. Human beings never do anything we perceive as bad for us long-term. Once we are convinced a certain action is the "best" for us, we are *not* free to do or act otherwise. Everything we do, we do with the best of intentions. We are incapable of freely choosing to do evil. We need to somehow persuade ourselves that our action is good in order to do it. Consequently, rationalizations are a common phenomenon. Clearly, the New Millennium is an evolving experience, not an end state.

Acting in Our Perceived Self-Interest

In his *Summa Theologica,* concerning the goal of the human person, Thomas Aquinas writes, "Whatever someone does, he does for the good." In other words, every human being is absolutely, and without exception, oriented toward the "good" as he or she perceives it—a perception of goodness determined by a very personal value system. Hence, the New Millennium Worldview assumes that no one ever acts without the intent of doing good. No one could ever do something for the "bad," as he or she perceives and judges it.

U.S. President George W. Bush, in commanding troops to invade Iraq, valued promoting democracy in that Middle Eastern country. He sincerely believed he acted on behalf of the Iraqi people as well as the American people. Based on his values and his judgment, he could not act otherwise without new information, information contrary to his understanding of the situation at that time. In this sense, he was not free to act differently without new information to change his mind.

We Act on Purpose

Although we don't often think about it, all of our actions have purpose. We may be unaware of what our purpose *is* in every single action, but nevertheless, whatever we do, we do on purpose. Our purpose is influenced by our perceived mental, emotional, spiritual, and physical wants and needs. Every time we do something, anything, we are doing it for the purpose of achieving some valuable benefit as we perceive it. All actions we take are for the purpose of satisfying our self-interest. In the eyes of others, our perceived self-interest may be difficult to see—because their values may be quite different from our own.

Individuals are not free to *not* act in their own perceived self-interest. We do what we think will result in the most satisfying (or least costly) outcome at any moment in any specific situation. In each case, we do a conscious, or unconscious, cost-benefit analysis. Then, we do what we determine gives the greatest benefit at the lowest cost. To behave this way is natural. To act otherwise would be illogical and senseless.

A garden plant automatically reaches in the direction of the sun. That is its nature. The plant cannot act differently. A hungry lion instinctively eats what the lion perceives as good. It cannot do anything different. As human beings, if we perceive something as good, we will naturally do what seems good to us. We cannot do otherwise, according to New Millennium Assumptions.

Lack of Clarity

The direction of our best interest is not always immediately apparent. What is in our perceived best interest often lacks clarity. Unlike plants and animals, we are able to perceive many alternatives because of our ability to think and feel. Moreover, our wants, thoughts, and feelings are continuously changing. We are also sometimes driven, in part, by our unconscious mind.

Examining Alternatives

Implicit in our effort to determine the best alternative is the recognition of our limited capacity. We cannot consider *every* alternative. As we have seen in Chapter Three, it is not possible to know everything. In terms of systems thinking, we are incapable of seeing the whole picture no matter how hard we try. Thus, in each situation, we look at all the alternatives available to us, and then we must act on the alternative we believe is best for us based on our limited information and our values. We don't actually know, however, what is best for us in a given situation. Therefore, all of us make mistakes, sometimes terribly harmful mistakes. A good example, in my mind, and in terms of my values, is President George W. Bush's invasion of Iraq. Had he known of a better alternative way of achieving his goals, he would have been motivated to act differently.

The more intellectually and emotionally mature we are, the more alternatives we are able to envision. Similarly, the less mature we are, the fewer alternatives come to mind; this results in tunnel-vision and often closed-mindedness. Children appear to make more mistakes than mature adults, albeit less costly, normally, because their situations are less serious.

Another result of not being able to see the whole picture is: We are limited in our consideration of *all the implications of each alternative.* This ignorance results in mistakes. While having good intentions, we don't always do what is best for ourselves, which results in feelings of regret when we become aware of, and admit, our mistakes.

In addition, we often conclude we don't have *time* to consider all alternatives. If we're shopping, for instance, and we have found an attractive jacket at a reasonable price, we question ourselves whether we should continue looking. Even though there may be a more flattering jacket at a better price in some other store, we consider the extra time and effort needed to look for it, adding in the possibility of not even finding it. If we believe the effort of additional shopping isn't worth the possible benefits, we stop shopping and buy the jacket. We no longer look for alternatives.[1] We then convince ourselves that we did the smart thing. When this experience is repeated often, our behavior becomes a habit.

Habits

Habits operate at a level below our awareness. Acting out of habit enables us to focus our attention on other, more pressing matters. Habits are "thoughtless," and a way to economize our time.

When our habits keep us from considering more beneficial alternatives, habits work against us; unbeknown to us, they are not in our self-interest. Were we aware of this dysfunction, we would change our behavior. It's this lack of consciousness that causes us to sleepwalk through life.

Changing Minds and Behaviors

Once the "benefit" of a certain action is clear, like the plants and animals we automatically take the path we perceive is best. As stated, if new or contradictory information comes along, we're motivated—unlike plants—to change our minds so that our new behavior will be in line with our perceived self-interest. Not wanting to admit a mistake, however, keeps many of us from examining new information that may be contrary to our original judgment. If a friend tells us the same jacket could have been purchased at another store at two-thirds the price, we may rationalize by saying that the quality of that jacket is probably not as good. Many of us have been brought up to believe that it is embarrassing to admit we've made a mistake, that we were wrong. Hence, we vehemently defend our decisions in order not to admit we made a mistake.

Sometimes, however, we do change our minds. As behaviorist B. F. Skinner discovered, all organisms will change their behavior if convinced they'll achieve a more satisfactory situation or improve a less-than-satisfactory condition. New and significant information is the major reason we change our minds, along with the motivation to avoid pain and seek pleasure, again in accordance with our values.

Equal Alternatives

What do we do when our available alternatives appear to be equally good? On the rare occasions when we're faced with equally positive (or negative) outcomes, and if the means to achieve those outcomes appear equally satisfactory, only then do we freely choose. In such situations, it's the same as flipping a coin. We make a free choice, but it really doesn't matter which alternative we choose. Each one is equally good or equally bad. Hence, the notion of free choice, in the New Millennium, is meaningless.

If an individual is given the opportunity to visit Hong Kong or Paris, both being of equal appeal to the person, she will normally delay the decision while searching for information suggesting that one city is better to visit than the other. A state of "analysis paralysis" ensues until a preferred alternative emerges, or until the point when further delay would prevent either trip. If one is about to lose the trip to Hong Kong or Paris altogether, and still no information clearly points to a preference, then one is motivated to "choose," perhaps by flipping a coin, one destination over the other, since not to go at all is an unacceptable alternative. Again, free choice exists in this situation but is meaningless, because neither destination is perceived to be better or worse than the other.

Self-Interest and Selfishness

Question: If we always do what we believe is best, are we not therefore selfish? The term "selfishness" is a catch-all phrase which fails to differentiate between different motivations. Tony de Mello, a Jesuit priest and Buddhist interpreter from India, describes three different kinds of "selfishness." (Here I have paraphrased de Mello's three points and have provided most of the examples.)

Selfishness exists[1]

1. When we give ourselves the pleasure of pleasing ourselves:
   - Enjoying a delicious meal at a restaurant
   - Studying and achieving an A in a challenging mathematics exam.
2. When we give ourselves the pleasure of pleasing others:
   - Preparing a healthy and delicious meal for a friend

- Helping someone get a job
- Changing a political structure to ease the gap between the poor and the rich.
3. When we please others to avoid experiencing a bad feeling:
   - Interrupting the pleasure of watching an intriguing TV drama in order to deal with someone else's concerns—as when a teacher abandons the TV to listen to a student's problem on the telephone, so as not to be disliked by the student or to avoid getting into trouble with the school administrator
   - Giving money to the poor so others will not perceive us as stingy or greedy.[2]

De Mello's third category denotes actions based on avoiding pain; the pain of being disliked by the student, the school administrator or the pain of not being seen as generous (given that generosity is a value we hold dear) is avoided. Our motivation is to avoid displeasure, rather than to receive pleasure.

Avoiding displeasure does not produce the same result as achieving pleasure, according to de Mello. A teacher endures displeasure by interrupting television viewing, to answer a call for help by a student. But we doubly lose out because we lose the pleasure received when we wholeheartedly assist a student. We also pay emotionally because of our resentment in giving up the television program. Plus, the student does not receive our best from our merely halfhearted attempt to answer her need. In doing our perceived duty out of resentment, fear, guilt, or shame, we find that the result is less beneficial, to both teacher and student, than if we had acted for the purpose of receiving pleasure. True, we have avoided being known as lacking generosity, but there is little joy in doing our duty. Yet we believe that this is in our self-interest, and better for the student, than refusing to respond to the student at all. We are selfishly doing what we want to do.

Acts of Sacrifice

Action taken from a sense of obligation rather than pleasure or joy, de Mello's third type of selfishness is considered a "sacrifice" in the Pre-Modern and Modern Worldview stories. Doing our duty and sacrificing our lives for our country is considered noble. Changing a baby's diaper out of a sense of duty, or even out of love for the child, is called a "sacrifice" or an "altruistic gesture."

In the Pre-modern and Modern Worldview stories, we perceive ourselves as victims when we "sacrifice" for others. We believe we give up what we want, even though it's painful, so that others will find us noble, nice, or loving. We do our duty, we are "respectable"—but not all that happy about it! We won't rush to do it again. In fact, next time we may well seek to be unavailable.

Calls for sacrifice, doing one's duty, and acting out of moral obligation have been largely ineffective within the Pre-Modern and Modern Worldviews. Sermons, lectures, and commandments calling upon us to generously give to the poor often sadly fall on deaf ears because these pressures are painted with a brush of pain rather than joy. "No pain, no gain," athletes are advised. "Be noble and altruistic, make a sacrifice—give up your life for your country." These admonitions are not attractive to most people, for in heeding them we see ourselves being sacrificial to others, and "giving up" something we like, such as our personal time. We tend to resent what we're doing. And our resentment often increases if we don't receive recognition and appreciation for our "sacrifice." Ultimately, we're not likely to again "make the sacrifice" to assist others. When many people have this same experience over time, the planet suffers from our unwillingness to care for our neighbors, as demonstrated in the assumptions of the Pre-Modern and Modern Worldviews.

In addition to our dissatisfaction and feelings of resentment, we also lose out on the pleasure that one can experience in serving others. The teacher missed out on the pleasure of assisting a student. We, too, miss out on the joy of giving of ourselves if we fail to recognize that what we're doing is actually in our self-interest, because giving is its own reward. Living for others is neither a sacrifice nor altruism. Cheerfully giving to others is singularly selfish—which is a good thing in the New Millennium, because it truly brings us pleasure and joy.

Values

We base our actions on our value system, always acting in accordance with our perceived values—a system formed by our upbringing and our continuing socialization. In the words of Peter Dawson, "The only difference between the benefactor and the scoundrel lies in the value system upon which each base their actions."[3] This view considers the motivation of the lawbreaker's action to be identical to what motivated Mother Teresa of Calcutta, India—namely, what "appears good" to the one and what "appears good" to the other.

Having been Mother Teresa's friend, I can testify that she found great joy in giving herself for the benefit of others. She did not see it as a sacrifice. In relieving the pain of others, she believed she was relieving the pain of Jesus, whom she loved. In her mind, her opportunity to bring relief to another was a blessing, not a sacrifice. Her action was an act of love and it brought her immense joy and gave huge significance to her life.

Perceived Negative Behaviors

What about people who "intend" violence such as rape, robbery, or murder? What about the actions of Osama bin Laden, Saddam Hussein, Pol Pot, or Hitler? Pre-Modern and Modern Worldview thinking labels these people as terrorists, deviants, and evil people, identifying the persons with their behaviors. In degrading language, they are dehumanized; we avoid seeing them as being like ourselves and find it impossible to experience empathy toward them.

The New Millennium Worldview perceives actions of violence, rape, robbery, and murder as having harmful consequences. Society must be protected from persons who do such things. Emerging Thinkers and Feelers do not, however, view rapists, murderers, and robbers as evil persons. We judge their behaviors to be seriously wrong because the consequences are frightfully damaging. However, we see the persons performing the evil acts as good and deserving of respectful treatment, because we assume we are all one. By valuing these persons, and trying to imagine how they view the world, we find that our actions toward them are motivated by respect and love. We don't seek to punish these individuals, but to find a way to rehabilitate them (see Chapter Eleven). Our positive language of appreciating differences enables us to empathize with them in their suffering and pain. We realize that individuals who hurt others are typically victims themselves and their actions are projections of their own pain.

According to the assumptions of the New Millennium Worldview Story, when we treat someone as if they intended to do evil, we're making a very serious mistake. We are failing to understand that no one intends to do evil. For example:

- A destitute person may see the money he steals as his ticket out of a life of poverty or the means of survival for one more day. His intention is to get out of poverty or simply to survive.

- A rapist may believe (often unconsciously) his aggressive actions are a way of proving his strength, domination, and power, based on the way he was brought up. (Let's be clear: this is not an excuse!)

- A murderer may be convinced his deeds are necessary for his own survival. His intention is to survive, and therefore killing another is justified in his own mind as self-defense, or as gaining an opportunity of which he perceives he was unfairly deprived.

- An employee of a munitions factory needs to support his family, so he persuades himself that his work is a patriotic act.

- A pilot may drop a bomb on the perceived enemy and, at the same time, kill innocent women and children. He justifies his action of killing innocents as necessary "collateral damage" in seeking to do his part to end the war.

Almost certainly, Osama bin Laden thought he was acting in the best interest of Islam when planning with his associates to destroy the World Trade Center in New York City. Pol Pot, who mercilessly killed two million of his own Cambodian people (as portrayed in the film *The Killing Fields*), was an ideologue who believed he was bringing into existence a communistic heaven on earth, in which everyone would share in the riches of life. Hitler, too, believed he was doing Germany and the world a favor by mercilessly killing Jews, gypsies, communists, and the disabled. He believed that destroying defective fetuses in the womb or disabled babies after birth was a responsible act, assuming that it would otherwise cost the state an enormous amount of tax monies to care for these "imperfect" human beings.

In Hitler's view, by using disabled babies for research, the Germans might find ways to make the "Aryan race" even healthier and stronger, thus helping millions of people. Others, including myself, possessing a different value system, may view such thinking as "rationalizations" and these behaviors as heinous. Whatever the case, all those mentioned above, and all of us, do what we do because we perceive that it is somehow *good* for ourselves, and perhaps for those we intend to help. Even people who commit suicide apparently perceive their deaths as the least of other evils confronting them.

New Millennium Thinkers and Feelers conclude that each of the individuals described above view, or viewed, their respective situations based on assumptions and values learned and internalized throughout their life. The New Millennium Worldview assumption is that, had these people been brought up differently, had they been conditioned by New Millennium Worldview assumptions, they would have thought, felt, and acted in a vastly different manner.

In the Emerging Worldview Story, we realize that mentally healthy persons do not get up in the morning intent on doing evil. Whatever negatives follow from our actions, in retrospect, we perceive our behaviors as mistakes for which we have deep regrets.

Motivation—We Always Do What We Want

Emerging Thinkers and Feelers realize that no one can motivate us to do anything. We will always do what we want. If you put a gun to my head and demand my wallet, I will give you my wallet. I am *motivated* to save my life, but I am not motivated to give you my wallet—rather, I am "moved" to give you my wallet. I am motivated by an inner drive to do what I perceive is best, namely, save my life. We are always doing what we want. Nobody can *make_us* do *anything* we don't want to do. Once New Millennium Thinkers and Feelers realize this, we feel strong and powerful, even joyful. No matter what happens, we never consider ourselves "victims"!

We understand that the way we perceive reality at present is based on what we were taught by word and example as we were growing up. We "cannot" think and feel otherwise without waking up and learning from new experiences (such as reading this book). Our motivation to perform or avoid certain actions depends on the level of desire for, or dread of, a particular outcome. Perceiving that our actions will lead to a strongly desired outcome, we are automatically highly motivated.

Once a student values an education more than anything else (because of her upbringing), and she believes diligent study will very likely result in considerable learning and growth (based on past experience or observation), she will be motivated to study hard. Goals and action plans will be set, based on these values and beliefs. The student is then *not* free to choose to waste time, and sees no alternative but to study. The student is also *not* free to change her behavior without new information, and is convinced that what she is doing is the best thing to do. The student is motivating herself to do everything possible to achieve the goal of acquiring as much learning as possible. See Figure 6.1

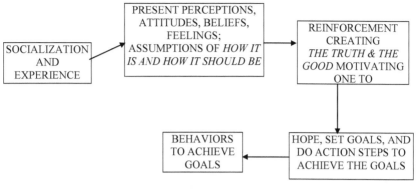

Figure 6.1

We determine our best course of action-at-the-moment by perceiving its anticipated benefit if we should continue or change our behavior. The "goodness" of the benefit is based on our values, which, similar to our beliefs about what is true, derive from our past and ongoing socialization and experience.

Values such as immediate gratification and perceived ease of accomplishment may be important to poverty-stricken inner-city youths who rob a convenience store. Rather than trying to find part-time jobs, or unable to find any, they see the alternative of quick money as *the* best one—if such action fits the youths' conditioned value system, and if they believe they will not be caught.

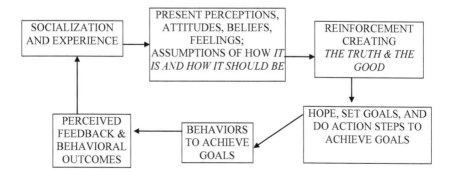

Figure 6.2

If a perceived positive outcome actually occurs as the youths expected (they get the expected amount of money and don't get caught), then they're pleased with themselves and their behavior. They are convinced of the "goodness" of their actions, reinforcing their socialization and increasing the probability that they will rob again. Over time, this repeated behavior becomes a habit. See Figure 6.2.

If, however, the results of their actions are *not* what the youths expected, they then may be motivated to change their behavior. If they get caught, their past experience of robbing is not reinforced. Now, they may be open to a change in their thinking, feeling, and behavior, and will perhaps be open to other means of achieving their desired goal of having money to spend. Fast learners understand and change their behavior quickly; slower learners need to be caught many times before it occurs to them that their strategy is ineffective. See Figure 6.3.

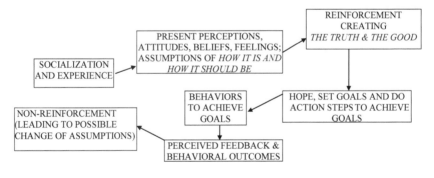

Figure 6.3

The Role of Community in Determining What Is Best

What happens when the New Millennium Worldview community perceives some behaviors as harmful or contrary to the effective functioning of society, as when youths rob a convenience store and are caught?

First of all, in the New Millennium Story, the youths are not punished. The community seeks to educate them. The intention is to influence them to reevaluate their goals and discover a more effective means of achieving what they want. The educational process may seem like punishment to the teens, but, in the minds of their caregiver educators, it is not. Through the competence of the caregivers, and their kindness and respectful treatment, the teens may well wake up and come to understand how changing their behavior, as in earning money through a meaningful job, is in their own long-term self- interest (See Chapter Eleven, on lawbreakers.)

On the other hand, certain young people may perceive an activity as beneficial to the community *before* members of the community recognize it. In this case, the young people seek to find positive ways to demonstrate, or persuade society of, the benefits of change. Young people may see that a war currently being waged is not ultimately in the community's best interest. Perhaps through protests as a catalyst to dialogue, youths may educate the community to realize that nonviolence is a more effective means to achieve peace than violence. Rather than blind uniformity, similar dialogues can address such issues as abortion, affirmative action, human rights, gay marriage, redemptive violence (for example, the belief that it is not wrong to kill in the pursuit of peace), and other controversial challenges and opportunities.

Education

Punishment usually results in resentment and turns people into sneaks or, at best, brings *external* compliance only. If the youths who robbed the convenience store are punished, they are not likely to change their attitudes. Upon being released from prison, they're more likely to repeat their negative behavior, gambling that they will not get caught the next time.

From a New Millennium perspective, genuine education changes such behaviors and underlying attitudes, enabling one to internalize new and appropriate behaviors. One comes to reevaluate past actions and is motivated to act differently.

New Millennium Thinkers and Feelers realize we're all "lifelong students." We continually want to learn and facilitate the learning of each other; further, to facilitate the learning of others we need to understand and appeal to their wants, to their self-interest. (See Chapter Ten on Education.)

We understand education to be an influence-process. And we rarely influence others unless we ourselves are open to being influenced. When we genuinely listen to and consider another person's thoughts and feelings, we become open to the other's point of view, and possibly to changing our own minds. Through dialogue, learning occurs in both parties.

But learning takes place only when we are *ready* to learn. To repeat an ancient Buddhist saying: "When the student is ready, the teacher will appear." We are ready when we appreciate that it's in our self-interest to study and learn something in particular, as, for example, to learn to swim, ride a bicycle, or drive a car. We become our own teacher, while being open to ideas and information from others.

The greatest challenge exists when people are not aware of their own wants, or not aware of when it is in their best interest to change. In this book, I have called such lack of awareness "going through life sound asleep"! New Millennium Thinkers and Feelers are *not* disheartened by this sleepwalk through life. Various means of consciousness-raising can be used. Note, for instance, the advertising industry. Advertisers create huge markets by convincing people they "desire" a product which didn't even exist a month before. The consumer then looks to purchase the product, perceiving it is something he wants.

Consciousness-raising occurs through many venues other than advertising. News stories, magazines, television, films, books, and personal experience can heighten awareness. Events such as demonstrations can sometimes trigger a wakeup to different perspectives. Regardless of the method, successful efforts include appeals to the intellect (information) and appeals to the emotions (desires and wants). Once we wake up and begin to think and feel differently, we change our behavior.

Unconditional Love

As human beings, we are never totally independent, as we have seen in Chapter Five. We are dependent on others for our well-being and happiness. We are creatures who want to grow. We perceive others as instrumental to our growth and necessary for the fulfillment of our desires. Since we are not completely self-sustaining, the motivation for all human behavior is to satisfy our wants and desires in and through others.

The Pre-Modern and Modern Worldview stories focus almost completely on our personal human needs. We do things for others based on some condition—namely, their worthiness of our kindness or generosity, or our desire that they will return the favor. Reciprocity is one of the highest values: "I will pay you a just wage on condition that you give me an honest day's work." A mother, though, might claim, "I love my daughter unconditionally; there is nothing she could do that would cause me not to love her." The existing condition, however, is that it is *her* daughter, not someone else's child. She doesn't love *every* child unconditionally, regardless of what they do or how much they get on her nerves. Under previous paradigms, such selfless love is normally reserved only for *her* child, or her grandchild.

New Millennium Thinkers and Feelers are motivated to love everyone, no matter what they do. Everyone's family is *our* family! We love everybody unconditionally, because we assume we are all one. We do, nonetheless, like certain people more than others, which is perfectly normal. Liking and being attracted to others is conditioned by distance and time. Our affection for them is limited by the twenty-four hours a day we have available, and by their proximity. (See Chapter Seven on Intimacy.) It follows, then, that the significant-others in our life, our intimate friends, receive most of our time, especially if they're near at hand and not on the other side of the planet. Thus, because of our finiteness, it may *appear* that we love—in the sense of being attracted to—some more than others.

CONCLUSION

The New Millennium Emerging Worldview assumes we automatically move toward what we perceive as being good for ourselves. We aren't free to do what we perceive is bad for us.

Moreover, everyone has good intentions—each person is always doing what is perceived to be in his or her own self-interest. Recognizing the good intentionality of people does *not* lessen personal responsibility, however. On the contrary, it makes it easier for us to accept personal responsibility for consequences, both intended and unintended—because we ourselves are not condemned as "evil" when harmful consequences result from our actions.

Recognizing that other people always act with good intentions has enormous implications for each of us personally. We now recognize that we, too, act according to our perception of what is best. Just as we no longer condemn people as evil when harmful consequences occur, so we no longer condemn ourselves for our mistakes. We recognize that an action with evil consequences doesn't make a person evil. The psychic cost of admitting our errors has been removed. We are more likely to recognize and admit our mistakes and act more appropriately in the future, since we expect to be understood and forgiven rather than punished. In turn, we understand and forgive others. Forgiveness acknowledges that what has happened in the past cannot be changed, and forgiveness enables the forgiver to trust again. It is extremely difficult to trust again after we've been disappointed; but, as New Millennium Thinkers and Feelers know, it is possible.

Significantly, if our own behavior results in negative consequences for ourselves and others, we do not blame others. We accept the responsibility to learn from our mistakes. We recognize we are trying to do well, even if we miss the mark. We treat ourselves with compassion and understanding, just as we treat others with compassion and understanding. We expend our energies in learning and in adjusting our behavior, rather than in denial, defensiveness, and guilt.

In seeking to change our behavior, we understand that we need to change our assumptions and perceptions with regard to how we look at life and what we value.

One change worth considering is to accept the validity and practicality of the Four Basic Assumptions, and to note how our behavior changes as a consequence.

The following eight chapters tell stories of what happens when we wake up, accept these challenges, and make these assumptions: a wonderful opportunity to learn more, and an invitation to our imagination. A new story for all of us to behold! Enjoy and trust the process.

CHAPTER SEVEN

The Story of Intimacy

In India, when people meet and part they often say, "Namaste," which means: I honor the place in you where the entire universe resides; I honor the place in you of love, of light, of truth, of peace. I honor the place within you where if you are in that place in you and I am in that place in me, there is only one of us. . . "Namaste."
Ram Dass
Spiritual Leader

Love alone is capable of uniting living beings in such a way as to complete and fulfill them, for it alone takes them and joins them by what is deepest in themselves.
Pierre Teilhard de Chardin
Jesuit Priest and Anthropologist

Loving people live in a loving world. Hostile people live in a hostile world, but it is the same world. How come?
Wayne Dyer
Spiritual Counselor

The more you love—be it others, yourself, the world, or what truly matters to you—the more you experience love. By loving deeply and fully we fill ourselves with compassion and generosity. Giving love changes our experience, how we think and feel about our world.
Bruce Elkin
Organizational Consultant

What Is Intimacy?

Intimacy, in the New Millennium Worldview, is a relationship with one's self, or with others, in which our innermost, deepest, and most sensuous being is recognized, accepted, affirmed, and shared openly and honestly. Intimacy leads us to a deep sense of connection, a sense of communion and shared identity—without losing our own self. Such a relationship is manifested in our desire to share time and space and activities with intimate others, experiencing what we call friendship. The more intimate the relationship, the deeper and more loving and affectionate the friendship.

Intimacy is a significant key to a good, useful, and satisfying life. Organizational consultant Niels Christensen suggests that there are three types of intimacy:

1. Intimacy with one's self, in the sense of being comfortable in one's own skin.

2. Intimacy with other human beings in relationship, as described above.

3. Intimacy with one's larger surroundings, whether one calls this nature, the universe, or God. (See Chapter Fourteen.)

Like so many other things, these three types of intimacy are interdependent and interconnected; each is a cause and a reflection of the others. Christensen further states that "Human beings long for intimacy of all three types."[1]

Intimacy Is Different from Love

In the New Millennium, we understand love as: seeking the good of the beloved. Although we love everyone, we are intimate and affectionate with only those whom we like, people we find attractive. The more we like them, the more attractive they appear to us, the more we desire to spend time with them, the more we want to be around them. Intimacy is measured by the amount of time and space we seek to share with intimates. Able to be in only one place at a time and having only twenty-four hours in a day, we recognize that our ability to be with the people for whom we have affection is limited. We can love everyone, but are capable of being intimate and affectionate with only a significant few. Intimacy, unlike love, is a relationship which goes beyond seeking the happiness of another. Intimacy with another means we wish to share our lives in many ways—with co-workers, friends, sexual lovers, spouses, and family. To be intimate with them presumes that we love them. When we marry another, we are saying, "I like and love you so much, I want to spend most of my time and space on earth with you."

Intimacy in Action

To be intimate means to share with another, openly and honestly, our own story: our feelings, thoughts, and wants—in other words, sharing what is important and what is going on within us *now* , as well as sharing our significant history and our hopes for the future.

At one end of the intimacy continuum is complete nonexistence, that is, being closed and self-protective; at the other end of the continuum is deep intimacy, being totally open and honest—with varying degrees of intimacy and honesty in between. (See Figure 7.1.)

CLOSED _____ OPEN

Self-Protective   Honest
                                                         Willing to Risk
No Intimacy   High Intimacy

Figure 7.1

The more secretive and confidential we are about our lives—particularly about our feelings, thoughts, and desires—the closer we are to the Closed end of the continuum.

The more our life is an open book—the more we honestly and concretely express our feelings, thoughts, and wants to another—the closer we come to the Open end of the continuum.

Being open and honest in expressing our positive feelings for others leads to reciprocal intimate responses and feelings of affection; this in turn brings us gifts of meaning and joy.

A few examples of sharing our feelings with others:

- "What joy! Oh, Bruce, I'm so happy you and Jody are engaged!"
- "I'm experiencing feelings of sadness and depression as I can't help thinking about all the women and children dying of starvation in the Pakistani flood!"
- "You're scaring me to death talking about suicide all the time."

When feelings come too close for comfort, we sometimes use sidestepping as a defense mechanism preventing intimacy.

Suppose Joan says to Peter, breathlessly: "Peter, I love you. I want us to spend the rest of our lives together," only to have him respond with the question: "What is love?" Peter's impersonal response is a defense mechanism to hide his fear of intimacy. He is "playing head games." If Peter were truly open and honest, he would immediately tell Joan how he feels; he would say whether or not he shares a similar love for her. She would hear what he thinks and how he feels about her at this moment. He might respond:

"Oh, Joan, I so wish I had the words to tell you how much I love you, too!"

or:

"I'm really touched by your love for me. I wish I felt the same, Joan, but I'm sorry, I don't."

According to psychologist Marshall Rosenberg:

An intimate connection at the heart level is an action of giving—not a feeling. We call it love. When we give from the heart, we do so out of joy that springs forth whenever we willingly give in order to enrich our own or another's life.[2]

This kind of giving benefits both giver and receiver. Receivers enjoy the gift without worrying about the consequences; we realize the gift is not given out of fear, guilt, shame, exploitation, or a desire for forgiveness. Givers automatically benefit from enhanced self-esteem, the result of seeing our efforts contribute to our own and someone else's well-being. We givers feel better about ourselves. We realize that the secret of happiness is to give.

The Process of Intimacy

Two people come together, drawn by some common interest which carries their initial contact beyond casual acquaintance. Perhaps they both like to collect seashells. Together, they wander along the beach, shoulder to shoulder, searching for shells and carefully placing them in a child's pail they have found.

Soon the relationship reaches a turning point. As they sit on the sand, the pail between them overflowing with seashells, they begin to carefully inspect the shells. Suddenly, they look up and gaze affectionately into each other's eyes: an invitation to intimacy. What will they do? If frightened by vulnerability—fear of revealing their feelings, thoughts, and desires—they might quickly look away, or look down at the seashells. If so, their relationship becomes stuck at the level of sharing shells.

But if they both risk continuing to gaze into each other's eyes, what then? If one of them takes the risk of opening up just a trifle, what will happen? At first, a small opening appears in the armor all of us wear to protect ourselves from a scary world. A bit of the person is revealed—a feeling, a thought.

In turn, if the other person reveals a similar feeling or desire; an intimate encounter results; a deeper connection between the two is made. As the opening in the pair's protective armor widens, both stand exposed, figuratively naked and vulnerable before each other. Nothing is hidden; nothing is secret. At this moment their relationship has progressed beyond sharing shells (ideas and common interests) to sharing *selves* (their wants, thoughts, and feelings, and what they passionately care about).

When we open up and share our inside selves with another, together we discover ever more deeply who we really are. Feelings bloom: feelings of genuine affection for one another and the wish to spend more time together.

Often, unlike the story above, the process of becoming intimate friends takes considerable time and energy. Yet the experience becomes so meaningful and joyful that we realize that being intimate is truly in our own self-interest; then we are motivated to invest our time and energy.

Pre-Modern and Modern Worldview Stories of Intimacy

The assumptions of Pre-Modern and Modern Worldviews make it difficult to be intimate with ourselves or with others. Placing little value on introspection, we tend to avoid paying attention to what we think and feel; we're seldom aware that our outside behaviors are caused by what is going on inside us. At best, we review our past to learn from our mistakes, and use these past experiences to be more successful in the future. In the present, we act unconsciously—sleep walking through life most of the time. As a result, when we're alone, separate from others, we often feel lonely or bored. Quite frequently we seek out others, and even enter into destructive relationships, simply to escape being by ourselves, lonesome and bored.

When we Moderns are among other people, we tend to pay attention to those who pay attention to us. We also notice those we believe can be of benefit to us, or those who may possibly hurt us. For the most part, all others become invisible.

A person's worth is often measured by external criteria such as strength, good looks, education, income, status, the size of one's house, or the cost of one's car. In this case, another's worth and attractiveness implicitly relate to what the individual can do for us. The higher the individual's potential to benefit us, the more worthy he or she is of our attention and respect.

If we're affluent, we're less likely to need the attention of others. We surround our homes with fences or live in gated communities. We see little value in spending time sitting on front porches, chatting with neighbors.

Because Pre-Modern and Modern Worldviewers strongly suggest that there is only one right answer to controversial issues, people seeking friendship are advised to avoid discussing controversial topics such as religion and politics. Conversations revolve around personal health, sports, the past, and the weather. When disagreements arise, attitudes of "peace at any price" are encouraged and practiced to ensure that we get along with each other. This behavior usually results in acquaintances, superficial relationships lacking passion and depth.

Intimacy in Our Current World Crisis

In his book *Global Shift*, psychologist Edmund Bourne discusses a key element of the global crisis in relation to the *lack* of intimacy:

> It is not an overstatement to say that our current world crisis can be viewed as a primarily *masculine crisis*... Our very way of life is in trouble, as evidenced by the widespread disconnection, alienation, and social fragmentation many of us currently experience. Large numbers of us feel fundamentally disconnected—from nature, from community, from our families, from spirit, and from ourselves. Addictions, to everything from drugs to overwork to unbridled consumerism, are grasped at in an attempt to fill the existential gap, but a basic emptiness remains. We are well-connected electronically, but often disconnected from our own hearts and souls ...
>
> Old paradigms based on traditional masculine values of separateness, hierarchy, and control are gradually giving way to worldviews embracing traditionally feminine values of interrelationship, integration, balance, holism, cooperation, and love . . . not that a feminine-oriented worldview is replacing the masculine . . . The emerging world order reflects a *marriage* of masculine and feminine principles and values.[3]

Many of us Pre-Moderns and Moderns think of ourselves in terms of the traditional masculine paradigm, in black-or-white dualistic terms—good-or-bad, strong-or-weak, tough-or-vulnerable. Taught to make judgments regarding what is objectively proper, we try to hide the bad, feminine, weak, vulnerable self. We wear a mask, pretending to be someone other than who we actually are.

We fear that if others really knew us—knew our bad, feminine, weak, vulnerable self—they would not like or respect us (because we ourselves don't like or respect that part of us). And so we're cautioned not to air our dirty laundry for everyone to see. Moreover, we're encouraged not to say or do anything that others might consider inappropriate. "What will the neighbors think?" is an example from the fountain of taunts that ensure conformity. But hiding our "other" self is an obstacle to genuine intimacy. It makes it difficult for others to relate to us with empathy and compassion, giving the impression that we've "got it together" and don't need anybody!

Fear of judgment or punishment motivates us to hide, not only our feelings, but our perceived weaknesses, along with our mistakes and their consequences. We hide our illness or apologize for being sick, lest we be seen as weak and vulnerable. To be needy or to have made mistakes, *especially* for males in virtually all world cultures, is to be one step down in the competitive game of life. If we want to compete, our weakness and neediness must be hidden at all costs. Depending on others is an obvious sign of weakness. Power, strength, and independence are the highly valued virtues.

So often when we realize that we're in need, we are our own worst enemy. Since we see needs as weaknesses, we pretend to be strong, to be *un-needy*. We use ritualistic behaviors such as responding with "Fine" or "Good" when asked, How are you?" Our society instructs us to hide our thoughts, feelings, desires, and even values, especially if they might be judged as negative.

Punishing Ourselves

We believe that it is normal to feel ashamed of ourselves when we don't measure up to our own values and prescriptions; and this, naturally, adds to our unhappiness. We hear our mother's voice echoing from the past when caught doing something of which she disapproved: "You ought to be ashamed of yourself!" or "Act like a man!" or "The trouble with you is . . ." Some of us are led to punish ourselves by doing penance. Our self-esteem plummets. Listen again to our self-talk: "If others really knew me, they could never love me. I'm too awful! I don't deserve anyone's love."

"Guilt is the gift that keeps on giving," said humor columnist Erma Bombeck. New Millennium Thinkers and Feelers have a sense of humor. The ultrawealthy industry mogul Pierre S. du Pont once said, "You have broken the Fifth Rule, you have taken yourself too seriously. What are the other rules? There are no other rules."[4]

Distancing Ourselves

When we're fearful of being hurt by negative judgments, blame, or punishment, we tend to distance ourselves from others. Distance makes sense, because we believe we're all separate from each other anyway. "Stay away from those who might hurt us," we tell ourselves. We then wonder why life is so lonely and boring. Fear of being hurt, physically or emotionally, motivates us to be careful, under the excuse of being prudent. Hence, in leaving one another, we project our own fearfulness, saying, "Take care!" We are too afraid to encourage one another instead to "Take a risk!"

Blaming

When we don't get what we want in a relationship, our tendency often is to blame the other. We assume that finding fault will solve our problems. Looking for the wrong in others and seeking to "fix" them is typical behavior in the Pre-Modern and Modern stories. Even when we simply express an observation such as "You're looking beautiful today," it's often interpreted as blame or criticism, as though implying: "You don't look beautiful **every** day."

Complaining

Complaining about others in order to get them to change is rarely effective, yet Pre-Modern and Modern thinking encourages this behavior. Evaluating, criticizing, labeling others as lazy, selfish, or not dependable makes sense to us when others fail to behave as we think they "should." This is done with considerable skill by all parties and with no winners. When we advise, "You should study more," or "I should stop smoking," we mean well; yet "should" causes frustration or anger in most of us. Then we wonder why our love and concern, packaged as "shoulds," are neither accepted nor appreciated by ourselves or others.

Punishing Others

Through the eyes of Pre-Modern and Modern Worldviews, we tell ourselves that it is prudent to punish those who grievously offend us. "They deserve to be punished," we conclude. "Otherwise, how will they ever learn?" "Punishment is the natural consequence of bad behavior!" For some of us, it's even a natural law. Do we not neglect our duty if we don't play God, making sure others who act differently from us learn their lesson and pay for their sinfulness and crimes? "How else will offenders learn to refrain from their misbehavior?" we state with conviction. Assuming coercion and control are required to prevent future occurrences of evil behavior, we give little or no thought to reconciliation, restoration, and rehabilitation.

Believing that people who hurt us deserve punishment or payback leads to a tendency to analyze and draw conclusions about who is right and who is wrong. Convinced that those who don't agree with us, who don't see people and events the way we see them, are *wrong*, we conclude that they deserve punishment for "the error of their ways."

Punishments such as wife- and child-beating are rampant throughout the world whenever and wherever people buy into

Pre-Modern and Modern thinking and values. Thus, in these cases intimacy is rare.

Recently, in a supermarket, a mother pushed two toddlers in a grocery cart while looking for items to purchase. One toddler struck the other, who instantly began to wail. The mother, not having seen the smack, asked the wailing child, "What's the matter?" The little girl pointed to her brother and stammered through her tears, "He hit me!" The mother then shouted, "I'll teach you to hit!" and struck the toddler who had hit his sister. Thus the mother reinforced the boy's assumption that it is okay to hit. She taught both of her children that "might makes right" and "force rules." She failed to teach them peace and understanding, though doubtless she would prefer that they be kind and intimate with each other. In her ignorance, she has taught them instead to be violent. Instilling forceful punishment bodes ill for intimate child-parent relationships.

Sex

In Pre-Modern and Modern Worldview stories, sex is most often separate from intimacy and affection, and may even be separate from romantic love and the institution of marriage. Males in particular often seek only pleasure, denying and frustrating a loving sexual relationship. Sex, then, being easy to come by, rarely has anything to do with commitment or fidelity. In many places, sex workers give their clientele sexual gratification with no more emotion than when shaking hands or preparing dinner. Many people have sex for money, even with people they dislike and distrust.

Separated from intimacy, sex under Pre-Modern and Modern assumptions is emptied of much of its meaning and purpose. The result is a culture of sexual boasting, exhibitionism, and pornography. For many Pre-Moderns and Moderns who seek intimacy, sex is fraught with disappointment, mistrust, and unhappiness.

Advice-Giving

In response to those who do have the courage to bare their soul, Pre-Modern and Modern Worldview socialization teaches the avoidance of feelings and places the emphasis on thinking. A typical thinking method is to give advice. Advice given under the guise of wisdom is a quick and easy method to avoid dealing with the pain of the other. More often than not, people already know what they're going to do to rid themselves of pain or avoid it in the future. Advice is not what they need. What they want and desperately need is understanding, empathy, and compassion. Empathy and compassion, however, take time, skill, energy, and a belief in their value. Being empathetic and compassionate also means being open to responses other than what we believe is best. Empathy and compassion assume others are capable of addressing and solving their own issues. Pre-Moderns and Moderns rarely assume such maturity! They insist on giving answers and fixing problems. As a result, intimacy is more the exception than the norm.

Yet our very nature cries out for intimacy with others. If we were meant to be alone, there would only be one of us on earth. Being vulnerable and sharing our pain, difficulties, and joys with another person fulfills our basic need for companionship, understanding, and intimacy. The tragedy is that so many people are hurting while Pre-Moderns and Moderns tell them they must be independent and strong—that their issues and desires are too unimportant to concern others. Thereby, many learn to suffer alone and in silence, bereft of intimacy.

The New Millennium Story of Intimacy

The Four Fundamental Assumptions of the New Millennium Emerging Worldview Story have a profound influence on our experience of intimacy. These assumptions make it possible not only to love everyone, but also to be intimate and experience affection with the significant others in our lives.

We Are Forever in the Process of Discovering

Imagine how intimate our lives can become when we assume that no one knows the *whole truth*. Our minds are open. We're fully awake. We continually come to know ourselves, sharing our stories and learning more about others. We listen without judging or giving advice. Our behavior opens the door to intimacy and affection.

Fully knowing others is beyond our ability. We actually prefer it this way, finding joy and fulfillment in the mystery of the other because it leads us to constantly discovering the wonder of the other. Uncertainty in the relationship with another is an opportunity, not a disability.

"For my part I know nothing with any certainty, but the sight of the stars makes me dream," said Dutch master painter Vincent van Gogh. Far from being a source of confusion and anxiety, uncertainty challenges and energizes us. When sharing our time with a significant other, we are continually discovering what, and how, we think and feel. Far from being bored, we find that our interest is touched; we feel alive and stimulated! The more we discover about our friend, the more exciting it is! We are filled with joyous pleasure as our relationship grows ever more intimate.

We Continually Create Our Own Reality

In the New Millennium Story we create our own reality; we focus on what is positive about others, appreciate their qualities, and visualize them living up to their potential. Out of love, we don't look for what's wrong so that we can fix or improve them. No one is perfect, so it makes little sense to focus on the negative. Such an approach leads to low self-esteem, resentment, and defensiveness. When we look only for the good in the other, we enhance our relationship by discovering beautiful qualities in ourselves and in the other.

Actively paying attention to others and appreciating their achievements causes them to seek to become even better. When we have high expectations, people live up to our expectations.

It works like magic! Our belief in them gives them confidence in themselves. And this belief and confidence in them becomes a self-fulfilling prophecy! When we seek and find what is positive in others, ignoring negatives, it results in relationships of genuine intimacy and affection.

Similarly, when we pay attention to and appreciate our own achievements instead of focusing on our failures, we not only continue to improve, but we also build our self-confidence. This, too, is a self-fulfilling prophecy. We express our dreams, our affirmative vision, in the present tense: "I'm a lovable person. I can bring happiness to myself and others. What a good feeling!" These persistent affirmations, in just a short time, become my ongoing reality!

Creating our own reality rescues us from a life of complaining and whining and gives us the courage, motivation, and self-discipline to change, thereby experiencing greater intimacy with oneself and with others.

We Are All One

New Millennium Thinkers and Feelers assume that we are all one. All forms of life are accepted and valued because of oneness with, and contribution to, all of us. With this realization, all aspects of being—humans, animals, plants, and inorganic matter—are integrated, with their varied age, color, gender, ethnicity, and size, into our holistic sense of life. In this process, aware of our oneness, we resonate with the music of our ancestors and the yet unborn. This fuller and deeper understanding of the essence of who we are enables us to be intimate with ourselves, with others, and with all of creation.

Self-Acceptance

In our New Millennium story, we assume that there are no *good-selves* and no *bad-selves*, just *our-selves*. We are all unique in this world! Our task, we believe, is to develop our own unique qualities and to appreciate the unique qualities and potential of others.

We begin by recognizing who and what we are: a unique expression of creation. This is a huge step toward self-acceptance. Second is the understanding of our personal responsibility for our actions. Next comes the conscious awareness of our interrelatedness and interdependence with all things.

Acceptance of Others

We assume, being one with everyone, that our mission in life is to accept and affirm the lives of others, because in so doing we enhance our own lives. Our purpose for existing is not to help others, which suggests dependence. Our mission in the New Millennium is to create opportunities for others to help themselves. "Give a man a fish and he will eat for a day. Teach a man to fish and he will eat for a lifetime," says the lovely old proverb. When others do the same for us, interdependence ensues. Together, we create an environment enabling all of us to have our wants and needs met more often than not, through accepting, affirming, and serving one another.

Because of our oneness, we realize that what is in one person's self-interest needs to satisfy the self-interest of everyone. At the same time, we understand that our oneness doesn't mean we're all *the same*. Our differences create excitement in our encounters. We complement each other, making up for what is missing in one another and consequently enriching the relationship.

We Always Do What We Perceive Is Best

In the New Millennium Story, we automatically move toward what we perceive as the best course of action. In any given situation and moment in time, we act in our perceived self-interest and assume the same of others. We conclude that no one deliberately seeks to hurt us; this gives us the potential to relate intimately with anyone.

Should we be hurt by another, we assume the person did not realize what she was doing, or did not intend to hurt us. Then we strive to better understand how the incident occurred and how it can be resolved and eliminated in the future. We take responsibility for, and seek to change, our own behavior, while at the same time seeking to be good to those who hurt us. In so doing, we contribute to, or restore, intimacy.

Intimacy Implications of the New Millennium Story

Assuming that people always do what they think is best, we focus on where they are coming from, their upbringing, their motives, and their feelings in the moment. Rather than diagnosing and judging them, we empathize, placing ourselves in their shoes. A shift occurs when we can say to someone who, given his information and consciousness, has made a mistake and is suffering for it, "I would have done exactly what you did, if I were in your shoes. My heart is filled with sadness as I identify with your pain."

The following is a powerful example of an Emerging Worldview response from parents helping their daughter with a troubling experience. It was written by one of my students and is used, anonymously, with her permission.

> The hardest day of my life was the day I told my Mom I'd had sex for the first time. It was the best, worst, and longest day of my life. I was ashamed and didn't like myself at all. I felt dirty. For a couple of weeks I'd been wrestling with the decision to tell my mother. What can I say, how do I tell her? I knew I had to tell her just because I was hurting so bad inside; I wanted and needed her love and understanding.
>
> My mom and I share everything and this was supposed to be a wonderful experience that I thought I'd want to share with her. Instead, I was afraid. I thought she'd hate me and think less of me. I convinced myself she would never again think of me in the same way. I was sure she would stop loving me.
>
> I now realize that all the emotions and fears I projected onto my mom were really my own. I fought with myself for a long time. When

I finally got up the courage and told her what I'd done, I cried and cried as she calmed me down and asked loving, caring questions. I was so ashamed and miserable about my behavior, regretting what I'd done.

She expressed her disappointment but she also surrounded me with love and the strength I needed. She was happy about our trust in each other and our close relationship and the fact that I had the courage to share this with her. She knew I was growing up, but didn't want it to be this quick. She understood my needs, feelings and emotions, but I'm not sure I did. We kissed and hugged.

As I lay in bed, my sadness and fears came back. Then I heard the garage door, I knew my dad had come home. I froze in the bed. We're a very close family and I knew Mom would tell Dad. That didn't bother me, but his unavoidable disappointment in me did. Thoughts raced through my head—What should I do? How can I look at him again? I'll pretend I'm asleep, no, I'll face him!

I slowly repeated The Lord's Prayer and went over the comforting thoughts I learned in Sunday School. I could hear my dad's footsteps coming up the stairs. I hid under the covers. I heard my door open and Dad call my name. Are you awake? I was crying, but I said yes. He walked over to my bed, gave me a big, warm, long hug and whispered in my ear, "Remember, God loves you and I love you very much, so does Mom—no matter what you do, we're always loving you. Go to sleep and we'll talk tomorrow."

I didn't want to let go of him; I felt so safe in his arms, as if everything was okay, normal. I cried myself to sleep knowing my parents loved me. I'll never forget that night as long as I live.

The days that followed were difficult, but each day was a constant reassurance of the love, support and understanding in my family.

As I look back now, I realize I was immature and couldn't handle a grown-up situation. I know that night reinforced a bond in our family. And now I know I can share with my parents and express anything and everything.

Loving Ourselves

We've discovered in the New Millennium Story that loving and becoming ever more connected to ourselves is truly a stimulating experience; it leads to feelings of intimacy. Truly loving and appreciating ourselves enables us to take risks and be responsible for our actions. Love of self results in feelings of high self-esteem and a new self-concept, which leads to greater self-confidence.

We look forward to spending time alone because we love ourselves. Awake and alone, paying attention to ourselves, we are centered. "I got it together!" we say. We experience intimacy. We feel connected. We discover that being alone is an enriching experience. Loneliness is never an issue.

Loving Others

In assuming we are all one, we love everyone and presume that others love us as well. We feel loved and experience joy in loving others. An extra dividend is found in not being afraid of other people. We look forward to meeting new people and enjoying their company. We see the potential for intimacy in everyone, including strangers.

Self-Awareness

In relationships, we pay attention to what is going on within ourselves. Wiping the sleep from our eyes, and using both our eyes and our intuition, we observe what is happening with others. For example, my "I" observes "Me" talking too much and not listening to my companion. My "I" remembers the Turkish proverb: "If speaking is silver, then listening is gold"—then my "I" directs "Me" to be quiet and actively listen to the other person. My goal in being intimate is to share what's happening inside me in the "here and now." This goal includes enabling my intimate companions to do the same.

Another aspect of self-awareness is authenticity. Engaging in Emerging Worldview assumptions, we become our authentic selves, fully awake and conscious of specific feelings at any particular time and place. We may experience feelings of depression or happiness, but these feelings do not constitute our essence. We say: "I'm not a depressed person. I'm a person who is experiencing feelings of depression." The *feeling* is not the person; the *person* is not the feeling. In the New Millennium, we assume we can control these feelings. No matter what happens, we are capable of feeling cheerful and grateful, if we want to; and these feelings quite naturally spill over onto our significant others! We are accountable for how we feel. It is up to us.

Empathy

When I was in graduate school, the wife of one of my professors died unexpectedly after a brief illness. I went with two fellow students to the professor's home to express our condolences. While we were there, the chairman of the professor's department, his manager, entered the home and slowly walked toward him. With a heart full of empathy, the chairman was able to identify with what the grieving professor was feeling. The chairman threw his arms around him and began to cry. Immediately, our professor started to cry, too. Oblivious of us students, these two grown men stood in the center of the living room embracing each other and weeping. I'll never forget this moment of genuine intimacy.

Alcoholics Anonymous

Another moving example of intimacy is a typical Alcoholics Anonymous (AA) meeting. AA is a fellowship of men and women who, to overcome their common addiction to alcohol, share their experience, strength, and hope with each other. AA was founded in 1935 and has over two million members in 150 countries.

Upon entering an open meeting, a stranger is immediately greeted with words of welcome. No one is perceived as a thug, scumbag, or outcast, no matter what they may have done. Members approach, shake hands, and introduce themselves in a friendly manner, genuinely conveying acceptance.

Once the meeting begins, each person shares a moment of silence and asks God (as each chooses and uniquely understands God) to help friends and loved ones, especially those who are sick or in the hospital. Strangers are recognized individually as the group responds in unison with "Hi, Joe," together with energetic applause. In other words, people genuinely pay attention to each other. No one is ignored.

One member leads the group in reciting the Twelve Steps toward Sobriety. Another individual reads the AA policy statement, which addresses the anonymity professed by the group. Almost everyone present stands and recites the Serenity Prayer with fervor and conviction:

God, grant me the patience to accept the things I cannot change,
The courage to change the things I can,
And the wisdom to know the difference. Amen.[5]

In many meetings, "leads" then begin to tell their story. They share experiences of loss and tribulation caused by drinking. They literally "go to confession" to the larger community. They also share how they came to AA and the many lessons they've learned, such as the power of God's love, gratitude for people in their life, and what is truly important to them now. Often they stress the importance of facing consequences and tell how they grew and became better persons. Everyone in the room rejoices at each person's triumph over alcohol—in a sense giving absolution, the blessing of forgiveness—because every alcoholic realizes that they have hurt themselves, their families, and the entire community by their mistakes. The listeners express gratitude to the speakers for such intimate sharing.

One can hardly witness such a meeting without feeling comfort, warmth, and inspiration. A group of people are connected by the common goal of staying sober. Through their vision, they grow to support and respect each other. Members pray to the God of their choosing and search for peace of mind.

A common theme among AA members is the willingness to humbly accept themselves and others. They speak of their intentional avoidance of self-pity, resentment, and guilt, explaining that their plight was caused by their own actions, for which they alone are responsible. Refusing to blame others for their mistakes, they exude appreciation for their accomplishments and those of their colleagues. An amazing experience of group intimacy transforms everyone in the room.

CONCLUSION

New Millennium Emerging Worldview assumptions have awakened in us a new awareness. Being aware that we are all one enables us to transcend our fear of being open and honest with others. We feel no need to compete with or be better than others. We become more generous, because when we give to others we give to ourselves. We find delight and meaning in the many intimate relationships we cultivate.

No matter what mistakes we've made in the past, we don't wallow in self-pity. Rather, we assume we can create our own reality through visualizing lives filled with love, caring, and meaning. In other words, we can change if we genuinely want to change. These assumptions enhance our ability to become intimate.

The key requirement for intimacy is to get at the feelings, thoughts, and wants behind our observations. In the New Millennium Story, all parties find it easy to openly and honestly express their feelings. In the end, people usually work out a win-win settlement which reinforces intimacy. This is possible because we're neither competitive, nor afraid of being intimate. We take full responsibility for our own intentions and actions, but not for the actions and feelings of others.

The Emerging Worldview Story assumes that we are all in the process of seeking good. When good doesn't materialize, we blame neither ourselves nor others. We realize that our failures arise from the lack of knowing what is in our long-term best interest. We no longer feel guilty or blame others for negative experiences in our lives. Out of compassion, we are open and honest about what we want to do to improve. We similarly respond to the intentions, feelings, and desires of others, creating a greater climate for intimacy with them.

Our ability and willingness to be open and honest with ourselves enables us to be so with everyone else, limited only by our time and energy. With this understanding, we at times find joy in being alone; at other times, we find joy in being with others in an intimate and affectionate way. We joyfully acknowledge uniqueness in others, as well as ourselves, and join in celebrating their successes. We experience joy in becoming the best we can be and rejoice in witnessing the success of others. Our joy over their successes creates healing and growth in them *and* in us—an authentic, long-lasting, and deeply satisfying experience of intimacy. Give it a try!

CHAPTER EIGHT

The Story of Wellness

He is the best physician who is the most ingenious inspirer of hope.
Samuel Taylor Coleridge
English Poet, Critic, Philosopher

Helping, fixing and serving are ways of seeing life.
When you help, you see life as work.
When you fix you see life as broken.
When you serve, you live life as a whole.
When we serve we understand that this person's suffering is also my suffering, his joy is my joy.
Frank Ostaseski
Founding Director, Zen Hospice Project
San Francisco, California, USA

If our lives are to be healthy and our spirits to grow, we must be dedicated . . . And the more clearly we see the reality of the world, the better equipped we are to deal with the world.
M. Scott Peck
American Psychiatrist

When health is absent, wisdom cannot reveal itself,
art cannot become manifest,
strength cannot fight,
wealth becomes useless, and
intelligence cannot be applied.
Herophilus of Chalcedon (335–280 BC)
Physician to Alexander the Great

What Is Wellness?

Wellness has become a metaphor for wholeness. In the New Millennium Story, we define wellness as: the state of being physically, mentally, socially, financially, and spiritually healthy—not simply being in a state free from disease and infirmity. It involves a complex interplay among the physical, psychological, social, emotional, and environmental aspects of the human condition, or what is described as a systems approach to wellness. Wellness is an integrated functioning of body, mind, emotions, and spirit which enables each person to experience a meaningful and joyful life.

Pre-Modern Worldview Story of Health

The primary purpose of the Pre-Modern Worldview Story still exists today: It is to cure people who are sick. A secondary purpose is to prevent people from getting sick. Sickness, in the Pre-Modern Story, may be due to spiritual and/or physical causes. Cures or treatments include spiritual and physical interventions. Prayers, rituals, and exorcisms are used, as well as medicinal plants, herbal mixtures, and other remedies. The healing process itself remains a mystery.

Alongside of this sense of the mysterious is a knowledge of healing practices and of plants with medicinal properties. Many of these plants are now used in pharmaceuticals.

Predominantly hierarchical and patriarchal, with an emphasis on paternalism, the Pre-Modern Worldview Story is structured with God (or gods) at the top of a pyramid. God selectively reveals the "whole truth," and determines the quality of human life, which is mostly fixed. (If one is born with a disability, one will remain disabled until one's dying day. Only a miracle from God can change this.) Pre-Moderns also believe God determines when and how people die. Whatever happens is God's will, the way the things are supposed to be. See Figure 8.1.

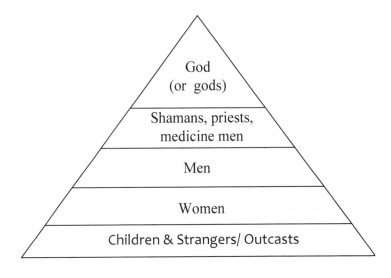

Figure 8.1

The intermediaries between God and humankind are shamans, medicine men, or priests—all of whom are typically male. Acting as instruments of the divine, these mediators intervene in daily life, performing ceremonies of healing. God is believed to directly heal the sick through miracles, but more often through these intermediaries, who have the most wisdom and knowledge, forming an elite class. Knowledge and wisdom are considered their sacred truth, giving them power over society. Carefully guarding their knowledge, they only reluctantly share it with those lower in the hierarchy. Any knowledge or wisdom deemed necessary to heal is passed on to men. Men, in turn, instruct females, children, and strangers.

Results of the Pre-Modern Worldview Story

Religious intermediaries focus on two key aspects of Pre-Modern healthcare: the body and the soul. The soul gives life to the body, which disintegrates and eventually dies in the belief that the soul lives on forever. Death is the gateway to eternal life. To lose one's soul by spending eternity divorced from God, family, and friends is a loss which eliminates all meaning from life, here or in the hereafter.

Sickness, in the Pre-Modern Story, is often considered the result of sin; e.g., people with AIDS are simply being justly punished for sinful behavior. Pre-Moderns believe that individuals who break God's laws or human laws commit "sins" and are punished by God in this life in the form of sickness. The assumption is that they "should have known better and therefore are responsible for their own illness."

Disabled persons, too, are considered sinners and are deprived of equal and special opportunities in education and employment. Segregated from everyone else, they become outcasts and receive little or no compassion. Spending tax money to provide easy access to public buildings and transit for disabled persons is more the exception than the rule.

In some countries such as Haiti, children born with a disability are believed to be cursed and contagious; this leads to parental infanticide, or placement of the child in proximity to people the parents hate, so that their adversaries can experience a voodoo curse.

In the end, many adults experience a feeling of peace and security because they believe that God is in control. If they obey God's will by carrying out prescribed rituals, God, who is a "He," will be merciful and bestow blessings upon them, leading to good health.

Modern Worldview Story of Health

The Modern Worldview Story focuses on "illness" and the treatment of diseases with the intention of saving lives. Health Departments are Disease Departments. Diseases are studied mostly to learn how to cure, rather than prevent, illness. Even so-called "preventive healthcare" focuses on symptoms and conditions, thus allowing further illness. Little or no emphasis is given to unhealthy lifestyles which lead to continuous medical treatments. Moreover, Moderns believe that sick people and the high cost of healthcare contribute to the Gross National Product (GNP).

In the Modern Worldview Story, *reason* and biomedical technologies replace God at the apex of the pyramid. See Figure 8.2.

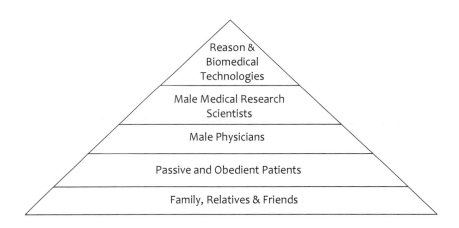

Figure 8.2

Priests, medicine men, and shamans have been replaced, by medical research scientists, typically male—the new custodians of "the truth." From their lofty perch near the top of the hierarchy, they transfer knowledge to typically male physicians, who apply the research to the quest for cures for their patients' diseases. Patients are programmed to be passive recipients of their physicians' diagnostics and treatment, assuming that all physicians know the "whole truth"—or are closer to it than anyone else. The patient guilelessly follows the doctor's orders, believing "the doctor knows best and means well."

As Modern medicine becomes ever more institutionalized, physicians must also contend with insurance companies and health maintenance organizations (HMOs), which largely control the provision of healthcare. Company administrators direct middle-managers, who direct the primarily female nurses and helpers. See Figure 8.3.

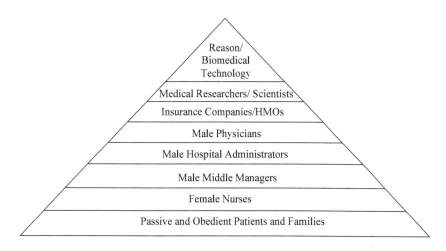

Fig. 8.3

Physicians

For their patients to have faith in them, physicians need to be seen as experts, medically infallible. Ironically, because of the financial constraints exacted by the insurance companies and HMOs, physicians often find that they are prevented from treating their patients in accordance with the best medical procedures and care available. Given that most have become doctors for the purpose of saving lives, many doctors experience extreme stress at being unable to do their best for the patient. Threats of malpractice suits add to their stress by questioning not only their competence but also their commitment. Discouraged and disgusted, many doctors leave the medical profession.

Nurses

Nurses, mostly women, are often expected to think and act "like men." As the scientific content of the nursing curriculum increases, feminine qualities of nurturing, intuition, and empathy are less valued, yet are the very reasons for which many entered nursing. Because of the traditional female roles, both patients and their families expect nurses to be nurturing and compassionate. Patients are particularly concerned about how much the nurse *cares*, much more than about what she *knows*. Nurses struggle with this conflict in their perceived roles.

The pressure for efficiency puts further strain on nurses because they are called on to care less and produce more, to cut costs and increase profits. Nurses are expected to accept orders from above without question and apply them to patients. Acting on one's own is largely prohibited, with fear of lawsuits further enforcing this prohibition.

Results of the Modern Worldview Story

Progress *has* been made under Modernist thinking and behavior. Life expectancy for someone born in 2000 is eight years longer than for someone born fifty years earlier. The mortality rate for coronary heart disease has declined by 45 percent since 1980.

The rate of disability among senior citizens has declined by twenty percent in the last twenty years.[1] Most of this progress is due to advances in public health—particularly in the areas of community development and sanitation, which are still desperately needed in poor countries.

The four leading causes of death—heart disease, cancer, diabetes, and strokes—were virtually nonexistent sixty years ago. It is suspected that polluted air and water, chemicals in our food, and the stress of contemporary life account for this turn of events.

Modern healthcare is also effective in managing crises such as acute infections and trauma. In genetics, technology has advanced the discovery of individual genetic variations, enabling physicians to customize medicine: two patients with the same disease, such as diabetes, receive different medicines based on their distinctive DNA.

The Human Body Treated as a Machine

Modernists tend to favor a single way of explaining the world. The systemic, spiritual approach to health is superseded, in Western culture, by a highly specialized and technical delivery system. This view conceives of the human body as a biological machine, whose owners bring it to the doctor for repair. It has many parts which can be taken apart, repaired, or replaced, and then, unlike Humpty Dumpty, put back together again. For example, high blood pressure is fixed with medicine that lowers blood pressure; soon the person has a heart problem and medicine is given to "cure" that problem; later, the medicine causes the cholesterol count to go up—for which another drug is given. A friend of mine is taking twenty-two pills a day. It all started with a blood-pressure symptom.

Patients are referred to, related to, and treated as a disease-type. They are labeled Cancer Patient or Diabetic or Paranoid Schizophrenic. Once labeled, you are a disease, not a person with a surname and a given name.

The Need to Be Right

In the Modern Worldview Story, people are uncomfortable with probabilities and seek certainties through scientific approaches to medical care. This allows them to *have patience* as scientific remedies are applied to them. Refusal to acknowledge that "the cure" is uncertain is a manifestation of fear. Researchers cling to the illusion that scientific theories are "facts" and often resist acknowledging contradictory evidence.[2]

Sadly, patients don't care to believe that their "cure" depends on the degree to which they change their lives. A magic bullet, often in the form of pills or treatment, is a cure-all, leaving no need to change behavior, attitudes, or lifestyle.

Extreme Costs of Healthcare

As described above, most healthcare bestowers in the Modern Worldview are tightly controlled by insurance companies and HMOs. These companies are intent on cutting costs and increasing their bottom line. Making money is primary. Healing the sick is the means to an end. It is in the interest of modern healthcare that people get sick. Lack of attention to, and appreciation for, the prevention of disease is the consequence.

Purchases of healthcare equipment are motivated by the need to keep up with technology and/or the need to practice defensive medicine. All is done in the name of staying competitive. When a doctor or health group invests in expensive equipment such as MRI machines, they use them often, to justify their cost; this leads to the over-prescribing of MRI procedures, regardless of the patient's need. Seeking to stay competitive drives out neighborhood hospitals and clinics, the major healthcare resource for the poor, while escalating the cost of healthcare.

Under the guidance of the American Medical Association (AMA) and its approach to scientific medicine, research scientists who adhere to the Modern Worldview believe their healthcare ideas to be the "truth." Healing practices not_sanctioned by the AMA are condemned as superstitious or as the work of unscrupulous fakes. Many of these non-sanctioned approaches are referred to as "alternative medicine." And most of these alternative therapies are not covered by HMOs or health-insurance policies. Patients seeking these types of treatment pay out of their own pockets.

Preventable Diseases Exist Throughout the World

Space does not allow for describing the tragic healthcare situation across the globe. One specific example, however, is Africa. Nearly all of Africa suffers from inadequate healthcare. In *The End of Poverty,* Jeffrey Sachs writes:

> More than one million African children and perhaps as many as three million people die from malaria each year. This horrific catastrophe occurs despite knowledge that malaria is completely preventable through the use of bed netting and other environmental controls.[3]

To prevent and treat a child's disease successfully, it is necessary to understand the child's social setting, requiring a systems approach. Destitute African parents are not capable of providing treatment for their children. Often they themselves suffer from disease or malnutrition and lack the ability to follow through on a recommended course of treatment for their children. African parents need assistance, to help their children as well as their nation.

It is not just a question of providing bed netting and pure water. A holistic approach is required in order to provide a healthy environment. Working holistically will require a compassionate, and passionate, intention to do so on the part of the world community.

Providing increased financial assistance to developing countries is not a high priority in the Modern Worldview Story. According to Sachs,

> Foreign aid to poor countries plummeted during the 1980s and 1990s. In 2002, aid per person in sub-Saharan Africa fell from $32 per African in 1980 to just $22 per African in 2001. This happened during a period when African pandemic diseases and conditions such as malaria, AIDS, and unsafe drinking water, ran rampant—the needs for increased public spending were stark.[4]

The AIDS Epidemic

In the time since the identification of the Human Immunodeficiency Virus (HIV) in 1981, the virus has spread worldwide. In 1990, an estimated 10 million people were infected. By the end of 2004, the numbers had climbed to 78 million. Of those 78 million, 38 million have died. And at the end of 2007, 33 million were living with the virus. At least 25 million HIV-positive people live in sub-Saharan Africa. Adherence to Modern Worldview assumptions finds only 500,000 being treated with antiretroviral drugs.[5] Even more horrifically, in 2008 Africa had over 11 million AIDS orphans.

In many hospitals in Africa, with the majority of beds occupied by AIDS victims, less space is available for those with other illnesses. Overworked doctors and nurses are stretched to the breaking point. Healthcare systems are unable to provide even basic care, causing an exponential rise in deaths from traditional diseases. Life expectancy is dropping, not only because of AIDS, but also because of the deterioration of overall healthcare.[6]

The sad news is that the epidemic could be stopped if the international community supplied the necessary financial aid, with methodologies for using it. Unfortunately, Modern Worldviewers focus on individualism, competition, and materialism, leaving little money for those judged as the unworthy outcasts of society.

The Emerging Millennium Story of Wellness

Dramatic changes are now occurring in healthcare. New Millennium Worldview Thinkers and Feelers are enlightened persons who view themselves as wellness seekers. They take serious responsibility for their own health and the health of others, in terms of both preventing illness and in treating it. The results are wellness and feelings of personal empowerment throughout the world community.

One proponent of the Emerging Worldview of Healthcare is U.S. President Barack Obama, who stated:

> Making sure every American has access to high quality health care is one of the most important challenges of our time. The number of uninsured Americans is growing, premiums are skyrocketing, and more people are being denied coverage every day. A moral imperative by any measure, a better system is also essential to rebuilding our economy—we want to make health insurance work for people and businesses, not just insurance and drug companies.[7]

President Obama's healthcare legislatio of 2009 was complex and controversial. He and his administration and supporters took on a gargantuan task, which resulted in conflict between outside groups on both sides, an increasingly heated battle accompanied by growing public unease.

The plan passed and was signed into law in March of 2010. It became the next step in the direction of universal healthcare throughout the planet.

We Are Forever in the Process of Discovering

Wellness seekers, in the New Millennium, place emphasis on learning how to live, instead of assuming we already know how to lead a healthy life and prevent illnesses. We realize that the medical profession does not possess the "whole truth" and there is more than one viable option for living a healthy, meaningful life and preventing or curing diseases.

Wellness seekers and wellness team partners hold only pieces of the "truth." No one has all the answers to wellness; no one acts as though there is certainty in the universe or as though correct diagnoses can be found. Hence, we call it "the practice of medicine."

By understanding that no one knows the "whole truth," we cease to be dogmatic about our approach to wellness, open to experimenting with alternative ways of promoting wellness and preventing illness. We use complementary interventions such as homeopathy, reflexology, diet, herbal therapy, vitamins, and positive thinking.[8] We also use meditation and prayer, mindfulness training, self-hypnosis, laughter, and energy exchanges. We join support-group sessions and do moderate exercise such as yoga, tai chi, or qigong (chi gong). These activities have become conventional and prove amazingly effective.

Wellness seekers no longer expect a medical professional to be our surrogate parent with all the answers. Without expecting the doctor to provide the magic bullet, we take primary responsibility for our own health. Concern for each other's wellness has prompted the development of wellness teams composed of both health professionals and significant others. This New Millennium thinking has completely changed the healthcare structure and will be discussed later in this chapter. We research our health concerns through the Internet (open source) and the news media, which provide a plethora of wellness information and, thereby, increased awareness and understanding.

Wellness advocates and our wellness team partners seek to discover how we can make effective contributions to promote wellness for ourselves and the community at large. Open dialogue and flexibility are vital in this process.

We Create Our Own Reality

Since 1974, when research at the University of Rochester revealed a connection between the immune system and the central nervous system, mind-body (brain-body) science has expanded. Mounting evidence points to a direct correlation between mental and physical well-being, making it possible for *wellness seekers* to participate in creating our own wellness. People have come to realize that our internal states, our feelings about what is happening to us, are directly related to becoming well. This recognition expands the understanding of the mind-body connection and has opened the field of medicine and healthcare to the fields of psychology, psychotherapy, and spirituality.

We are bringing to clinics and healthcare facilities new methods and techniques, considered inappropriate by Modern Worldviewers, methods such as visualization. A new way of structuring the whole wellness process has emerged.

Wellness seekers in the Emerging Millennium Story understand the power of thoughts and feelings. We use awareness and conscious mental skills to alter our mind-body capabilities, resulting in less need for invasive procedures. These mind-body capabilities are known in the Modern Worldview as the "placebo effect."

Placebos, aka sugar pills, have no known scientific effect. For years doctors have administered sugar pills, containing no healing power, while telling patients they are taking a newly discovered medicine. A high percentage of patients, believing the doctor, actually get better. This effect has long been evident, even though it's unexplainable in modern medicine.

New Millennium Thinkers and Feelers use this placebo dynamic to our benefit, knowing we can create our own wellness and the wellness of others. We've learned how to be well by holding a vision of ourselves as truly healthy and happy. Prior to surgery, we're confident we're in good hands and the surgeon is capable. Believing in the physician's amazing skill, we visualize ourselves getting better and living a meaningful life, and we usually do.

On the other hand, when people are filled with fear that the surgeon won't be able to get all the cancer, or that something might go wrong and we may not survive, this negative energy depletes our immune system, often becoming a self-fulfilling prophecy. We realize that those who hold a vision of themselves as distressed, trapped, or unable to get well, become and remain ill. Each vision tends to create its own reality. We know from past experience that when we say to ourself, "I'm depressed," the body responds at the cellular level and we become and remain depressed. In the New Millennium Story, we avoid such negative self-talk, speaking positively about our age, health, and future. We appreciate the power and energy of visualization.[9]

Every day, many times a day, using self-affirmations of feeling strong and filled with energy, we focus our mind and heart on our own well-being. We picture ourselves vibrantly rising from bed each morning, enthusiastically greeting the day, and living out the rest of the day with energy and joy. We envision specific parts of our anatomy healing, overcoming any and every handicap. Our positive attitude, coupled with self-discipline and thoughts of gratitude, results in long-term health and meaningful living.

And we do the same for others, visualizing them being well, overcoming illness, and living strong, happy, meaningful lives. When individuals do become ill and need medical attention, their significant others consciously visualize them recovering and living a vibrant life, which then often occurs.

We Are All One

Since we assume we are all one, in the New Millennium we believe that it is in our own self-interest to develop and implement healing practices that promote our own wellness *and* the wellness of others. According to psychologist Edmund Bourne,

> Each of us is a "cell" in the collective body of humanity ... By cultivating peace and healing in your own life, you become an exemplar of healing and peace for others.[10]

—causing them to unconsciously feel what you are feeling.

In New Millennium thinking and feeling, interventions are no longer illness-driven, but rather focus on maximizing the wellness of each and every person. We're proactive wellness seekers, not reactive patients. All of us deliver wellness to one another. On learning that one of our fellow human beings is ill with cancer, we realize that all of us are stricken with it. The person with the illness is carrying the sickness for us all. It takes the whole community to assure wellness for everyone.

In the Emerging Millennium Story, we assume our bodies to be "at one" with our environment—fellow human beings, animals, plants, and other organisms. Key emphasis is placed on the study and enhancement of the natural resistance of the human immune system to bacteria, rather than identifying microorganisms and developing medicine to kill them.

The manifestations of wellness stem from the connection and interplay of mind, body, emotions, and spirit living in harmony with the environment. A holistic and ecological concept of wellness, both in theory and in practice, has superseded the biomedical model. Healing and wellness lie outside the limited scientific framework and are understood not simply in reductionist terms.

The human body is not approached as though it were a machine needing repair or having spare parts, but rather as a living organism capable of restoring itself. For us to experience total well-being, every organ and tissue depends on the health and well-being of every other organ and tissue. If even one of them fails, it has a negative impact on the entire body. Learning to take care of our bodies, then, wellness seekers have become *whole-body-minded*, paying attention to both organic and functional conditions.

We Always Do What We Perceive Is Best

The New Millennium Story assumes we always determine and act upon the best alternative, based on our values. We rarely choose. (See Chapter Six.)

We always do what we perceive is best for our own wellness and the wellness of others. We don't compete with others, only with ourselves, as we seek to continually improve our own well-being and that of others. The key is continually learning more and more about the human body and its environment, so that our perception of what contributes to our own wellness and the wellness of others actually *does* contribute. For instance, when Moderns believe that eating will numb negative feelings, a person may eat inappropriate food in huge amounts.

The New Millennium Story changes the way we think and feel; we consciously eat nutritious, organic foods and participate in a regular exercise program. We don't seek to numb our feelings, but to intensify them; this gives us energy to face our challenges. When we change our thinking and feeling, to take responsibility for our health, we consciously do what is needed for us to be well.

No Blame or Punishment

In the New Millennium Story, wellness seekers are not blamed for being ill. When we happen to sneeze, we receive genuine expressions of concern for our well-being. We do not, as In the Pre-Modern Worldview Story, respond to a sneeze with "Gesundheit" or "God bless you," responses based on the myth that sneezing is the closest we come to death before we actually die. Modernists avoid even those expressions.

In the Emerging Worldview Story, no one is blamed for creating cancer, even if they expose themselves to chronic stress and carcinogens. Even smokers are not blamed for putting themselves in harm's way. It is assumed that if people who smoke, drink too much, take drugs, or fail to exercise or eat healthy food had known exactly what they were doing to themselves, they would have refrained from starting the unhealthy behavior and would have acted to promote their own well-being. Nor are they blamed for not knowing better. It is assumed that a good reason exists for their ignorance. We assume that if they had known better, they would have acted differently.

Alcoholics are not viewed as evil, weak personalities or social misfits by the community. They aren't judged or punished, even if their intoxication has led to a tragic accident in which others were killed. In the New Millennium Story, alcoholics are accepted, loved, and seen as being in serious need of healing, even though abominable consequences have followed from their drunken behavior. Energy and effort are directed toward healing the illness of alcoholism, not toward punishing individuals for their actions. If every effort fails to help the alcoholic overcome the addiction for example, that person may lose the right to drive—not as punishment, but out of love and concern for his safety and the safety of the community.

It's assumed that we who initially experiment with mind-altering substances, becoming chemically dependent on them, perceived them to be personally beneficial and not harmful. The same is true for those of us who partake of excessive food or smoke cigarettes. If we're warned of the dangers, it is presumed that we don't believe the warnings. It's possible that past experiences of being misinformed, or lied to, have resulted in disbelief—because research keeps changing. For instance, scientists at one time warned us that butter was dangerous to our health, and people were urged to switch to margarine. Further research now shows that margarine is even more dangerous to one's health than butter. No one ever knows "the truth" for certain.

The reasons for people's drug addiction, destructive behaviors, or other obstacles to wellness are not the significant issue. The reasons are important only because that knowledge eventually contributes to wellness. In the New Millennium Story, energy is focused on creating wellness for those who suffer from an addiction.

Wellness seekers (who sometimes, as part of the wake-up process, are not even aware that they are seekers of wellness) are invited and expected to work with wellness partners in a collaborative effort similar to the Alcoholics Anonymous approach. The objective of the cooperative approach is to become responsible and accountable for one's own wellness and the wellness of others.

A second objective is to truly understand the personal and social damage that addiction and other illnesses have on our relationships. A person's family and the common good of the entire community suffer. According to Joseph Califano, former Domestic Affairs Chief under President Lyndon B. Johnson and Secretary of Health, Education, and Welfare under Jimmy Carter, substance abuse costs Americans one trillion dollars per year.[11] Substance abuse is implicated in poverty, violent crime, soaring healthcare costs, family dissolution, child abuse, homelessness, teen pregnancy, and AIDS. Substance abuse is definitely *not* in the community's self-interest.

Emerging Worldview Thinkers and Feelers have awakened. We realize that our individual actions can seriously damage the health of the community. We have committed ourselves to being well and contributing to the wellness of others.

Sobriety, or just saying no to drugs, nicotine, or alcohol, is not the final goal. Wellness—a life of continued health, meaning, and joy—is what we seek. A society of fulfilled, productive individuals contributing to one another's wellness we assume is certainly a goal worthy of community effort.

We are aware that we can't change others, only ourselves. Once we're able to take control of our own lives, we influence others by living healthily ourselves and by examining various approaches to healthy lifestyles with wellness team partners. Our goal is for all of us to make progress beyond just avoiding disease.

In the process, we are motivated to delay immediate personal gratification; we come to appreciate the benefits of long-term wellness. Far from being a sacrifice, it is an enlightened move. We always pursue what we believe is "well" for us; we cannot do otherwise. It is not a choice. Through the process of seeking wellness, we give ourselves a gift.

Results of the New Millennium Story

In the New Millennium Story, the focus has moved from treatment of illness to seeking wellness. Indeed, wellness now has become the highest priority. More than eighty percent of the practice of healing focuses on wellness and preventative measures, while treatment of acute infections and trauma interventions amount to less than twenty percent. As a result of disease prevention, the cost of healthcare has dramatically dropped by more than fifty percent.

When Emerging Worldview Thinkers and Feelers speak of being well or healthy, we're not speaking only of freedom from sickness and pain; we're also describing the high energy within us (physically, emotionally, and spiritually) because we're in the process of achieving a healthy community environment.

We promote wellness in the New Millennium by encouraging a well-balanced, nutritious diet, exercise programs, positive thinking, and the education of the community on the benefits of "getting high" by living up to our potential, rather than by substance abuse. The wellness profession, government, athletes, and others are modeling this behavior. The community has developed a better understanding and appreciation of the vision of wellness.

Opportunities for maintaining and improving one's well-being can now be found in the use of vitamin supplements and inexpensive, healthy, organic foods. Lots of parks with clean air are free to the public, as well as affordable athletic facilities and spas. This thinking and feeling shift, in the New Millennium Story, has occurred largely because we woke up and changed our values through education.

The shift has further resulted in an increase of wellness information, insightful innovation, and creative understanding of health and healing practices. By shifting our awareness, we find ourselves concerned with the wellness of everyone in the community.[12]

The wellness process is successful when it produces results desired by wellness seekers—results validated by the combination of experimental methods and scientific research—occurring in a way that engages the seekers and their belief systems in the service of wellness and healing. To achieve this for everyone, fundamental changes have been made in the structure, organization, and processes of the wellness system.

Team Structure and Organization

In the New Millennium Story, the hierarchical and patriarchal pyramid approach to healthcare no longer exists. Instead, an egalitarian circle, similar to a round dinner table, has become the new model. See Figure 8.4.

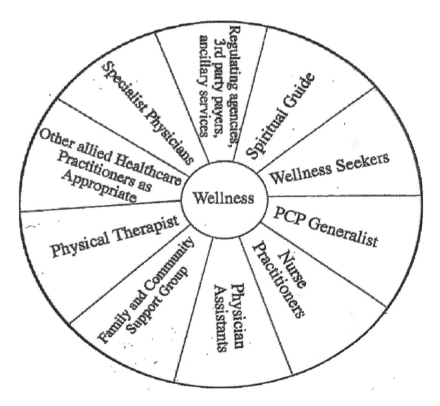

Figure 8.4

At the center of the circle is "the wellness of the individual *and* the community." The wellness experience is still a mystery because we are continually in the process of discovering new and more effective practices for creating and improving a healthy quality of life and for healing the ill.

People are *no longer referred to as patients,* but as *wellness seekers.* Hospitals are now called Health Centers. Comprehensive wellness services are delivered across the entire continuum of life through coordinated wellness teams. Team members are partners and have an equal opportunity to provide input. By removing individuals and the community from the bottom of the hierarchy, we have formed a circle. Each partner plays an important role in the awareness process. Within this structure it's normal for a partner to play more than one role. The role of wellness seekers changes from passive to active members of a wellness team. The partnership of the entire team contributes, to different degrees and in different situations, to the well-being of each wellness seeker.

In the New Millennium Story, professional restrictions placed on team members by their "bosses" have been removed. The medical professionals, wellness seekers, and healthcare community work together as partners. Each team member is recognized for his or her contribution to all wellness seekers' good health. The physician or other medical professionals recognize immense value in the team approach.

Wellness seekers and the wellness team share all pertinent information openly and honestly with one another. Emphasis is placed on keeping everyone informed. Transparency prevails because there are no judgments, and no one experiences shame or blame.

The most effective systemic healing practice at any particular moment is the sum of all the insights and efforts of the wellness team. Although the physician is often the most knowledgeable in terms of healing processes, the physician does not function as the sole leader of the team. Leadership is shared and continually rotates in the group, depending on the nature of immediate issues being addressed. Physicians are no longer chiefs in a vertical system, but partners in a networking circle of wellness seekers and wellness teams. Renowned social ecologist and management consultant Peter Drucker postulates a definition of partnership in which all partners are equal.

Likewise, the New Millennium team shares a common purpose with mutually-agreed-upon goals. Members share all information and cooperate—without giving or taking orders—rather than compete with each other, as they work in a synergistic process toward the well-being of the wellness seeker.[13]

Additionally, an attitude of confidence and trust prevails because of the team's beliefs and positive attitudes. Convinced that they can overcome obstacles, they cooperate to realize their vision of wellness. The community believes that those who are ill can get better, and the team confidently acts in unison to the benefit of each wellness seeker.

It isn't unusual for friends and family to remain constantly at the bedside of wellness seekers—not only to participate in their care, but also to provide nutritionally appropriate food and ensure sensitivity to the wellness seeker's cultural and religious background.

Openness and Feedback

As we become more enlightened, we come to understand how the self-interest of others may at first appear to conflict with our own self-interest. But, committed to open communication, wellness team partners know they can state their opinions, thoughts, and feelings without fear. Differences of opinion and perspective are welcome and valued. Openness to all opinions and feelings, such as systemic, analytic, and intuitive reasoning, plus honest, caring feedback, permeates the team's organizational climate. Such openness facilitates wellness within the team, while enabling efforts toward optimal wellness for all wellness seekers. T-groups and other forms of team-building training are provided to increase and enhance these kinds of interpersonal skills.

Wellness: A Celebration

Laughter, joy, and trust are the norm within a culture of seriousness and commitment to high standards. Jokes, however, are not told at the expense of groups or individuals. Making fun of others is not an accepted practice for eliminating stress.

Dialogue contributes to agreed-upon policies. Rules, procedures, and processes enable team partners to do their jobs with ease. Technologies and medical resources are shared, and profits are kept to acceptable minimal levels in order to maintain affordability of care. Successes are recognized and celebrated. Partners feel enthusiastic and energized by their work. Hard work is balanced by leisure time and pure fun, both of which are essential to the process and to good health.

Wellness: A Community Affair

Wellness and healing are realized through relationships. In the New Millennium Story, we are wellness providers to one another. Our essential nature serves and heals each and all. Intimacy is a strong antidote to illness, as well as a means to recovery. Touch is recognized as a continual source of wellness and a powerful healer.

Emerging Worldview Thinkers and Feelers believe that intimacy and companionship serve to keep our immune, nervous, and endocrine systems at optimal functioning. Through the expression of emotion afforded by intimacy, the immune system is strengthened positively, because we feel secure, cared for, and worthy of love.

Recognizing that we are cared for and worthy of love has a profound effect on how we think and feel about our surroundings. Wellness seekers look for and find ways to build a community network. As part of our wellness plan, wellness seekers gather and furnish social support of friends, family, church, synagogue, mosque, clubs, work colleagues, support circles, and neighbors.

Wellness Training

Medical education emphasizes integrative medicine, a new field of medical practice and research. Based on the premise that the body can heal itself if given a chance, wellness practitioners are trained in the use of all modes of treatment that demonstrate evidence of efficacy.

Wellness training is an ongoing educational experience for wellness seekers, wellness-seeking practitioners, and the community. Learning is directed toward developing a healthy lifestyle and a meaningful life, not simply toward avoiding sickness. We also actively seek to belong to the wellness teams of others and to promote a healthy, wellness-oriented community. We grow up learning to take care of one another, but only when others *need* our assistance. Inter-dependence replaces dependence and independence.

Our primary teacher is our own experience, shared with others. We're both encouraged and motivated to have our own wellness program: to be our own doctor. We access assistance through the internet's open source by entering vital signs, symptoms, and our history. We're able to gather assessments worldwide, and then bring this information to our team partners, who share their thoughts and insights.

Wellness practitioners begin and end by making themselves models of healthy living, as they practice what they encourage others to do. For instance, wellness practitioners not only avoid smoking, but have implemented in their own lives health-producing activities such as appropriate exercise, a diet of fruit and vegetables with some protein, and visualization.

Healthcare professionals' training focuses on a generalized-practitioner approach. Each practitioner knows each wellness seeker intimately, including his or her extended family. They look at the entire picture, not just the symptoms of illness.

Healthcare professionals are prepared and trained to support, not to control. They understand the intertwining of mind and body, appreciate and use the emotions, and recognize the value of lived experience and supportive insights.

Their training and learning combines the philosophical and natural sciences. While it is based on empiricism and the latest in medical technologies, spiritual values are also taken into account. New types of healing centers combine the sacred and the scientific.

Medical research and technological advancement continue to be emphasized in medical schools as we search for the best prevention and healing practices. We discover, for instance, the effects of free-radical oxidation in the body, thus fore-stalling potential heart disease and cancer. Insights and greater understanding arise from concepts, perceptions, and values that are in a constant state of flux. In this process, we see more clearly and understand more about wellness.

If student practitioners have the motivation to serve others and the intellectual ability, plus a compassionate and empathetic personality, nothing can prevent them from becoming a physician or any other type of wellness practitioner. All potential physicians and wellness practitioners are welcomed and encouraged. Incentives encourage individuals to practice in rural areas and in distant lands. Under New Millennium assumptions, no creative mind is lost because of financial or social restrictions that exist under the Modern Worldview. Students intern in some capacity from the moment they begin their healthcare education. In this way they broaden their educational experience, and the community benefits from their education sooner than it can in the Modern Worldview Story.

Wellness seekers want to be treated as human beings. They want to be addressed as whole persons, not simply machines that need to be fixed. Thus, professionals are trained to attend to the feelings and spiritual beliefs of the wellness seeker. The key is learning how to take time, pay attention, and actively listen to the whole person, in order to arrive at a thorough understanding of what is happening physically, emotionally, and spiritually.

Healing Centers

Healing centers (hospitals) are hospitable. Both the architecture and the smiling staff manifest the feeling of a sacred place that is both lively and joyful. Since the bottom line is not the foremost indicator of success, adequate pay and leisure time enable staff to maintain a pleasant and loving attitude toward those whom they serve, as well as toward visitors and one another. They are never too busy. They literally have ample time and energy to be of service.

Wellness seekers do not perceive healing centers as places to go to die, but as places to reinforce wellness. Visitors and wellness seekers come to these centers at will, entering and leaving as they desire. They have access to any area of the healing building and don't need to be referred by a medical practitioner.

If they seek assistance with weight loss, for instance, they may go to the nutrition or exercise area.

Universal Healthcare

In the Modern Worldview Story, many people who needed health insurance coverage found it cost-prohibitive. In the Emerging Millennium Story, however, a government-mandated single-payment program provides universal coverage regardless of circumstances, thus ensuring cost-effective healthcare for everyone. The cost structure has been designed so that, as a caring enlightened community, we provide affordable coverage to both children and adults alike.

A national partnership provides opportunities for individuals, communities, and wellness professionals to work together to maintain and improve the health of everyone in the community. A good example of this is the way in which dentists and oral healthcare specialists are now providing treatment for everyone without exception, because we realize that there is a link between oral health and total well-being. By preventing oral diseases, we're preventing far more expensive illnesses and saving immense amounts of money.

Social Security

In the New Millennium Story, people are no longer afraid that Social Security benefits will run out by the middle of the twenty-first century. The arrival and acceptance of new immigrants, with their desire to work hard and find fulfillment, are contributing to Social Security funds. Moreover, governments throughout the world appreciate the contributions of senior citizens. The elderly know that if sufficient funds are not available in the Social Security program, the government will make up the deficit.

In the past, governments have had no difficulty with spending, and even borrowing, huge amounts of money to wage war. Now, defense expenditures are diverted to strengthen Social Security for the benefit of senior citizens, instead of contributing to the pockets of weapons manufacturers. Since we are all one, there's no need to spend heavily on armaments. (See Chapter Thirteen, on Politics.) Tax money is easily directed toward Social Security and the needs of senior citizens all over the world.

Life Transitions

Companies are no longer responsible for healthcare benefits or pension plans. As indicated above, governments cover wellness costs, and they make adequate provision for retirement under Social Security.

A vision of life has been created in which aging is a period of enrichment. No longer accepted is the Modernist view of aging as "decline." By focusing on aging as a time for continuing personal development, and the making available relevant resources and skills, we create hope and enthusiasm that empowers our senior citizens. By moving beyond *repair*, we emphasize enjoyable growth-enhancing activities for which poor seniors in particular previously had few opportunities.

In the New Millennium Story, we realize that all facets of a person's life contribute to, or detract from, wellness. Expanded services and opportunities for senior citizens exist, such as music, art, massage, recreation, beauty services, horticulture therapy, and personal care. These services enable senior citizens to grow, learn, and contribute, and to age with graciousness, dignity, and spirit.

A significant byproduct of this development is the ability to laugh at one's mistakes, set future goals, and overcome regrets. Tomorrow is another day, a day of accomplishment, a day to bring laughter and joy to one's great-granddaughter! These opportunities improve the day-to-day quality of life for senior citizens. The community goal is to keep individuals independent and to maintain the level of dignity and respect that they experienced when younger. Age enhances, rather than diminishes, this right to respect and dignity.

In addition, New Millennium Thinkers and Feelers provide household assistance to the elderly so that they can stay as long as possible in their own homes. Team partners assist with running errands, paying bills, preparing food, and acting as companions to those in need of companionship. Financial assistance, such as budgeting or monetary assistance, is readily available.

Friendships and personal bonds, developed throughout the years, are taken into consideration when one seeks housing facilities, should one no longer be able to live independently.

Suffering and Death

End-of-life care has changed. Emphasis is now placed on palliative care that stresses physical comfort as well as emotional and spiritual well-being, rather than simply providing curative treatment. The desire of the senior citizen to live comfortably with those whom they love is given the highest priority in the New Millennium Story. Aged and ill persons receive palliative care earlier, and home-based hospice services have been expanded. Fewer people die alone.

For Emerging Worldview Thinkers and Feelers, suffering and death are events both accepted as part of the human condition and appreciated as sources of emotional and spiritual growth. Wellness seekers understand that our physical lives on this planet necessarily come to an end. We have faith in an ever more meaningful and fulfilling existence beyond the grave. Sometimes suffering is an unavoidable prerequisite to dying. From a deeply spiritual perspective, and without being morbid, seniors give their lives over to death with a grateful attitude.

New Millennium Thinkers and Feelers therefore accept suffering and death as a meaningful learning experience, both for ourselves and for others. Our own suffering teaches us how to be empathetic and how to relate both physically and emotionally to the suffering of others. Suffering and death are an opportunity for the wellness seeker to experience meaning and joy by reaching out to serve others in need.

Neither feared nor detested, suffering and death are viewed as a positive means of self-renewal, a transformation process, a paradox in which destruction becomes the handmaid of a new creation.

Visualizing wellness, New Millennium Thinkers and Feelers now live as though our ultimate fulfillment is already present, as if we've already passed through death's doorway to a fuller engagement with the landscape of the cosmos. Wellness seekers experience peace even in the face of death and suffering.

CONCLUSION

In the New Millennium, the Emerging Worldview Story has had a significant impact on healthcare. Paternalistic, patriarchal, and hierarchical structures have collapsed. Individuals, the community, and the wellness profession have become responsible partners in preserving and providing wellness.

New Millennium healthcare is focused on enabling wellness seekers to develop healthy lifestyles while contributing to the well being of others in the community. Wellness seekers take primary responsibility for our own wellness. We act as participating partners on our own wellness team and the teams of others.

An improved tax structure ensures that no matter one's ethnicity or religion, preventative healthcare and emergency treatment are available to everyone throughout the world, without exception. For example, resources have been provided for researching a preventative strategy to arrest the spread of the AIDS epidemic: funds are available for deploying antibiotics; better health education enables world populations to better understand how HIV and other sexually transmitted diseases spread.

We learn how to act responsibly and promptly implement our learning.

In assuming that we are all one, we have made money available for treatment, prevention, and education. All three are integrated into a comprehensive plan. More than sufficient funds are available to wellness agencies for prevention and education as well as for effectively addressing crises as they arise. Sufficient money is also available for medical research, particularly in areas neglected in the past.

In Africa and other places throughout the world, malaria, tuberculosis, and the AIDS epidemic have been curtailed. Realizing that when one suffers we all suffer, financial aid from more affluent countries has supplied technology, medicine, medical personnel, and wellness volunteers who are all successfully preventing the spread of disease.

Education has been a major factor in raising awareness and understanding of how diseases are transmitted. In the case of HIV, people are tested regularly. While abstinence is important and strongly encouraged, people realize that condoms are necessary, pending the arrival of new technology to prevent the spread of HIV. Consequently, free condoms are supplied, and the infection rate has dropped significantly to minimal levels. People are back to work; food is plentiful. Children have parents once again and are joyfully attending school.

As wellness practitioners, we are excited by the new ideas, research, and discoveries of nonconventional therapies. We're convinced personal experience is valid. We distrust "objective" labels for bodily or psychological diseases. We trust self-regulation, the body's tendency toward wellness, the meaningfulness of experience, and the belief in transformation through crisis. We address the body-mind, emotion, and spirit as a whole, and the unity of the whole person with the environment. We believe in a systems approach.

As wellness providers, we work together in a totally integrated system. The result is a significant drop in healthcare costs. Wide use of complementary therapies has further contributed to cost savings. No human being is without competent and compassionate healthcare anywhere in the world.

Through a combination of creative education, coaching, and visualization, disabled people are no longer excluded and rejected in our communities. Money spent enabling them to develop themselves to their best potential has helped them to obtain work of merit and importance. The disabled have been empowered to contribute to the community and are truly an inspiration for everyone, disabled or not. We are all delightfully the beneficiaries.

CHAPTER NINE

The Story of Work

The supreme accomplishment is to blur lines between work and play.
Arnold Toynbee
Historian

Never continue in a job you don't enjoy. If you're happy in what you're doing, you'll like yourself, you'll have inner peace. And if you have that, along with physical health, you will have had more success than you could possibly have imagined.
Rodan of Alexandria

There is nothing better for man, than that he should eat and drink, and that he should make his soul enjoy good in his labor.
Solomon, speaking in Ecclesiastes 2:24

The good of the individual is contained in the common good; all work has the same value; the life of labor is the life worth living . . . I arose with the dawn, ready to reduce these principles to practice.
Mahatma Gandhi
Political and Spiritual Leader of India

What Is Work?

In the Emerging Worldview Story, work is defined as: the behavior which enables human beings to survive and thrive as we manage our lives on this planet and lovingly contribute to the common good.

Surviving relates to the lower levels of Maslow's Hierarchy of Needs, in which workers earn the basic necessities of life, such as food and shelter (physiological needs), without fear (security needs). See Figure 9.1.[1]

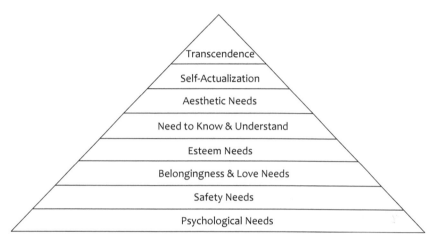

Fig. 9.1

Thriving means going beyond such necessities and experiencing acceptance and friendship within, and outside, the workplace (social needs). It also reflects finding fulfillment through one's work emotionally, intellectually, and spiritually (other-esteem, self-esteem). Beyond satisfying our esteem needs, humans are motivated to learn and understand, to appreciate and enjoy beauty (aesthetic needs), and to do what we were created to do in life (self-actualization needs). This means becoming our authentic selves, realizing our potential, "being all that we can be," as management consultant Joe Batten says.[2] Maslow believed that we are motivated further, to transcend ourselves, to connect to something beyond our egos that empowers **others** to find self-fulfillment, thereby realizing our potential. Meaningful work is not just about *me*, it is about **us**.

Workers feel empowered if they are making progress toward fulfillment. We experience freedom, responsibility, and feedback while performing meaningful and significantly valuable activities, and realize that we are proud and happy to do so. Through work, we make a living *and* find fulfillment and joy in life as we make the world a better place. When this happens, according to historian Arnold Toynbee, "The lines between work and play are blurred—and this is the supreme accomplishment!" The Greek philosopher Aristotle wrote, "Those who work with pleasure always work with more discernment and greater accuracy." We do excellent work *and* we enjoy ourselves because we are doing what we want and doing it with competence.

To do nothing is not meaningful to most people. We find it demeaning to live off the efforts of others, to receive and not be able to give. Giving of oneself, being of service, is its own reward. Moreover, the greater the significance of the gift we give, the more fulfilling it is for us. If I regard myself as valuable and I give *myself*, I am giving a valuable gift and experiencing transcendence. (See Chapter 7 on Intimacy)

Business, that is, corporate enterprise, is the focus for this story about work because of its ubiquity and because issues found in enterprise apply to most organizations—bistros, the corner store, theaters, zoos, social profits, kosher taco stands.

Pre-Modern Worldview Story of Work

In the Pre-Modern Story, existing among all societies, but dominant among the poor nations, God, stands at the pinnacle of the hierarchal pyramid. See Figure 9.2.

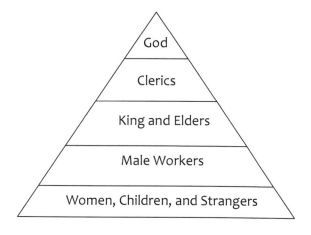

Figure 9.2

"This hierarchy began with God—its apex—and extended down to the lowliest creatures and plants," says psychologist Dr. Edmund Bourne:

> In this hierarchy, ordinary humans were subject to the authority of the church (vested in the pope and bishops), and women and children were subordinate to men. Few questioned the relative order of authority in this hierarchy because it was believed to be the revealed will of God... [O]bedience to God required not questioning the reality of this cosmic order. Indeed, the church maintained the authority to prosecute and persecute those who publicly raised questions about the nature of the world that it legislated.[3]

God reveals "the truth" to the clerics, *His* representatives on earth. They, in turn, interpret and bless "the truth" for the king and the elders, who control most properties and resources. They perceive themselves as God's prescribed guardians of *His* creation and of "absolute truth." The King rules over the male population, and they in turn control the women, children, and strangers in the land. Strangers are: slaves, the poor, immigrants, outcasts of society—all those who struggle to barely make it. They are at the bottom of the heap and, in the Pre-Modern Worldview Story, they deserve to be on the bottom; otherwise God would not have placed them there. For these individuals, work is demeaning, yet a necessity if they are to stay alive. Life, in most cases, is judged to be a trifle better than death.

Most Pre-Modern workers accept their situation because they are taught to believe it is God's will that they occupy lower and less significant positions in the hierarchy, and to believe they would have otherwise been born into rich families or given great talents. With low self-esteem, workers convince themselves they don't deserve anything better; power and authority are neither experienced nor expected. The one exception is the home, where the father, imitating the "bosses" at work, rules with an iron hand. "Spare the rod and spoil the child" is the prevalent assumption and practice of the Pre-Moderns.

Further, Pre-Modern Worldviewers believe the purpose of life is to please God by being obedient to *His* precepts and, in so doing, achieve nirvana, peace, and happiness in life after death. Survival and a little pleasure from family, sex, alcohol, sports, and other games are the most workers can expect out of life. Many of them imagine winning the lottery, thereby being free from life's bondage for the rest of their lives. Driven by this hope, the poor are the major purchasers of lottery tickets in countries throughout the world. Belief in luck, both good and bad, and miracles from God, dominates the thinking and behaviors of Pre-Moderns.

Work as Punishment for Disobeying God

For the Jews, Christians, Muslims, and others, work is viewed as punishment for disobeying God. The story in the Bible recounts Adam and Eve being discharged from the Garden of Eden for doing what God told them not to do. Based on this story, Pre-Moderns believe humans must "earn their bread by the sweat of their brow," interpreted as: Work is punishment for offending the divinity. Many people with a Pre-Modern Worldview, based largely on their interpretation of the Bible or the Qur'an, assume that the more righteous one is, the more prosperous one is, and, therefore, the less work one needs to do. Health and wealth are signs that individuals have found favor with God based on their present and past good behavior. Riches are perceived as blessings from God and rewards for doing God's will.

Implications of the Pre-Modern Worldview Story of Work

Assuming one "has to" go to work to live, creates a tendency to seek out the easiest jobs and do the least work possible. For Pre-Moderns, Monday is the worst day of the week because one "has to" return to work after a weekend off. Wednesday is "hump day," with the week half over, and Friday is "sweetest day" because the workweek is over. Friday night is "party night," allowing a sleep-in on Saturday morning. On Sunday, in mainly Christian countries, one "has to" go to church.

Economics

In the past, economics was based on agriculture as Marc Luyckx pointed out. (See Chapter 2) The kings and the elders maintained control of the primary resources: land, crops, and livestock. Today, control is related to money gained from oil, other investments, and speculation. Profits from such sources were, and continue to be, channeled upward to the corporate aristocracy, who enjoy wealth, power, and prestige without physical effort. Wealth is then passed down through generations in the "royal" families. From the perspective of effort, inheriting money is no different from welfare.

Women

Pre-Moderns believe women are meant by God to be subservient to men. The female, consequently, is largely restricted to working within the home and to mothering. This latter is extolled as one of the highest professions. Women must be satisfied with the role of taking care of their husbands and children, a chore which is often more physical than intellectual.

Mobile Workers

Beginning with the Industrial Revolution, circa 1750, laborers have left the countryside, heading for the cities in search of jobs. In poor countries, workers not only migrate to the cities, but often leave for wealthy countries, most finding jobs in factories, some backbreaking farm work, or as domestic workers. Pay is minimal, and without healthcare, insurance, or pension. Many factories in Asia and Central and South America pay what amounts to a few dollars a day, while the owners of the factories amass enormous profits. Work is typically labor-intensive, with a constant demand for greater and greater productivity. Workers are valued for their brute strength or dexterity, and decisions are made without employee input. A similar situation exists for immigrant farm workers in the United States.

Punishment

Obedience is promoted as the highest of virtues. Management expects workers, like children, to "do what they are told" and "be seen and not heard." If they do not comply, punishment ensues. A good worker is one who blindly follows orders without bothering management with questions or requests.

Workers are given identification badges, stand in line for lunch, ask the supervisor for permission to go to the bathroom, follow a dress code, and bring in a doctor's note when they miss work because of illness. Time clocks prove accountability for time at work. Often, workers are searched as they leave the premises to ensure that they do not steal.

A thirty-year-old U.S. Marine, having returned from the war in Iraq and gotten a job at a local steel mill in central Ohio, reported: "I was leading combat troops in Iraq, and now I'm picking up scrap metal. They even have rules for walking through the parking lot."[4]

Enclosed by forbidding high walls topped with barbed wire, workplaces in many poor countries which I have seen with my own eyes are only a step away from prisons. Unannounced visits to the factories by outsiders are banned and impossible. Joel Bakan, former law clerk to Chief Justice Brian Dickson of the Supreme Court of Canada, describes conditions in many poor, and even rich, nations, throughout the world:

> Behind these locked doors, mainly young women, workers are supervised by guards, who beat and humiliate them on the slightest pretence; and fire them if a forced pregnancy test comes back positive. Each worker repeats the same action—sewing on a belt loop, stitching a sleeve—maybe 2,000 times per day. They work under painfully bright lights, for 12–14 hour shifts, in overheated factories with too few bathroom breaks and restricted access to water (to reduce the need for more bathroom breaks), which is often foul and unfit for human consumption in any event... Young women work to about age 25, at which point they're fired because they're used up. They are worn out. Their lives are already over and the company has replaced them with another crop of young girls.[5]

Further, in coming to work, with their minds not needed, employees daydream. They do not expect to have a voice in making decisions about their jobs, or the products they are providing, or the operation of the company. Hence, they are passive and live in constant fear of being punished for the least infraction.

These sweatshops are justified thus: They are a step up from begging in the streets and malnutrition or starvation. Those at the top of the hierarchy believe that tasks will not be accomplished unless those in control, the "male bosses," personally see to their completion. "Subordinates" *need* to be punished and threatened. They're perceived as incompetent, incapable of self motivation, and irresponsible—especially when they are of a different gender, skin color, or nationality.

Immigrant Use and Abuse

In Hong Kong in 2007, over 500,000 women worked as domestic servants, and in Singapore another 150,000. In Japan more than 100,000 "Philipinas" are employed, mainly as nightclub entertainers or sex workers. Most come from impoverished villages in the Philippines, Indonesia, and Sri Lanka. Much of the Philippine economy is based on the money these women send back to their native land from work done in wealthier countries. I met women with teaching and nursing degrees who told me they earned more money as domestic servants in Hong Kong than they could earn teaching children or nursing the sick at home in the Philippines. They confided to me that they saw their children and husbands once every year or two. Yet they confessed to feeling blessed to have a job and proud that they could provide for their families back in the Philippines.

Modern Worldview of Work

In the Modern Worldview of work—dominant among the world's affluent countries in the twentieth century—money, measured in corporate profits, has supplanted land as the coveted resource and has replaced God as the most valued reason for human existence. Members of boards of directors and chief executive officers (CEOs), the corporate aristocracy, have become the tribal chiefs and high priests in the hierarchical pyramid. See Figure 9.3.

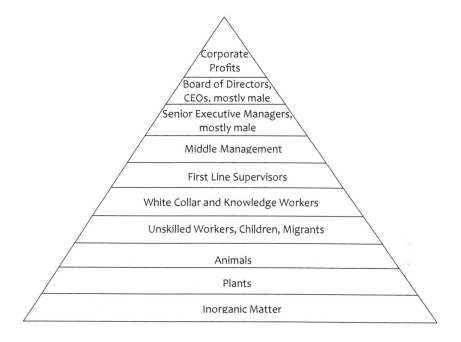

Figure 9.3

Middle management and first-line supervisors rank lower in the pyramid. Their role is to operationalize the strategic plans of their "superiors," making sure all workers below them are compliant and docile.

Some workers come to work with the hope of achieving power and wealth by climbing the rungs of the hierarchical pyramid. One possible step in the process is to study for a master's degree in business administration (MBA). Sometimes this strategy brings success in achieving power and wealth.

Animals, plants, and inorganic matter are to be used and abused depending on the wants and needs of those above in the hierarchy. Many animals are simply killed for sport.

Corporate Greed and Questionable Morality

Greed and questionable morality tend to define the corporate world's culture. Corporate greed is the reason for corporations' existence and the incentive for most company activities. According to Joel Bakan,

> [T]he law forbids the corporation to have any other motivation for its actions. It is literally against the law for a corporation to assist workers, protect the environment, or save consumers money, unless it can be demonstrated that such action benefits the bottom line of the corporation.[6]

Corporate legal teams and lobbyists work incessantly to promulgate laws that favor business, in the belief that what is good for business is good for everyone. They maintain a neoliberal philosophy, convinced that everyone's success is best served by the market, with the firm belief that government and the public sector should exert little or no influence on business. They are paid handsomely to limit government's interference, as well as that of the public.

Potential harm to others—workers, consumers, communities, and the environment—is viewed as mere collateral damage. Neoliberal philosophy, according to Noam Chomsky, acts as though "people who work for corporations are not human beings, but human resources," simply tools to generate as much profit as possible. He writes that a "tool can be treated just like a piece of metal—you use it if you want, you throw it away if you don't want it."[7] People are, thus, not considered true assets of a company, but rather are perceived as "costs."

People who manage corporations are not evil. As a professor of business, and an organizational consultant, I have met and worked with many managers in the United States and other nations of the world. I have never known a person who was guilty of malicious intent. Meeting managers, I am taken with their thoughtfulness, even kindness. Their intention is to do what they believe is good for business and for the nation. The assumption is: What is good for business and good for the nation is good for *them*. Seeing themselves as devoted, patriotic citizens, they perceive that they are contributing to the common good. My experience with university and hospital administrators is the same. They intend to be ethical and competent, in the belief that their actions are contributing to the betterment of society, even when the bottom line is the foremost value. Unfortunately, I have not found it much different in the Church. Parishes are closed for financial reasons regardless of the feelings of the faithful parishes.

Implications of the Modern Worldview Story of Work Women in the Workplace

Slowly, and with reluctance on the part of management in many cases, women are being granted workplace positions of power and influence, but only in certain professions. For example, in the Catholic Church, women are not allowed to be priests. In most companies women receive lower pay than men doing the same work; further, they regularly experience everything from lack of promotions to sexual harassment. Kim Gandy, President of the National Organization for Women (NOW), stated that "Women in the United States make up less than 15% of Congress and law-firm partners, 12% of big-city mayors, 9% of state judges, and one-percent of Fortune 500 CEOs . . . In most industries the higher up one looks, the fewer women can be seen. Looking downwards in the hierarchy one sees a greater number of women. It means far more women are likely to live in poverty than men."

A 2008 Grant Thornton International study reports that the highest percentage of women in senior management, 47 percent, is found in the Philippines. The lowest, 7 percent, is in Japan. In 34 percent of private businesses worldwide, no women hold senior management positions.[8]

In Saudi Arabia in 1985, I found a beautiful new corporate office building designed by a Chicago architect. The outer walls of the edifice were practically all glass. A waterfall within was a reminder of the preciousness of water. Nowhere in the building, however, could be found a women's restroom. The personnel director revealed to me that, apart from his wife and children, he sometimes goes months without hearing a woman's voice. In frustration sometimes he calls London just to speak to a female secretary.

Blind Obedience

Both female and male employees who are below senior executive management are programmed to believe in "the truth" handed down from the corporate aristocracy. Having learned never to publicly question this truth, they "do as they are told" if they want to keep their jobs. Promotion to higher hierarchical rank, climbing the ladder of success within the company, together with monetary increases, is the anticipated "carrot," the reward for compliance in terms of "doing a good job." "Going along to get along" is the common result. Whistle blowers who point out ethical transgressions are considered disloyal and are treated as such.

Lack of Ethics

A positive bottom line tells top management that the corporation is correct in its actions, even when the actions do not adhere to society's rules and laws. After all, "A sucker is born every minute."

Thousands of companies have experienced the results of such leadership, and thereby contributed to the conditions that motivated the U.S. government, in 2008, to approve a massive economic bailout in order to avert another Great Depression.

The inequities of the subprime mortgage crisis that began in 2007, combined with the 2008 commercial-paper fiascoes and deregulated credit-default swaps, have put the whole world into a capitalistic crisis and a state of fear unparalleled since the Great Depression of the 1930s. According to the International Monetary Fund, the "world economy is now entering a major downturn in the face of the most dangerous shock in mature financial markets since the 1930's."[9] This bungling behavior by Modern Worldviewers has caused a breach of trust—without which capitalism cannot exist—leading to debacles such as the famous cases of Bernard Madoff swindling $50 billion from investors; the Enron Corporation manipulating electricity at the expense of its clients and employees; American International Group/AIG's receipt of up to $180 billion in federal bailouts, $93 billion of which was funneled to Goldman Sachs Group and a host of European banks, while AIG itself rewarded its managers with $165 billion in bonuses—the same managers who issued billions of dollars in derivatives insuring risky assets.[10] And Citigroup, another recipient of US taxpayers' money in 2008, posted five consecutive quarters of multibillion-dollar losses but nevertheless in 2008 rewarded its CEO, Vikram S. Pandit, with a compensation package valued at $38.2 million; this in addition to the $80 million Mr. Pandit received for selling his hedge funds to Citigroup in 2007.[11] No wonder the American electorate is angry and threatens to "throw the bums out" referring to previously elected officials.

The Sky's the Limit on Margins

Deregulation has opened the door to more monopolies and less customer satisfaction. To better control the market, companies seek to buy out their competition. Once successful, they overcharge or maximize the margin for their products, as much as they perceive the market will bear. Price depends on supply and demand rather than on the intrinsic value of the product.

Business students are taught to achieve, and managers are rewarded for, the highest margins possible. There is no upper limit, even if the product costs the customer one hundred times the company's costs for producing it! Such results are praised and rewarded. If such practices are challenged, the response is that immense profits eventually bring competitors into the business—ultimately driving down prices: proof that the capitalistic system works.

Business schools teach students techniques designed to achieve these unlimited margins. The more effectively CEOs promote an increase in the bottom line, the more often they are brought to campus to lecture; this suggests to students that these modern-day heroes are to be admired and imitated.

The corporate aristocracy is exceedingly well paid. In the U.S. between 2000 and 2005, productivity grew by 2.3 percent. However, employment rates and median family income dropped. In the same years, corporate profits soared by 50 percent.

Only the corporate aristocracy benefited from this prosperity. According to Lowell L. Klessig, emeritus professor of integrated resource management at the University of Wisconsin, Stevens Point:

> A good Chief Executive Officer deserves to be paid well. But does any CEO deserve to be paid more each day, including weekends, holidays, and vacations, than an average employee of the company is paid for a full year? Reality is even more outrageous. On average, American CEOs earn 411 times what their employees earn. Some CEOs earn more than 1000 times what their lowest paid workers earn.[12]

Customer Service

Even though many companies claim that their highest priority is great customer service, the reality is that the bottom line—profit—takes precedence. Automation has replaced the human element. When a consumer contacts a company by phone, it is rare to encounter a human being, especially one who is both competent and accommodating.

Global Implications of the Modern Worldview Assumptions Regarding Work

Under Modern Worldview thinking and acting, heavy emphasis is placed on competition and the destruction of the opposition; business has become, according to Juan Somavia, current Director-General of the International Labour Organization (ILO), more fragmented, protectionist, and confrontational. Half of all workers in the world are the working poor, living on less than two dollars a day per person. Because they work without social security or healthcare, parents conceive many children to ensure that they will be cared for in their old age or when they are too sick to work.[13]

About a billion people, including refugees, are homeless. The homeless dramatically represent the failure of Modern Worldview capitalistic assumptions. One-sixth of the people of the world are victims of the system's basic inequity.[14] In the year 2007, famine killed twenty-four thousand people every day. Over a billion people are hungry at this moment. Their hunger could be prevented if rich countries spent just nineteen billion dollars to eliminate starvation and malnutrition globally, a mere drop in the world's bucket.

In January 2009 the International Labor Organization (ILO) reported:

> The scenarios for working poverty suggest that the proportion of poor workers may rise, ranging from an increase of 1.5 percentage points to an increase of 4.8 percentage points in 2009. The latter case would suggest a return to a situation in which more than half of the global labour force would be unemployed or counted as working poor.[15]

Unable to find work at home, these victims of Modern Worldview assumptions contribute to immigrant tensions, human trafficking, and terrorist activities. Demands for greater investment in the military to protect against terrorism and to finance more effective immigration control are the result of Modern Worldview assumptions. Governments play upon citizens' fears of those who are different in race, nationality, and religion.

Discrimination abounds. Immigrants are blamed. No consideration is given to the fact that, if the people were employed in meaningful jobs at home, few would chance the dangers of becoming illegal immigrants—or even want to leave their own country. Modern Worldview assumptions blame and build walls, instead of searching for explanations and trying to understand immigrants' motivation.

The New Millennium Story

New Millennium Thinkers and Feelers, having changed and adopted the Four Fundamental Assumptions, realize that the reason we work is not only to make a living, but to experience meaning and fulfillment in our lives. We achieve these ends through participation and cooperation. In our New Millennium Story, we renounce competition between companies and among members of the same company. We resist authoritarianism with its command-and-control mentality. We embrace an egalitarian appreciation of the value of everyone's contribution. Subsidiarity, or pushing decision-making down to the person doing the job, is one of our highest values. Solidarity in which we network together to achieve the common good is another salient value.

Our purpose for being in business is to produce a quality product or service which enhances the lives of others and is available at a reasonable price. Profit, although necessary, is a byproduct. Profit is to the corporation what air is to the individual. We need to breathe to live, but we do **not** live to breathe. In our New Millennium Story, we realize that our companies exist for the good of all the stakeholders, namely, employees, suppliers, customers, government, and the local and worldwide community—not only for the stockholders and top management.

We Are Forever in the Process of Discovering

We assume there are no absolute "truths" we can know for sure. Consequently, in the workplace we do not argue over who is right and who is wrong. Instead, we seek to understand how, with our colleagues, we can look at an issue and see it in various different ways. Through dialogue, our purpose is to be open to other points of view rather than convincing other employees, customers, and suppliers of the correctness of our own view. Leaders and other employees seek to discover, through this dialogue, a shared way to work together for the good of the company and the community.

We Continually Create Our Own Reality

Most of the ideas for making organizational change in the Pre-Modern and Modern Worldview Stories revolve around "fixing what is broken." In the Emerging Worldview Story, little attention is paid to what is wrong or "the problem" with employees or organizations. Johann Wolfgang von Goethe has written: "If you treat a man as he appears to be, you make him worse than he is, but if you treat a man as if he already were what he potentially could be, you make him what he should be."

Hence, using the theory of Appreciative Inquiry, or AI, created by Dr. David C. Cooperrider,[16] we use our heads and hearts to create our own reality, based on what is already working well and on what we might do to activate an organization's potential. We look for successes rather than problems, and we work to amplify these successes.

Appreciative Inquiry assumes that everyone in the system is knowledgeable in one way or another. It further assumes that everyone is capable and wants to contribute their wisdom through co-creation. Everyone in the company and its environment (the total system) discovers, dreams, designs, and delivers what they themselves, and the others in the system, seek and co-create. We use visualization to appreciate the positive potential of one another and the organization, then create and realize our dreams. Again, Goethe inspires us when he writes, "Whatever you can do or dream you can, begin it. Boldness has genius, power and magic in it."

We Are All One

In the New Millennium Story, we have come to realize that, since we are all one (employees, suppliers, customers, stockholders, the government, and members of the local and worldwide community), what is good for the company is good for everyone, and what is good for everyone is beneficial for the company. We are one even with our so- called "competitors." We are not in competition! Together we cooperate and co-create for the benefit of all.

We realize that we all benefit when another company invents or improves a product or service. The successes of other companies are a challenge to our own ingenuity and creativity, as well as an opportunity for us to develop a product which serves others in an even more beneficial and cost-effective way. We do not seek to be better than other companies. We seek to build upon rather than tear down. We enjoy the challenge of seeking to improve our own capability to the maximum of our potential. The competencies and successes of other companies invite and encourage us to realize our own potential and to accomplish for the sake of all.

When a new and successful restaurant opens down the street from ours, this tells the world that this is the street to come to for fine restaurants. In Minneapolis, Minnesota, Nicollet Avenue has come to be known as "Eat Street." The better the new restaurant, the more it attracts patrons to the area. Hungry prospective customers visit our restaurant, as well as others on the street, seeking perhaps a varied ethnic menu and a variety of food preparations. The new restaurant is not a competitor. Rather, in manifesting the oneness and distinctiveness of the food industry, it becomes a catalyst to attract more customers to our street and our restaurant.

As employees, New Millennium Thinkers and Feelers have changed yet another of the foci. Where the focus was once simply on *my* success (prevalent in Pre-Modern and Modern Worldviews), it has been enlarged to include the entire business, all employees. We have changed rampant toxic organizational cultures and relationships into healthy "we-centered" environments. What is beneficial for others is automatically beneficial to each of us—or it is not beneficial at all.

Since we assume that we are all one, we realize that we are all interdependent and interconnected. Consequently, as employees, we co-create with and cooperate with the other employees, enabling all of us and the company as a whole to attain our full potential. We realize that competition is an "Us-versus-Them" attitude which erodes trust. It results in self-centered behaviors of command and control, blame, punishment, resignation, and negative self-talk. On the other hand, cooperation and co-creation increase trust and encourage a service-centered attitude toward one another inside the company and outward to the community. Complaining has been replaced by positive self-talk.

This is *not* an abdication of autonomy. It is analogous to the current system enjoyed worldwide by artists. Artists—film, sculpture, painting, writing, music— live isolated lives (as do the workers in Pre-Modern and Modern Worldview settings). This aloneness leads them to become members of what is known as *The Artists' Community*. This community crosses all disciplines; the painter supports the poet as well as other painters, the musician supports the filmmaker as well as other musicians, and so forth. This support includes encouragement, constructive critiques of each other's work, and input on marketing and distribution. Its manifestations are camaraderie, networking, and interconnection.

Likewise, with this assumption of oneness, company employees are able to find balance between what a single employee wants and what other company employees desire. We give the same priority to the desires of associates as we do to our own career and success goals. We show consideration and empathy for one another while maintaining a realistic focus on the organization's survival and growth. In so doing, we assume that we actually help ourselves when we are of service to others.

We Always Do What We Perceive Is Best

Every employee seeks to do a good job; the result is that more than ninety-nine percent of employees actually *do* a good job. Neither managers, workers, suppliers, customers, nor anyone else, wakes up in the morning with the intention of hurting themselves or their own place of work. People see work as a means of contributing to the community and supporting their families, in the process of experiencing fulfillment and transcendence.

Implications of the New Millennium Story of Work

We Manage Our Thoughts and Feelings

New Millennium Thinkers and Feelers are aware of this well-accepted concept: *How we feel influences how we think.*

And, in turn, our thoughts influence how we feel. By consciously integrating our emotional and intellectual lives, we are able to distinguish between thoughts and feelings. Recognizing that all feelings are good, even anger and sadness, we are not afraid in the workplace to reveal: "I feel pleased and excited by the research you did on this report!" Or: "After all the hours spent on this proposal, I feel disappointed and frustrated that it was rejected!"

Aware also of the feelings of others, we encourage our colleagues to open up and are sensitive to *nonverbal* actions and reactions. In highly emotional situations at work, we assume that no one knows the absolute "truth"; therefore, we disagree vehemently and still refrain from becoming disagreeable! Amiable behavior toward colleagues in disagreement comes from knowing that neither position is absolutely right. Hurting another, physically or emotionally, makes no sense.

Relationships at work go beyond mere acceptance of one another; they take on a satisfying intimacy.

Communication

Communication is no longer a matter of semantics. Words are significant expressions of employees' values. Words such as "superiors," "bosses," and "subordinates" perpetuate Pre-Modern and Modern Worldview stories. "Partners," "associates," "managers," "facilitators," "servant leaders," and "reports" (for people who *report* to managers) are in vogue among New Millennium Thinkers and Feelers. The term "associates" includes *all* who work for an organization. Managers, even CEOs, are associates, equal to janitors and food servers. We function differently and play different roles in the organization, yet everyone makes a significant contribution.

Further, referring to employees as "associates" rather than "subordinates" is expressive of a respectful and appreciative orientation to others and to ourselves. Our words dissolve dependency and stress interdependence. Meaningful communication assumes that we are all equal (but not the same), and we all deserve mutual respect. No longer believing we are "allowed" to do things, we become "enabled" and "empowered," thus performing competently and willingly with confidence.

Problems Are Replaced by Challenges and Opportunities

The word "problem" is hardly or rarely uttered in the workplace. Employees speak of challenges and opportunities. No longer are "problem-solvers" placed on a pedestal. Team-players, who build on the positive qualities and accomplishments of others, are the ones who are acclaimed and imitated.

Gratitude

In response to a "Thank you" for doing a colleague a favor, we hear "It's my pleasure"; we do *not* hear: "It's my duty," as in a communist state, and *not:* "No problem," as is common among students and others in the Modern Worldview.

Cheerful Service

Service is rendered with a cheerful spirit because we assume that we are all one: interdependent and interconnected. When we serve one another, we assume we are enhancing ourselves. We have come to appreciate that the secret of happiness on this earth is being for others. It is the major reason we are "in business."

Non-Profits Become Social-Profits

"Non-profits" no longer exist. In the Emerging Worldview Story, we realize that social-profit organizations make substantial contributions to the community—which enables all of us to *profit*.

Work Is a Privilege

Associates perceive that they no longer "have to" go to work, nor "should," nor "must" do a particular job. Associates "get to" go to work! We are "invited" and "empowered" to do certain tasks, rejoicing and grateful for the challenge and the learning involved.

Feeling Powerful

When we leave our workplace, we no longer wish others, "Have a nice day!" suggesting that having a nice day is a matter of chance. Now we strongly urge, with enthusiasm and sincerity, "Make it a nice day!" Implied is: Each of us has the power and the responsibility to create our own happiness. If we are not happy today, we do not blame our spouse, our business associates, or the weather. We realize that only we ourselves determine how we feel about anything that is happening in our lives. No one else has the power to "make" us happy or "make" us angry. We are in control of our feelings! We believe we are responsible for how we feel every moment of our life, and this belief empowers us.

Feelings

In response to the very intimate question "How are you?" in the New Millennium Story one rarely hears "Fine." Emerging Worldview Thinkers and Feelers realize we are a complexity of emotions. At any given moment we could be experiencing happiness, excitement, and fear along with a host of other feelings. We may, for instance, be grieving because of our mother's death, but also feeling relieved and grateful she is no longer suffering, feeling comfortable with a friend as we talk about Mother and her death, and feeling happy she lived as long as she did.

We do *not*, moreover, identify with our feelings. In the New Millennium Story it is abnormal to hear someone say, "I am depressed" or "I am happy." Managers and associates may say, "I am experiencing feelings of happiness" or "feelings of depression." When we experience *feelings of* depression or happiness, these do not constitute who we *are*. We refuse to identify with any feeling. I am not depressed! I may have feelings of depression. The distinction is of major importance in the New Millennium Story. Each of us is an authentic self who has specific feelings in the now, in any particular situation and place. We can control these feelings. No one can make us angry or happy. We are capable of feeling cheerful and grateful in the workplace, no matter what has happened. It is up to us.

Breathing

In difficult work situations or stressful meetings, as well as during other times throughout the day, we perform exercises enabling us to remain focused and centered. We take three slow, deep breaths, focusing our attention on inhaling energy and breathing out negative thoughts and feelings. Feelings of peacefulness come over us. We are able then to think clearly, responding with calmness; we are better able to appreciate others and be aware of their good intentions.

Taking Time

On the way home from work, many of us find a favorite spot where we can quietly commune with nature. We spend ten or fifteen minutes paying attention to the changing color of the leaves, the sounds of squirrels and birds, the smell of fresh air—all in the present moment. At the same time, we are aware of thoughts and feelings welling up inside us amid these welcome expressions of nature. Afterward, feeling at peace, we continue our drive home refreshed. Once at home, we lovingly greet and communicate with our family, leaving the challenges of the day's work for tomorrow.

Imagining

Associates express their dreams and positive visions of the company in the present tense, using the first-person singular "I" or "we," while eliminating all negatives and affirming all positives. "I have failed to make my sales quota" has been supplanted with affirmations such as "Our sales are over quota this quarter and we expect even greater customer satisfaction next quarter because we are doing [the following things]." Such statements are not lies or exaggerations. Our imagination does not know the difference. It cannot handle the negative. If I say, "I am not failing to reach my sales target," the imagination hears, "I am failing to reach my sales target." As a consequence, I then go on to fail to reach my sales target! Instead, one states, "I am making my sales quota, and it feels wonderful!" The persistent affirmation enables one, over time, to be a successful sales person.

Associates, therefore, in the New Millennium Story, persist in expressing their personal and company vision in the positive present tense. Our collective envisioning enables us to realize our dreams.

Cognitive Dissonance

Cognitive dissonance, or the apparent contradiction between present sales and our sales vision, provides the motivation and creativity to persist and persevere in actions leading to what we actually want. We either begin surpassing our sales total, or we cease our positive self-talk and our sales efforts decline. The dissonance, or pain of dishonesty, drives us to actually act one way or the other.

Leadership in the New Millennium Story

Leaders perceive themselves as servants of those who report to them. This concept was developed by Robert Greenleaf in his book *The Servant as Leader*.[17] Rather than the Modern Worldview's hierarchical chain of command, with emphasis on the power and dominance of the executives and docility and compliance on the part of the workers, New Millennium Thinkers and Feelers share responsibility, accountability, and respect—all heretofore accorded only to top management. The traditional pyramid is turned upside down. The leaders are at the bottom, supporting and serving the associates, rather than being masters served by the associates. See Figure 9.4.

EMPLOYEES

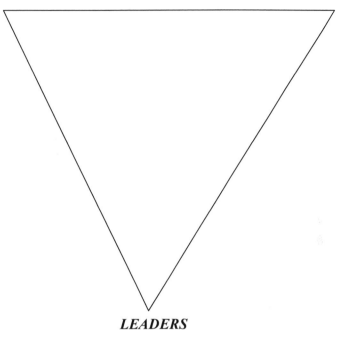

LEADERS

Figure 9.4

Relational, revolving, and involving, New Millennium leadership includes emotional intelligence, self-reflection, and a commitment to appreciating and connecting with others. Through trust, leaders employ skills such as: systems thinking, active listening, empathy, self-awareness, openness, influence (rather than control), foresight, flexibility, and community-building. In this environment associates grow personally, become less dependent on leadership, and become effective leaders themselves. Embracing feelings of empowerment, they strive to give more than they receive. "Power-over" becomes "power-with."

Leadership is inclusive, appreciates others, develops partnerships, encourages risk, and invites sharing. The result: associates are highly motivated to make the organization succeed.

Both leaders and followers develop, and implement, the company's plans together. They work cooperatively, even in the face of personality and workplace differences. The outcome is a human organization in which everyone shares in the responsibility of learning what is best for everyone concerned. The leadership pays close attention to the needs of all associates and seeks to contribute to their positive sense of self within the organization. This results in overall success in the marketplace.

Working Teams

In the New Millennium Story, associates work in teams, are accepted, and treat one another as equals. Managers are perceived, not as "bosses" or "superiors," but as colleagues and friends. Circles replace the hierarchical structure. Solidarity and subsidiarity supplant patriarchy and paternalism. Associates engage in examining the total system as they are invited to reconceive the organization as a whole. See Figure 9.5.

Figure 9.5

In the New Millennium Story, businesses recognize the value of having team members work together to address various challenges and opportunities. Diverse talents, knowledge, skill sets, and experiences derive from the benefits of cultural, religious, and age differences. All associates synergistically contribute to the company's benefit. Team membership is determined by the individual talent, knowledge, and skills needed for a particular project or situation. At times membership can include customers, suppliers, even government representatives.

Leaders Evolve and Revolve

Team members alternate as leaders according to who has the needed information and/or energy at specific project times. A revolving, evolving process results in more rather than less leadership. Senior managers and other management-team members take turns being the CEO, in behavior if not in title, in the same way that the leader of a wedge of migrating geese falls back when it becomes tired and another takes the lead.

When a team discovers an idea or method that works better than any of the others, the associates implement it with an open mind, continuing to look for even more effective and efficient ways to provide quality products and services at a price customers can afford. Profits are secondary, and the primary goal is truly to serve the customer.

A Service Orientation Has Replaced Production Worldwide

Knowledge, heartfelt actions, and technology enable the communication of ideas and values. Products, money, and natural resources are delivered across continents, resulting in cooperation with partners and customers in other nations. Information and feelings, not as truth, but as points of view, are shared freely across borders. For example, a project team might consist of a computer analyst in India; engineers in Korea, Canada and the United States; technicians in China; and sales associates in Israel, Pakistan, and Brazil.

Dialogue

Assuming ourselves to be one and not separate, associates in the Emerging Worldview Story are creating an environment of dialogue with the focus on interconnections and inclusion. We begin with the assumption that everyone means well, and we appreciate each other for who we are. We engage in behaviors which honor one another's uniqueness, in the manner of participants in the positive experiences of U.S. encounter groups and sensitivity groups of the 1960s. Valuable training time is given to encouraging participants to be open and honest with one another in the present moment, always with the intention of seeking what is best for one another. Openness is encouraged and rewarded, which enables associates to break through "the code of silence" and express personal thoughts and feelings.

We also openly share dreams for ourselves and the company, together with our assumptions, beliefs, and biases. We courageously confess fears about being excluded, rejected, or judged unfairly, or feeling stupid and looking foolish in front of others. Mutual accountability and shared responsibility result from this evidence of vulnerability, as each associate moves from "personal" self-interest to "mutual" self-interest.

Negative thinking is transformed into positive thinking. New possibilities for the future are discovered. Opportunities open up, expanding our minds and emotions in new and exciting ways. With this awareness, we create a sense of community, in which leaders and followers feel trusted, accepted, and valued. We thereby have the experience of being freed up to strive for a higher level of performance. We intend to do what is best for ourselves, others, and the organization.

The End of GDP

Economists and policymakers under Pre-Modern and Modern assumptions assert that national output in the form of gross domestic product (GDP) is the key indicator measuring economic development. The value of goods and services which are exchanged for money determines a country's GDP. The goal is to maximize both the amount and the value of these goods and services, with this assumption: The more economic activity there is, the better off we all are. Writing in *The Futurist* magazine, Dr. Robert Costanza critiques the GDP measurement of a nation's economy:

GDP is limited, measuring only marketed activity or gross income. It also counts all of this activity as positive. It does not separate desirable, well-being-enhancing activity from undesirable, well-being-reducing activity. [Bury: For example, an oil spill as in the Gulf of Mexico in 2010] increases GDP because someone has to clean it up, but it obviously detracts from society's well-being. From the perspective of GDP, more crime, more sickness, more war, more pollution, more fires, storms, and pestilence are all potentially good things, because they can increase marketed activity in the economy.

GDP also leaves out many things that enhance well-being, but are outside the market. For example, the unpaid work of parents caring for their own children at home doesn't show up, nor does the non-marketed work of natural capital in providing clean air and water, food, climate regulation, and a host of other eco-system services . . .[18]

In the words of U.S. President John F. Kennedy, "GDP measures everything except those things that make human lives worthwhile." For example, in Thailand GDP grows but wages do not, according to Sethaput Suthiwart-Narueput, a member of Thailand's SCB Economic Intelligence Center. He adds, "Focusing too much on GDP distracts us from the things that really matter: people's welfare and living standards." He asks, "Why doesn't the country's productivity and wage growth get equal billing with GDP growth?"[19]

Emerging Economic Measurements

The New Millennium Story assumes that people recognize the following as the purpose of the economy: to provide sustainable human welfare, *not gross income*. This purpose includes material well-being, while also understanding the limits of economic consumption. Hence, New Millennium Thinkers and Feelers prefer the Genuine Progress Index (GPI) to measure our quality of life. It separates the positive from the negative components of marketed economic activity while adding the value of nonmarketed products and services. For example, all the thousands of hours of volunteer work adjusted for income-distribution effects, and are recognized, valued, and counted.

New Millennium Thinkers and Feelers also prefer to measure our growth and development by Gross International Happiness (GIH). Behavioral scientist Runt Veenhoven has created a world database of happiness. GIH is based on equitable development, environmental conservation, cultural heritage, and good governments. His research concludes that there is more to life than making money. He found that General Well-Being is more important than Gross Domestic Product.

Veenhoven's Gross International Happiness research reveals what determines individual and collective happiness: high-quality education, good nutrition, freedom from fear and violence, gender equality, and, most important of all, the ability to be an agent on behalf of what matters to oneself and one another. In other words, personal freedom, with the ability and the opportunity to actually be of service to others—this is the root of happiness.

The VISA Story

The New Millennium Story is about ordinary people thinking and feeling differently about work. We consistently do extraordinary things, but *not* for the purpose of being recognized, applauded, or given more money. We do these extraordinary things because we assume we have been graced with the competency and opportunity to do so. We also perceive them as the "best," most effective deeds needing to be done. Dee Hock, CEO emeritus, explains:

> Imagine for a moment a business where more than 23,000 separate institutions from over 200 countries and territories and 355 million people use its products to make 7.2 billion transactions exceeding 650 billion dollars annually—the largest

single block of purchasing power in the world! People involved are, at one and the same time, its owners, its associates, its members and its managers. It exists as an integral part of the most highly regulated of industries, yet it is not subject to any regulatory authority in the world.[20]

This community actually exists. VISA is its name. It was created, and continues to be, one of the most poignant examples of the New Millennium Worldview in business today. Hock continues the description of this Emerging Worldview company:

VISA is a non-stock, for profit, Membership Corporation. It is an inside-out holding company, not holding anything, but being held by its functioning parts. It has a market value exceeding 150 billion, yet it cannot be bought, traded or sold, since ownership is held in the form of membership rights.

Each member owns a portion of the business it creates and is reflected in an individual's own stock. It has had no less than 20 percent and as much as 50 percent compound annual growth for a quarter of a century. Its associates receive mediocre salaries by commercial standards and are not compensated with equity [and] acquire wealth for their services. Yet those people selected their VISA name, completed the largest trademark conversion in commercial history in a third of the time anticipated, and built the prototype of the present communications system in ninety days for less than $25,000.[21]

When Dee Hock and his team of seven were asked in 1968 to look into what was happening to banks in terms of the beginning use of credit cards, their findings were shocking:

Bank after bank had issued credit cards. Operating credit and fraud losses were believed to be in the tens of millions of dollars. In actuality, losses were not in the tens of millions, but in the hundreds of millions and accelerating.[22]

The team realized that tinkering with the organizational structure, management styles, and processes was clearly not the way to proceed.

Reorganizing, reengineering and reinventing were the wrong "RE"! What was needed, in the most fundamental sense, was to re-conceive the concept of bank, money, and credit cards—even beyond that, to the essential elements of each and how they might change in a microelectronic environment.[23]

This entailed altering assumptions about work and *imagining* an altogether different kind of organization, from a systems perspective. They needed to *reconceive,* with their heads *and* hearts, a business far beyond where they were and what they had known.

Dee Hock sums up this amazing result: "Given the right circumstances, from no more than dreams, determination, and the liberty to try, quite ordinary people consistently do extraordinary things."[24]

As they began their work, Dee Hock and his team concluded they needed to broaden the measure of organizational success from the merely financial, to include social, ecological, and economic factors, forming a triple bottom line. It was a new way to think and feel about values. They left the Pre-Modern and Modern Worldviewers' stories far behind!

They recognized that, under the present circumstances, none of the individual banks could survive. Moving beyond the normal hierarchical structures of an obsolete capitalistic system, they made manifest a dream in which everyone who wants to work can have a job that provides for a decent living *and* brings fulfillment to the associates, who in turn realize that they can significantly contribute to the common good. To achieve this dream, Dee Hock and his team concluded that they themselves needed to model from the beginning the same behavior they wished to create. The process itself needed to be one of evolving, of reinventing almost everything as they went along. The present VISA community is the result.

In the New Millennium Story, highly supportive and collaborative environments exist for the purpose of encouraging extraordinary things to happen. Workers don't experience being used and treated like a piece of equipment. Being valued and achieving success result in high self-esteem and satisfaction among associates. The beneficiaries are delighted customers, suppliers, associates, and members of the community. Through the use of open source computer technology, associates have all the information necessary to do the work successfully. No more secrecy! No more confidentiality! No more asking for permission! Shared information and openness to everyone's ideas are the norm.

Since all associates share in the ownership of the business, everyone's livelihood depends on one another's competence and commitment. With this spirit of entrepreneurship, we are motivated to do whatever needs to be done to ensure high-quality products and services at a just and reasonable price, bringing satisfaction to all of our customers. Excuses such as "That's not my job" are no longer heard.

The Semco Story

In 1981, Ricardo Semler inherited his father's business in São Paulo, Brazil. The Semco Company was in every respect an example of the dominant Modern Worldview. Semco was a traditional manufacturing company, complete with a typical hierarchical structure. Command-and-control management style prevailed. Rules, rules, and more rules were in place for every contingency. Little thinking or decision-making was asked for or required of the workers.

At Ricardo's invitation, he and the workers set out to *reconceive* and *reinvent* the company. Thinking and feeling differently, they didn't focus on what the company was doing wrong, nor on all its problems. Instead, together they examined what the company did *right*. They dreamed about how they could make the company even better.

Believing in the human potential of Semco's associates, Ricardo sees his role as catalyst and cheerleader. He perceives himself as neither the CEO with all the answers, nor the only one with a company vision. Believing that it takes the whole company to create its own reality, Ricardo has the ongoing goal of having all Semco associates involved into reconceiving and re-creating an environment in which they are empowered to make meaningful contributions, and experience fulfillment in the process.

Invited by Ricardo to reconceive and reinvent the company, associates have indeed become creative and innovative. The old rules have been discarded: counting everything, regulating everyone, and keeping track of who is late. Emphasis is on associates' thought, judgment, and common sense. Free of all the numbers and rules, associates' goal is to think, innovate, and act as mature adults. Trust in both the integrity and the competency of the associates replaces old rules and regulations. As a sign of this trust, profit-sharing has become democratic. Associate assemblies now negotiate how the funds are distributed and have determined that 25 percent of corporate profits are to be shared.

When I visited the Semco factory in 2003, I found it messy and beneficently chaotic. Associates were working in clusters or teams. The workplace appeared disorderly, since machines were not evenly spaced. Associates were, and still are, responsible for secondary maintenance and for cleaning up their own work areas. It is easy to imagine why cleaning is sometimes lowest on their list of priorities.

Scoreboards above the shop floor indicate the workers' current production as compared against monthly goals they themselves have set. The scoreboards serve as feedback motivation for achieving their goals.

Once a team decides an issue, it stays decided, the employees told me, unless receiving new information, the team itself determines to change it. No approval is needed to make a change. Teams are held together by a natural system of collegial respect.

As workers learned to take more responsibility for their own work, the need for supervisors diminished. The ladder of success at Semco has become circular, going from twelve levels of management to three, with concentric circles replacing the traditional hierarchical pyramid.

Managers are evaluated by their reports every six months. Everyone sees the posted results. No secrets exist under the guise of confidentiality. Training sessions teach the associates how to give constructive feedback in a manner which enables the recipient to hear it clearly and profit from the ideas and suggestions offered.

Satellite Program

Semco associates believe that the best way to empower workers is to practice subsidiarity, which results in involving them in the decisions affecting them! Not believing in the economics of scale, Semco has divided itself into small factory/business units of approximately 250 associates. Everyone knows everyone else, and people address one another by their first names.

Because of Semco's determination to remain small, it is necessary to outsource work. The associates have developed a satellite program. Instead of contracting work to strangers, associates developed a process for contracting to themselves. Encouraged, and helped, to become owners of a satellite business, associates supply materials, equipment, and expertise to the mother company. At no cost, Semco leases to the associates the very machines that they operate at Semco.

Results at Semco

How did it work? Between 1994 and 2003, annual revenue increased from $35 million a year to $212 million. Ricardo Semler states:

> Our [associates], who each produced an average of $10,800 worth of goods a year in 1980, in 1993 produced $92,000 worth of goods a year

(adjusted for inflation), four times the national average. Associates at Semco have discovered their potential. They are continuing to turn their dreams into the reality they want.[26]

Semco has remained successful and has diversified, including the creation of: Semco Ventures, Semco Manutenção Volante (mobile maintenance services providing electrical and civil maintenance throughout Brazil), Semco–Pitney Bowes, Semco Bioenergy Project (which gave rise to BRENCO (Brazilian Renewable Energy Company), and the Semco Group as founding shareholder in Tarpon Investimentos (one of the first asset managers in Brazil to access the market).[27]

The Terra Bite Story

In the little town of Kirkland, Washington, USA, is a coffee shop named the Terra Bite Lounge. Located at State Street and Kirkland Avenue, this for-profit business appears to be a typical coffee shop with the usual variety of ways to drink coffee—except that at Terra Bite *there are no prices!* In the spirit of the New Millennium Story, especially in being seen as guests as well as customers, everyone is invited to pay what they wish, or skip it altogether. Associates pay absolutely no attention to the amount of money customers place in a metal box on the counter.

Terra Bite founder and owner Ervin Peretz, a 38-year-old Google programmer, trusts people. And experience has proven that his trust is well placed. People care about those who cannot pay the amount needed to keep the café afloat and generously pay extra. As a result, the coffee shop not only survives, but thrives.

Peretz puts his faith in people. He believes that they are basically generous and, at the same time, act in their own perceived self-interest. To give is its own reward. Generous customers pay more than the cost of a cup of coffee and a bagel-with-cream cheese. They also know that if they forget their wallet they can still stop by for a "magical mocha" and a croissant without paying a nickel, and without experiencing an ounce of guilt.

Since November 2006, Terra Bite has served up to eighty customers a day, averaging about three dollars per transaction. A playful spirit among the patrons and staff enlivens the atmosphere. Everyone feels welcome, poor and rich alike. Nobody is excluded.[28] Terra Bite is a social-profit enterprise which breaks even.

The Open-Source Story

As a result of assuming that we are all one and not separate from one another, the open-source approach has come into vogue in the New Millennium Story. Not only every associate, but literally, everyone who has an interest and the motivation, can now participate in the economic and social well-being of the planet. Dr. Arnat Leemakeej, director of the Master in Finance Programme at Thammasat University in Thailand, describes one example:

> One individual creates a small software product, with a source code and issues a license which enables anyone else who wishes to study the product with its source code, to freely add features and make improvements. Thousands of developers around the world join the collaborative development working whenever the spirit moves them, motivated by the pure joy from the challenge of adding value. With thousands of eyes looking for ways to improve each product and thousands of hands writing codes at the same time all over the world, the combined effort results in products that are improved and perfected at an amazing rate and re-released.[29]

Contributors are not motivated by financial gain or altruistic behavior. They are motivated by the excitement of the challenge and the pleasure of being part of an effort that improves the quality of life in our communities. All of us realize we experience joy and fulfillment when contributing to making something better. We discover that it is in our self-interest to participate.

For example, in Denmark, Rasmus Nielsen and his students applied the open-source approach to create Vores Oel, or Our Beer.[30] They released a recipe online, inviting others to experiment and help develop a better formula—in an industry where ingredients and processes are typically kept under strict trademark. It has been a huge success, and the recipe is shared among users for free! People want the beer, and a good experience was had by all who contributed to the recipe.

Within Companies

Applying the open-source approach to company processes, associates from all departments in an organization are encouraged to participate in product design and to work extensively on various projects, processes, and services. Depending on ability, energy, and interest, associates use many opportunities (outside their job description) to contribute to the greater success of the company. New and improved software products, reports Dr. Leemakeej, have been developed using this open-source approach. Examples include Linux, Mozilla, Apache, PHP, OpenOffice and others.

Associates testify:

We eagerly perform our personal responsibilities with greater enthusiasm. We feel both wanted and appreciated when we lend our creative, intuitive talents to other challenges within the organization. It is a fantastic joy to experience both our formal applied knowledge and our intuitive skills being valued and used![31]

New York Times columnist Thomas Friedman writes that Google Finance was conceived entirely by the Google team in India. Google engineers from around the world feed into that team instead of into Google's headquarters in Silicon Valley in California. "We don't have the idea of two kinds of engineers anymore," a Google associate reported, "ones who think of things and others who implement them." "Product development happens across the global campus now," another added.

Friedman gives another example, Enterprise DB, a U.S. company in New Jersey. In interviewing the CEO, Andy Astor, Friedman learned that the company's "primary development team consists of sixty Pakistani engineers in Islamabad, who interact with New Jersey headquarters via Internet-based video conferences utilizing everyone's ideas." They use the open-source data base called PostgreSQL.

Governments, scientists, and researchers worldwide are using the open-source approach to protect healthy people from contagious diseases, to develop vaccines, and to find cures for the already ill. Tapping into the enormous creative and innovative potential of thousands of people has resulted in improved products and services and has also resulted in affordable prices for everyone.

Professor Nicholas Negroponte at the Massachusetts Institute of Technology is the founder and chair of the social-profit OLPC, the One Laptop Per Child Association, Inc. Both China and Intel provide laptop computers so inexpensive that children in poor countries are able to possess a personal laptop designed with the child in mind. They are almost unbreakable.

Professor Negroponte's goal is to furnish one laptop for every child in the world. Each computer costs $100 to produce and deliver. People in wealthy countries pay $200 for their own, and a free laptop goes to a child somewhere in a poor country. Using batteries rechargeable by a hand-cranked device, children are able to use these laptops in areas where there is no electrical system. Enticed by the fun they have with the computers, Negroponte reports, fifty percent more children are coming to school. Many are learning on their own or being taught by their buddies in areas too impoverished to have a school.

In January 2008, I had the pleasure of observing excited children experiencing computers when Susie Krabacher[32] facilitated the beginning of this process for poor children in Haiti. They watched the demonstration impatiently—each of them wanted to try it!

Children all over the world are being trained to use the open resource approach. Because of OLPC, children have become global co-dreamers and co-creators of the future they envision. Being connected to what is occurring all over the planet, they broaden their own personal visions. Thousands of people in every corner of the world are now able to use their potential talents, bringing benefits beyond measure.

Mobile Workers

Standing tall in New York Harbor is the Statue of Liberty. It invites:

> . . . "Give me your tired, your poor,
> Your huddled masses yearning to breathe free,
> The wretched refuse of your teeming shore.
> Send these, the homeless, tempest-tost to me,
> I lift my lamp beside the golden door!"[33]

In every nation in the New Millennium Story, immigrant mobile workers are welcomed in this spirit. No nation carries the absolute authority to exclude people. Physical and political walls between nations, such as the Berlin Wall and the West Bank Wall in Palestine, are dismantled, along with "the fence" between Mexico and the United States.

By bringing in diverse cultures, nations not only have the opportunity to improve lives, but also to gain skilled workers. Technically skilled workers quickly become entrepreneurs, contributing to the development of the host country; other mobile workers tend to children, care for the sick and elderly, and harvest and prepare food. All add to the economy by purchasing goods and services. Taxes contribute to social security services. Immigrants' children often do exceptionally well in school, becoming assets to the community.

Local economies that were left behind improve because of money sent home to the mobile workers' native lands.

When residents and immigrant mobile workers interact, the differences in culture and language promote creativity and understanding. With the assumption that we are all one, we cooperate and benefit from the richness of each other.

Financial Crises No More

Under the dominant Modern Worldview in 2009, most nations in the world floundered under all-consuming debt. The United States of America owed eleven trillion dollars to China and to international bankers. Interest on this debt alone was estimated to be a billion dollars a day of tax payers' money. Great Britain, France, Italy, and other nations (referred to in this text as "rich countries") suffered from a similar financial calamity.

In line with the Emerging Worldview, the United States' financial obligation is being repaid rapidly, because of three changes in the monetary system:

First, the Federal Reserve Bank has been placed under the auspices of the Secretary of the Treasury. It is no longer a private enterprise.

Second, banks now can legally lend only as much money as they actually have in reserve. Financial markets *finally* are not able to control the government.

Third, the federal government not only prints our money, but it also manages the money supply in accordance with the Constitution, by spending only the money it prints and not borrowing from banks or other nations.

Consequently, the government is no longer paying a billion dollars a day in interest. Now the government spends the money it prints for the purpose of improving the infrastructure of the country. In so doing, it provides job opportunities for the citizenry. Now the growth of the financial economy serves the growth of the real economy, instead of the other way around. As a result, not only are bridges safer, but high-speed trains enable people to travel from city to city quickly and safely. Within cities, an efficient electronic transit system transports the populace inexpensively and pollution-free. New seaports and airports grace the nation. Roads free from potholes are commonplace.

Most especially, without borrowing and wasting money on interest payments, the government provides universal healthcare in addition to quality education with a personal touch, in both rural and urban areas.

CONCLUSION

In the New Millennium Emerging Worldview Story, cooperation replaces competition within and between businesses throughout the world. Emerging Worldview Thinkers and Feelers assume that the purpose of business is to serve the public with high-quality products and services, at a reasonable price, while providing a meaningful livelihood for associates through local, national, and international structures.

Workplaces are open to everyone who desires to work and receive just compensation, regardless of gender or social, racial, political, or religious background and beliefs. Businesses large or small are communities in which associates thrive economically, socially, and culturally via joint ownership and democratic governance practices. Associates actively participate in determining their companies' goals, roles, policies, and procedures.

Responsibility, democracy, equality, equity, and solidarity permeate organizational culture as associates adopt the values of honesty, openness, social responsibility, and service to others.

New Millennium Thinkers and Feelers realize that the words we use to describe ourselves, our activities, and the way we relate to one another are powerful—and have the force to change the world around us. We have therefore developed an appreciative attitude, seeking and finding opportunities and challenges rather than problems. We consciously act to enhance, rather than fix, what we observe.

We value and implement education and training to best advantage. All of us associates, therefore, have opportunities to grow and develop, experiencing the joy of both contributing to the success of the enterprise and seeing ourselves continually improve and mature in our careers.

CHAPTER TEN

The Story of Education

The real object of education is to leave a person in the condition of continually asking questions.
Mandell Creighton, Bishop of London
Ecclesiastic and Historian

It is important that students bring a certain ragamuffin, barefoot, irreverence to their studies; they are not here to worship what is known, but to question it.
Jacob Chanowski
American Educator and Philosopher

Good teaching is an act of hospitality toward the young, and hospitality is always an act that benefits the host even more than the guest.
Parker J. Palmer
American Educator
Senior Associate, American Association for Higher Education
Senior Adviser, Fetzer Institute

We teach nothing. We do not teach students . . . What we do, if we are successful, is to stir interest in the matter at hand, awaken enthusiasm for it, arouse a curiosity, kindle a feeling, fire up the imagination—and now she who is exposed in this fashion goes on her own way [to learn it].
Professor Julius Sumner Miller
Physics Department, University of Dillard and University of Sydney, Australia

What is Education?

Education, as defined in the Oxford English Dictionary, is

The systematic instruction, schooling or training given to the young in preparation for the work of life; by extension, similar instruction or training obtained in adult age. As such, it expresses the Modern Worldview assumption that the business of education is business.

In the New Millennium Emerging Worldview Story, education is defined as: an exchange process by which educators and students enable one another to think, analyze, synthesize, and communicate. Through this process, both student and educator discover new approaches with which to question and address personal and societal issues and actively develop and implement plans for a positive future. It is assumed, consequently, that if students and teachers do not continually change their way of thinking and acting, the educator is not teaching and the students are not learning. It is assumed that we are all lifelong learners, continuously seeking to change our values and beliefs, our worldviews. Ultimately, we use knowledge to understand, discover meaning, and positively and passionately change our behaviors. Along with Gandhi, the eminent teacher and peace activist of India, we seek "to become the very change we expect to see in the world."

New Millennium Thinkers and Feelers discover meaning and knowledge by being curious and asking questions. As Nobel physicist Albert Einstein has said, "Learn from yesterday, live for today, hope for tomorrow. The important thing is not to stop questioning."

Never ceasing to learn is never ceasing to ask questions. Through continuous questioning, educators and students alike unlearn obsolete ideas and values retained from our upbringing.

The esteemed Baha'i spiritual guide, Abdu'l-Baha, urges us: "We must be willing to clear away all that we have previously learned . . . [W]e must not shrink from beginning our education all over again, if necessary."[1]

When we in the New Millennium Story are willing to clear all away, then our questioning minds and hearts are open to new ways of reconceiving the universe. Seeking to be educated, we are eager and willing to realize our potential by thinking and feeling in a new and different way. Fortified with education, we take on the challenges with which the human race is grappling. We become wise enlightened persons, effectively able to take responsibility for our own lives.

Education versus Training

There is a distinct difference in the New Millennium between education and training. As defined by its Latin root *educare,* education means to reach inside individuals and pull out the greatness that has been lying dormant in them, rather than "install" in their empty heads unquestionable truths. It is more useful to assume that everybody can learn! No normal and healthy person is stupid! While all adults are knowledgeable about different subjects, we nevertheless are prone, sometimes, to do stupid things—because we don't know it all! We don't know the whole "truth"; we don't see the whole picture. Hence, we have the urge to continually educate ourselves in the issues we value most.

Education provides us with both information and the opportunity to learn from experience, particularly from our mistakes. Education enables us to come up with new knowledge and skills to address ever-challenging issues such as a cure for cancer or AIDS, or providing adequate food for starving populations, or ending dysfunctional conflicts and bringing peace to a world beset by violence. All are significant issues that invite and challenge us to be wise and creative in our efforts to discover new approaches to promote the common good. As we saw in the last chapter, work that contributes to the well-being of all is the only work that is truly challenging and fulfilling.

Training, on the other hand, is the learning of skills and techniques that others have already found to be effective in addressing past and present challenges. For example, a nurse learns how to draw blood gently from a person seeking wellness; accountants are trained to use T-accounts. (Every student accountant learns that the left side of the *T* is a debit and the right side is a credit—a useful tool developed by someone else to the benefit of all.) Thus, training teaches answers to other peoples' problems. Education teaches us to address challenges that still need to be addressed.

Through education we learn to question methodologies with open minds and to unlearn obsolete theories and practices as we discover new and more effective methods. This questioning of traditional theories and conventional practices includes questioning their purpose and goals.

Lifelong Learning

No formal training or education can provide students with all the knowledge and skills needed throughout a lifetime. New challenges continually appear because life continually changes, providing opportunities that require new information and rethinking.

The purpose of education, therefore, is not only to give students the tools to learn continuously, but also to endow them with heightened curiosity, the curiosity that motivates us to question and to seek more knowledge.

The Role of Educators

To become effective facilitators of knowledge, educators become passionate learners themselves. Their love of learning and love of their subject matter are contagious. Educators design and create an environment that is experience-based; supply information which is personally applicable to students; provide a process that enhances the learning styles of each participant; and seek to integrate discovered insights into the students' life experience. When this happens, students are eager to learn and enjoy the process.

Pre-Modern Worldview Story of Learning

Along with the church, schools are viewed as the center of community life in the Pre-Modern Worldview Story. They are designed to train young people in civic responsibility, self-discipline, and the value of hard work. Schools are expected to play the role of parent, making sure students learn proper values, learn what they need to know to make an honest living, and learn how to stay out of trouble. Civic leaders, school administrators, teachers and parents, all alike, assume that a value-consensus exists which necessitates teaching students "the good, the true, and the beautiful."

When public schools do not adequately provide this conventional knowledge, then home-schooling, voucher schools, charter schools, and many parochial schools develop, to better train students in the Pre-Modern Worldview's traditional values; these values are considered absolutely true and unchangeable. In the process, methods of teaching also reflect the absolutes of "true, necessary, and unchangeable."

Hierarchical Structure

The perception of public schools, in the Pre-Modern Worldview Story, is that God enlightens the school board, made up of civic leaders, who, in the patriarchal tradition, are typically men. These well-respected men direct the male school administrators and tell the female teachers at the grade school level how to teach, and these teachers train the students. (See Figure 10.1.)

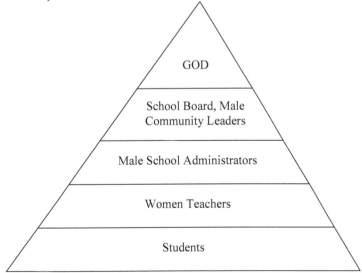

Figure 10.1

Purpose and Process

Pre-Moderns see teaching as a respected, almost holy vocation. In much of the world, sacred books, such as the Bible and the Qur'an, form a cultural background for the content of what is taught. Young students are instructed to treat teachers, as well as all adults, with the utmost respect. In addition to the schools, parents and other extended-family members function as co-teachers, preparing the young for successful lives and good citizenship.

Children are expected "to be seen and not heard." As passive recipients of the wisdom of their elders, they are to grow up to be loyal, patriotic citizens, ready and willing to do whatever their nation asks of them.

Results of the Pre-Modern Worldview Story of Education

Unlike the dialogue approach, patterned after that of the Greek philosopher Socrates, wherein teachers ask students what they think, the approach of Pre-Modern teachers is to *tell* the students what to think and how to behave. Believing they know the entire truth and what is good for the students, teachers do most of the talking; and students do most of the listening. Teacher-centered learning, in lecture form, rather than student-centered learning, prevails.

Classrooms are structured with the teacher up front, "the sage on the stage." Students sit neatly in rows awaiting the wisdom of the teacher. Teachers digest what they perceive as the most important material to be learned and provide the answers and solutions to issues of the past, present and future. Rarely, if ever, do they admit to not knowing something, which would be seen as a sign of incompetence. Students are expected to listen, take notes, memorize the answers, and feed back the correct answers to teachers' questions in written exams. Pre-Moderns today do not acknowledge that each student has a particular learning style. Most classrooms are set up for thinking-style learners who sit in rows of chairs or at square tables, taking notes from the sage on the stage.

In his research, Professor David Kolb of Case Western Reserve University discovered that people also learn by doing, feeling, and observing. Professors who change their teaching styles to match the predominant learning style of each student have been found to be far more effective educators.

Pre-Moderns today do, however, cling to the notion that education can be effective once again through *educational reform*. They believe that it is possible for a specialist to know and understand accurately and completely the complexities of this world and then break them down for all of us to understand and follow.

Modern Worldview Story of Education

The Modern Worldview Story of education is patriarchal, hierarchical, and heavily influenced by the Enlightenment period in the West and the Industrial Revolution. Education is business. Efficiency is the most important value, guided by rationality and standardization.

A New Hierarchy

God is supplanted at the top of this hierarchy by educational scholars, who are in possession of "the truth." (See Figure 10.2.).

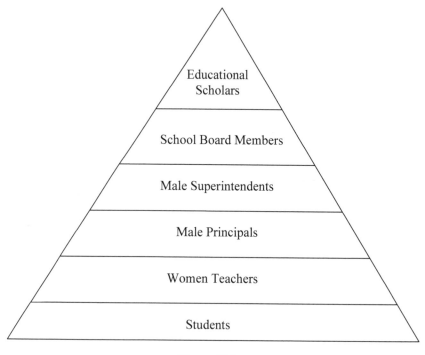

Figure 10.2

University scholars and researchers develop educational theories to influence the school board which, in turn, directs the male superintendent, who is viewed as the chief executive officer (CEO). He, in turn, controls the male principals.

Principals are similar to business managers and are expected to have supervisory skills. Their role is to make sure the predominantly female teachers work hard and teach the right things, according to government standards. If students do not meet minimum requirements, as determined by standardized tests, principals hold the teachers accountable. In addition, federal and state financial support is often tied to students' test scores.

Teachers are seen as being capable of teaching because they receive teaching degrees from universities. It is up to the principals, however, to determine what methods they will use to teach. Principals' judgment is rarely questioned publicly. They are responsible for setting clear standards, inspecting, judging, disciplining, and expelling if necessary. Principals have power over teachers, who learn to assert the same power over their students. Usually they treat the students in the way they are treated. Consciously or unconsciously, all live in fear of authority.

The curriculum is designed with standardized testing in mind, and is developed with the objective of preventing the teacher from teaching lessons that may not be on the test. As a result, many teachers feel powerless to contribute to a student's learning experience.

Purpose and Process

Schools operate something like factories. They are expected to serve economic, as well as cultural, purposes as efficiently as possible, as measured by the most graduates for the lowest cost. Students resemble products, whose quality is indicated by the grades they receive. They are judged and then divided into fast learners (college preparatory), slow learners (vocational school prospects), and nonlearners (troublemakers). The grading system assures that some students will fail. Teachers who insist that students *not fail* are seen as soft (lacking in rigor) and not supportive of school standards.

School structures consist of: lockstep grading systems, classes that meet on a regular schedule, and standardized grading periods with testing at short intervals. For a student to graduate from high school and college, he or she must earn a specific number of credit hours. Students who attend class and get adequate grades on tests are allowed to graduate and go out into "the real world."

Modern Worldview adherents focus on what students should know by a certain age, with the major emphasis placed on learning skills that will allow them to make a living. It becomes clear, to anyone who has doubts, that the business of education is *business*.

As in the Pre-Modern Worldview Story, Moderns present their teachings as *absolutely true*. Ambiguity is to be avoided at all costs; it is too inefficient! "Learn what you need to know to make a living, and get out into the 'real world' and go to work!" is the message students receive. In addition, to prove your worth you need to make more money than the next guy.

Results of the Modern Worldview Story of Education

Under Modern Worldview thinking, schools are normally satisfied with minimum competence, as opposed to maximum individual achievement and the full development of each student's unique potential. Standardized testing is seen as the easiest way to "objectively" assess whether a student has achieved minimum competence. This belief remains in force despite overwhelming evidence *against* equating the results of standardized testing with the ability to think deeply, ask meaningful questions, listen actively, and communicate clearly in oral and written form.

Modern teachers, like Pre-Modern teachers, possess all knowledge, and students need to absorb it. Lecturing is the expected pedagogy. The teacher acts as a speaker with a message. Students are treated as receptors who tune in to get the message. Since the curriculum is tightly scheduled, little time is left over for questions, much less dialogue. The student's head is perceived as a *tabula rasa,* an empty slate, upon which the teacher writes information.

Another metaphor: a student's head is like an empty bucket to be filled with the liquid of "right answers," *the truth* possessed and controlled by teachers. Students' papers and exams are awash in red ink, which highlights what the student did wrong, not what the student did right.

Standards

Teachers' goals are to turn students into "good enough" copies or clones of the teachers themselves. They present the material to the students as "the facts," and they expect the students to memorize such data, deemed knowledge, and reward them for doing so. To evaluate learning, students are tested to determine whether each has succeeded in becoming a "good enough" copy of the teacher. Clearly, an "educated person" in the Modern Worldview is one who can memorize and repeat the teachers' propositions.

In response to fact-laden courses, students retain just enough information for just long enough to pass the test, and tend to forget most of it afterward. Students rarely want to invest time in exploring the subject later on; and even if they did, the textbook would not be available, having been returned to the school for next year's classes. When students purchase their own texts, they tend to immediately sell the books back to the bookstore once the course is over.

Good Students

A student's responsibility is to "measure up to" the standards set by the teachers and the school system. A student achieves success when he or she conforms, stays in school, does not question either content or process, and eventually obtains a diploma or its equivalent.

Poor Students

When a student does not "measure up to" the standards set by the teachers and the school system, the student is threatened and punished. Threats and punishments range from detentions to being expelled from school, receiving a failing grade on a test, or flunking a course. When a student is seen as causing trouble in school, teachers are trained to respond with threatening phrases such as, "No!", "Don't do that!", and "Stop that or else!"

Because the expectation in both elementary and high school is that everyone be treated the same, no matter the potential or the disabilities of individual students, large classes of forty and even fifty students are the desired norm. However, classes in affluent neighborhoods tend to be smaller, numbering twenty to twenty-four students. While affluent districts' classes are not completely individualized, neither are they "cookie cutters."

Facing many students daily, teachers are often overwhelmed and exhausted. They do not have the time or energy to pay the needed attention to particular "low-achievers" or teach according to each student's learning style. Further, they perceive that meeting with students after class is impractical, because of sheer numbers and the time constraints.

Teacher-Principal Dynamics

Stressful demands and disagreements about teaching conditions regularly occur between principals and teachers. Principals' attempts to introduce new material or a new curriculum into the classroom usually fail—because teachers are rarely asked for input or included in the decision-making process. Resentment toward the administration often results. Teachers who express disappointment and dissent are regarded as troublemakers. Successful teachers are those who comply with the instructional model developed by the school system and the government. When teachers become unhappy with the way they are treated, they are often compelled to seek more money through the teachers' union as compensation for their frustrated expectations. That is to say, teachers are by and large willing to work for less pay if they are given freedom to be creative and innovative within the classroom. Without this opportunity, earning more money becomes important. Often the money is denied, and teacher strikes tend to follow.

Many teachers came into their profession motivated to give themselves over to assisting students. But large classes and formalized structures often take their toll, especially when counseling/parenting roles are neglected. Teaching becomes not an act of hospitality, but a chore. What began as an exciting opportunity to do something meaningful ends up being simply a job.

Modern Worldview assumptions resist raising taxes for purposes of educating students. The common attitude is: It's okay to "invest" in the military, but it is not okay to "throw money away" on education. If any money is found, it goes toward buildings and especially toward the latest technological equipment.

College and University Teaching under Modern Worldview Assumptions

Higher education, in the Modern Worldview Story, has become largely a for-profit institution. It is seen as an industry administered by corporate executives whose workforce is composed of faculty members dispensing knowledge as a product. Students are seen as customers. The goal is to be as efficient and profitable as possible.[2]

Student customers are persuaded that achieving a college degree will enhance their career opportunities and enable them to better live the "good life" for *themselves*.

Higher education is market-based and privatized for the alleged "common good." The goal is to deliver a name-brand product—doctor, lawyer, or professional athlete. Education serves as a training ground for the corporate workforce, for professional sports enterprises, and for cloned faculty members to continue the process ad infinitum.

Schools openly compete with one another for students, advertising how their graduates have succeeded in business as measured by large salaries, or by playing in the National Football League at even larger starting salaries.

For financial reasons, corporate administrators are intent on having the largest possible classes and fitting them into lecture-designed classrooms. The instructor becomes the "sage on the stage," instead of having students sit in circles, with the facilitator as "a guide on the side" encouraging dialogue.

The more adjunct or part-time instructors an institution can hire at low wages and without healthcare and pension benefits, while still meeting accreditation requirements, the more respect the administrator receives.

In the liberal arts departments, for example, upper-level courses are consistently eliminated when not signed-up-for by the required number of students. Lower-level courses are "managed," often by nontenured or adjunct instructors. Cutting costs and increasing productivity are key values, along with developing new revenue streams.[3]

While this mental model is widely represented in the United States, similar capitalistic models can be found even in China, with its socialist mindset.

In the spirit of privatization, for-profit international companies have moved into the professions and the master's in business administration (MBA) educational market worldwide. Through the use of the latest in marketing techniques, students are enticed into seeking business careers and professions such as medicine, law, and criminal justice. Answers and solutions to known problems (vocational training) are desired and taught. The objective is to simplify and solidify information so that "truths" are easily memorized and fed back on exams. Students the world over are led to believe the promise that if they learn the quick answers, it will lead them to the easy and affluent life found in the West.

Professors

Professors are virtually unknown by anyone except possibly the dean and their immediate peers in their own department or discipline. Most faculty members are psychological and intellectual strangers to one another. Professors largely hide in their offices and barricade themselves behind their credentials, their lecterns, their status, and their research. If they meet for lunch, it is time often spent complaining about students or the administration.

One would expect universities to be places of intellectual and emotional stimulation, with educators from across disciplines debating and dialoguing with one another, both privately and in the presence of students. Alas, it rarely happens. Philosophy, religion, and politics are subjects to be "avoided like the plague." Safe subjects such as the weather, sports, one's health, and complaints about students are the status quo topics of discussion in the faculty lounge.

At *teaching* universities or colleges, Modern Worldview professors are largely afraid of being judged negatively by their students, because student evaluations are the major criteria for receiving tenure. Professors are therefore not encouraged to try new forms of teaching, due to the danger of making a mistake, hurting the school's reputation, or being seen as a "hotshot" or a "show boat." Professors generally look for assurances and guarantees and thus fail to realize their own potential. Their tendency is to focus on negatives, seeing the problems, obstacles, and limitations which would result if they experimented with a new teaching style or presented material outside the required curriculum.

At *research* universities, professors see teaching undergraduates as a distraction from doing their research, publishing, and obtaining grants. The adage "publish or perish" weighs significantly on whether a professor receives tenure or is asked to leave. Being an excellent facilitator of undergraduate learning is rarely considered an essential criterion for tenure.

Students

Because of a distrustful academic culture, university students, like their professors, are full of fear, doubt, and anxiety—fear of failing, of not understanding, of having their ignorance exposed and prejudices challenged, or of looking foolish in front of their peers. Most of all, students are afraid of being themselves. To please their professors and the administration, students wear masks, pretending to be other than their authentic selves. Thinking and feeling differently is denigrated and sometimes punished.

"Good students" are docile students who accept without argument "the truth" as it is placed before them. Critical skills and questioning of the truth not only are undervalued, but are considered inappropriate professional behavior, and a potential negative when students apply for a high-paying job after graduation. Unwittingly, students learn trickery, how to be condescending, and how to exploit power relationships in order to be successful in their careers. They are advised to be silent or dishonest about what they think and feel, under the guise of being diplomatic and effective.

Students mostly see education as a means to a short-term outcome, such as being able to get a good job in the "real" world.

Questions like "Will this material be covered on the exam?" or "Will this major get me a high-paying job?" are the ones which students have been taught to ask, by both their instructors and their parents. With emphasis primarily on pragmatic utilitarianism, one can find little sense of colleagueship or mutual caring. Friendships that last long after graduation are the exception, rather than what is expected and encouraged, particularly in the United States. The opposite is the case in Taiwan. Chinese students are so strong on relationship that classmates find a special place in each other's hearts that lasts a whole lifetime; they can be likened to blood brothers and sisters.

The New Millennium Story of Education

Simply changing four fundamental assumptions causes the New Millennium Education Story to differ strongly from the Pre-Modern and Modern Worldview stories. Using our imaginations, we can see the amazing difference in purpose, structure, content, process, standards, and impact on students, teachers, and society.

We Are Forever in the Process of Discovering

Because we assume we are always in the process of discovering, we are open to *reconceiving* school systems on the primary, secondary, and university levels.

To reconceive means not only to change the goals, rules, processes, and procedures, but to change our fundamental assumptions affecting our beliefs, values, knowledge, and relationships—resulting in radical changes in behavior. Consequently, reconceiving in the New Millennium Story means changing school systems to serve entirely new purposes. To the extent that people wish, the whole community is invited to become democratically involved in the transformation. The whole system participates in determining the end goal and the means to achieve it.

In the classroom, teachers are facilitators. They do not teach "the truth." They seek to ask significant questions that enable students to learn, grow, and remain flexible to changing their minds. Rather than providing answers, teachers encourage students to think and come up with their own conclusions, which are understood as "beliefs" or "hypotheses" rather than truths.

We Continually Create Our Own Reality

Community leaders, parents, students, and educators, in the New Millennium Story, visualize and co-create school systems through group dialogue that supports individual and collective development and growth. Using the same processes, school administrators, principals, educators, students, and support personnel use the outcomes of community gatherings to redesign curricula and structures. Rather than being consumed with what is wrong with schools, they focus on what has been effective and on the strengths of the system. Everyone works together, using imagination to frame and define a learning organization that encourages and makes possible students' dreams and aspirations. A shared vision emerges, which meets the desires of most members of the school and the community.

Educators firmly believe in the concept of the self-fulfilling prophecy, by which "the expectation of an event tends to cause it to happen." They believe they can educate students in what students themselves believe they need to know. Teachers also believe that students have the capacity to learn what they want to. Educators experience students in the process of learning to think, analyze, synthesize, and communicate.

Educators further recognize that pluses and minuses exist for every idea, feeling, and value. Rather than focus on the negative, they "accentuate the positive."

We Are All One

In the New Millennium Emerging Worldview Story, we assume that we are all one. An educator is one with his or her students. A high school is one with its neighboring elementary school. The administrator of a school in France is one with the administrator of a school in India. Assuming this, we all work together to create school systems that act as fountains of opportunity, growth, and learning in every part of the world. We think globally.

New Millennium Thinkers and Feelers act locally by seeking to understand and implement changes in their school systems and in their communities. These changes are designed to satisfy desires and to support what are perceived to be the best interests of all students, schools, the community, and society. Everyone is welcome to contribute their talents to this effort. We assume that a society that loves its children has a future!

We Do What We Perceive Is Best

Assuming that we always do what seems best, we assume it is in our self-interest to support positive-change efforts. We do not look at one student, a group of educators, or one school as the cause of problems existing in the school system. Rather than fixing "her," "him," "them," or "it," we approach each issue by focusing on the school system holistically. We all come together to influence school systems to continue to change and question, to become institutions of genuine learning.

At the classroom level, we do not see students as disobedient or troublemakers. We see them as possible mavericks with something to teach us and as young people who cannot get their wants met in the present educational environment. We then focus our efforts on discovering ways to meet these students' needs and desires.

Standards

Teachers in the Pre-Modern and Modern Worldview stories tend to threaten and punish students who do not behave in accordance with the teacher's prescription. In the New Millennium Story, the goal is always for students to learn.

Emerging Worldview Thinkers and Feelers do not believe that threats and punishment are an effective way to encourage and enable students to learn. When students make mistakes and are disruptive, for example, we explore the reasons. We assist the students in learning what to do differently the next time. "Differently" does not simply mean not doing something again. It means devising a more effective way to act in the future. When a student loses his temper and strikes another person, for example, the system's response is not to expel the student from school, but to enable him to learn and practice nonviolent strategies in confronting perceived injustice.

When we live in a threatening, punishing environment, we tend to hide our errors and failures, or blame others for our mistakes, often making things worse.

In the new Millennium Story, educators experience being appreciated themselves, and they work to understand and appreciate their students. They seek to form caring, mutually respectful relationships free from the fear of punishment and humiliation. Forming lasting relationships with their students helps them to internalize positive values and behaviors. When, for example, a student experiences stressful times, teachers exhibit positive and understanding behavior. Students respond positively, being receptive to the educator's influence, and realize that positive behavior is in their own self-interest.

Results of the New Millennium Story of Education

The purpose of education in the New Millennium Story is being achieved through changing the four fundamental assumptions. Adults and children alike, across the globe, are growing and developing, living successful and meaningful lives, and contributing to the common good, while tapping into an ocean of compassion.

- Children are receiving a basic education; they learn to read and write, and are competent in mathematics.
- Children also learn to get in touch with and value their feelings.
- Students are learning to challenge the "given-ness" of the world.
- Students are learning to seek, and are competent in, leadership roles, developing the social skills necessary to influence one another.

- Tax monies support schools in such a way that every student has competent educators and proper equipment equal to those of every other learner.

In the New Millennium Story, staff, students, parents, business and civic leaders, city and county officials, union leaders, state legislatures, clergy, and citizenry all join together with energy to visualize, create, and support a school system desired, designed, and developed by the community through participative decision-making.

Education through Feedback

New Millennium school systems are welcoming, encouraging, and continually open to the process of learning from feedback. Because school systems are dynamic and organic, they invite and sustain change over time. Dreams, aspirations, and goals are welcomed and eventually realized.

Educators come together to share and discover ideas and interventions whose result is that students learn to think and to be aware of their feelings as never before. A significant reason for this is that the students see faculty members exhibiting similar behavior among themselves and with the students—becoming aware of, accepting, and managing their feelings.

Educators, parents, and administrators discover effective methodologies to enable students to become more proficient in math, reading, and writing as a prelude to discovering their own creative ideas. They are able to achieve this through dialogue, with openness to the ideas of others and no fear of change.

Dialogic Inquiry

Educators are viewed as professional facilitators with competence equal to that of other professionals in society, and are paid accordingly.

Educators also integrate multiple learning styles. The use of multiple learning styles eliminates the Pre-Modern and Modern positive and negative spirals which reinforce the belief that one is "smart" or "dumb."

The Socratic method—teachers asking students questions—is alive and well, with students also asking questions. Together, educators and students alike have discovered that we learn best by leaving ourselves open to dialogue, acknowledging that we do not know "the truth."

Through dialogic inquiry, New Millennium educators lift up and reframe what their students are saying, creating benchmarks of how far they have come and how far they get to go toward whatever they are seeking to learn.

Fights over who is right and who is wrong are not an issue in dialogic inquiry. Every time we enter into dialogue with another, we appreciate that we all have opinions that were formed by the way we were brought up and programmed. We respect the beliefs and values of the other, since each of us sees, affirms, and seeks the good according to the experiences we have had in our lives. Out of compassion, we learn to bracket our own temperaments and ideologies, both liberal and conservative, in order to have empathy with one another.

The Process

Wisdom- and knowledge-centered learning environments use experiential activities in and out of the classroom, as well as reflective moments, group dialogue, role playing, simulations, and mentoring, with some lecturing. Educators enact staged dramas to introduce students to the lives and ideas of great thinkers. Students are invited to comment and give opinions, stating what they think, in a spirit of dialogue.

Educators design learning opportunities, not as "busy work" but as opportunities for discovery, creativity, and achievement. Examinations or performance appraisals are given, not as instruments to demonstrate superiority, but as learning tools to give students feedback on their achievements and directions for further study.

Students are not clients or customers, but explorers, with their educators, on an educational journey. Educators neither prescribe nor proscribe what students need. They explore topics that provide meaning, while meeting the challenges of society.

They see the students as creative individuals, capable of working with others. Students pool their research findings and have numerous opportunities to give knowledgeable presentations on various topics that integrate learning.

Student Feedback

Grades are not given, period! Comparisons are odious; so students are not compared with one another. Everyone is expected to be all they can be, to live up to their potential. Students commit themselves to supporting one another in this process.

When a student writes a research paper, since no grades are given, the teacher provides feedback in a way similar to that of a book or magazine editor, suggesting how the paper might be improved. The teacher writes this feedback in green ink rather than red, singling out the positive aspects of the work rather than what may be perceived as negative or wrong. Teachers offer opportunities for continuing improvement by editing and re-editing the papers before the end of the course. Students then save or seek to publish their work as evidence of their continuing improvement. In this way, feedback encourages students to continue their process of discovering and learning, rather than discouraging students from further learning via negative judgment, embarrassment, or punishment.

Interpersonal Climate

Educators give personal attention to students because small classes of twelve or fewer members are common. Teachers treat each student, no matter his or her nationality, color, or religion, as an equal worthy of concern and respect.

Emerging Worldview educators talk, joke, listen, notice, laugh, and encourage each student, continually emphasizing the positives. The educators' spontaneous, flexible, and nonthreatening interpersonal style, mixed with friendly humor, makes it easy for students to relate to them. They enable students to feel good about themselves by designing challenging, but achievable, learning experiences which result in high self-esteem, a positive self-concept, and strong self-confidence.

Because communities and school systems emphasize small classes, educators are able and willing to enter into each student's world so they can hear and discover each student's personal truth and values. The goal is not for a teacher to change the students by teaching them "the truth." The goal is to understand each student and therefore better facilitate a process by which each student discovers how to learn, grow, and work with others to achieve his or her unique potential. In this process, New Millennium educators discover what they themselves believe and feel, and are open to changing their own thoughts, attitudes, and behaviors as they continue to discover and learn; in this way they achieve their unique potential as educators.

As students, we are open to being influenced, because we see the achievable benefits of learning and changing. We conclude that the primary reason for studying is not to get a good grade and a good job, as in Pre-Modern and Modern Worldview stories. Our reason for studying is to find meaning and joy through a life of continuous learning, development, and contribution to society.

As a consequence, students believe they can be anyone they want to be and do anything they want to do, within certain constraints. Through self-awareness, they recognize their personal constraints (such as quadriplegia, dyslexia, blindness, or hyperactivity) and create their dreams within their boundaries. Students then come to envision themselves as:

- Medical researchers developing a cure for AIDS
- Lawyers protecting the natural wildlife in Brazil
- Educators co-creating an educational system for students in India
- Community organizers facilitating a process in which people are invited to participate in their own development in China
- Writers and motivational speakers promoting and implementing peace and justice approaches around the world
- Poets, painters, and moviemakers putting magic into life

Total Community Involvement

Education is a circular process in the New Millennium Story, as opposed to the hierarchal model of Pre-Moderns and Moderns. As shown in Figure 10.3, each of the various elements of the entire community both contributes to and receives wisdom and knowledge.

Figure 10.3

Everyone serves everyone else in seeking and discovering knowledge, because everyone knows something of value. We are all one, and therefore all of us have a stake in learning and growing as individuals and as a community.

All of us are in the process of discovering. Everyone's ideas have merit and are worthy of consideration.

Parents

Given that everyone in a child's environment has influence, parents play a significant role in education. They take an interest in what their children are learning and assist them when necessary. Over the dinner table, children hear their parents discussing significant issues of the day. Children see their parents regularly reading books and articles, attempting to learn and understand. Parents thus set a positive example by seeking to educate themselves.

Grandparents

Grandparents volunteer their time by coming to school and reading to the children and leading them in song, giving teachers a chance to rest and refuel. The seniors share their wisdom with the children and exemplify genuine love and concern for each child. Both the student and the grandparent benefit. The excellent outcome is manifest in today's Experience Corps which operates in twenty cities nationwide:

Experience Corps—a program that "brings older adults (55 and over) into public elementary schools to improve academic achievement of students . . .

A Johns Hopkins University study found that "Third graders working with Experience Corps members scored significantly higher on a reading test" than students who did not have this assistance. Referrals for discipline problems dropped by half in schools with the Experience Corps, while staying about the same in other schools. A separate study by Washington University in St. Louis also found evidence of improvement in reading skills (either a little or a lot) by more than 60% of the students who received tutoring assistance.

Washington University's research also found benefits for the older adults. "More than 85% of the volunteers felt their lives had improved" because of their work with youngsters in schools. More than 60% said it was "very true" that the program helped them feel better about themselves, and helped them use time more productively.[4]

The Educators' Approach

New Millennium educators enjoy their students, believe in them, have faith and hope in them, and therefore pay attention to them. In the classroom, educators exemplify their own love of learning. Their love of the student and the subject-matter becomes contagious.

Before class, educators express encouraging words for the day. Students are invited to write in a journal, from which educators come to know each student's authentic self. Through the journal and other activities in and out of the classroom, educators encourage their students to feel, to dream, and to create their own reality.

Educators recognize students and colleagues as whole human beings, each significant in their own right, each in a process of growth and development, and each with a potential for becoming well-integrated, mature, competent professionals. Instead of being overly helpful and giving students answers, New Millennium educators facilitate self-dependence by enabling students to look at available options and make decisions for themselves, by providing each student with the autonomy and opportunity to discover, develop, and pursue their own path toward learning.

In the Emerging Worldview Story we assume that no one knows the absolute "truth." Educators are not afraid to let go of certainty. Because we are all in the process of discovering, the Emerging Worldview educator also understands that each student sees the world through different eyes. Each individual's view is based on his or her cultural upbringing and other life experiences, as well as perhaps some predispositions at birth. The educator respects and values these differences.

Educators are open to students because learning is an influence-process. When students observe educators being open to learning from *them*, they in turn are more willing to learn from their educators. When educators learn from students, they are willing to create new understandings and to change the ways in which they facilitate learning. What results is a larger and expanded perspective for all.[5]

Questions like "How can we integrate all these ideas, opinions, and feelings to create a new approach?" replace questions like "Who is right?" or "What is the correct answer?" Educators are excited with their role in a student's development. Students in turn are eager to learn and are grateful and enthusiastic about their opportunities.

New Millennium educators are not discouraged by negative attitudes and their accompanying behaviors. Rather, they take the time to understand each student's background and reach out with empathy. Their being able to identify with students enables the students to trust. With trust comes a willingness on the students' part to think and feel differently about what has happened to them in their lives.

Professor Parker J. Palmer tells us how he started seeing the world through the eyes of his students in his book *The Courage to Teach*. One student in Palmer's class was a young man who sat in such a way that Palmer could not tell whether his eyes were open or closed. The student's notebook and pen were nowhere to be seen. It was a fine spring day, but the student's jacket was still buttoned, suggesting that he was ready to leave at any moment.

Palmer was bothered by this student's behavior and labeled him "the student from hell." He did, however, have the time, energy, and commitment to enter into conversation with the student from hell after class. Palmer writes:

> I will always remember the conversation that followed. The student's father was an unemployed laborer and an alcoholic who thought his son's desire to finish college and become some sort of professional was utter nonsense. The young man lived with his father, who berated him daily for his foolishness: "The world is out to get people like us, and college is part of the scam. Drop out, get a fast-food job, save whatever you can, and

settle for it. That's how it's always been, and that's how it'll always be." Daily this young man felt his motivation for college fading away... [He] asked, "What do you think I should do about it?" I do not know whether I helped him—but I know he helped me. He helped me to understand that the silent and seemingly sullen students in our classroom are not brain-dead: they are full of fear... This particular student—whose plight represents many others—forced me into a deeper understanding of the student condition, one that is slowly transforming the way I teach.[6]

In response to a classroom rich in love and conducive to human growth and development, students trust, admire, and identify with their educators. (The same dynamic exists in well-functioning families.) In trusting educators, students are open to educators' influence and are, therefore, open to learning and changing. Students begin to recognize their own potential, their own talents, and the positive possibilities of what they can become.

New Millennium University Results

In the Emerging Worldview Story, assuming that no one knows truth absolutely, we appreciate that our lives are capable of being re-created. We are grateful that our existence on this earth is not a boring set of givens which we must accept without question; this opens up higher education to the excitement of discovering ever new significant information and theories which revolutionize and enhance our intellectual, emotional, and spiritual experiences.

We conclude that higher education is for everyone who is interested in having a stimulating intellectual life. Those who have little interest in this are invited to pursue whatever stimulates them, with an eye toward serving the common good as well as their individual well-being.

For those, however, who are interested in delving deeply into the life of the mind and heart, higher education in the New Millennium Story is personalized and much too highly valued by the community to be left to the motive of profit. Learning for learning's sake stands equal to instrumental professional studies.

Rather than placing value on efficiency, colleges and universities are perceived as providers of physically safe educational experiences with manifold opportunities to imagine, think, feel, and communicate—and time for students to critically examine and investigate the past and present world while envisioning a world that will make their grandchildren proud of their accomplishments! As part of this experience, students assume that the university is an institution that values people over profits. They picture the university teaching and practicing the values of an open and democratic organization rather than those of a corporately controlled institution. Students see universities producing research which contributes to the long-term common good rather than the immediate gratification and tangibly quantifiable gains of corporate interests.[7]

Students are further encouraged to sink deeply into the study of the role of social justice with regard to globalization and to become ever more aware of our oneness, our interconnectedness, which motivates us to provide for the many instead of the few.

Studying abroad is part of almost every university education, enabling students to appreciate the pluses and minuses of other cultures and to understand their own culture far better.

Cooperative Learning

Educators in the New Millennium, joined with their subject and their students, use many techniques: lab exercises, fieldwork, cooperative learning, lectures, dialogue, and telepresence.

Cooperative learning, in itself, is a form of dialogue. It calls on students with differing abilities and experiences to discuss subjects and work together in productive ways. Cooperative learning develops basic skills in young people from a wide range of backgrounds, and at the same time develops skills in thinking and team effectiveness. Students literally teach and learn from each other. An example of cooperative learning is the National Writing Project, which involves the active participation of students and educators together, sometimes resulting in educator/student publications.

University students also assist professors in teaching classes, making presentations, doing research, consulting with companies, and writing books. The book you now hold in your hands is a joint project of cooperative learning with students at Baldwin-Wallace College in Cleveland, Ohio, at Southern California University for Professional Studies, at Burapha University in Thailand, and at Faculdade Catolica de Administração de Economia (FAE) in Curitiba, Brazil.

Team Learning

Working in teams, students place emphasis on co-creation. Team products are designed with the understanding that all students on a project team will receive feedback and share in the synergistic reward of realizing they could never have written such an excellent paper alone. Teams substitute competing for a good grade (Modern Worldview) with cooperating and co-creating for the intrinsic value of an appreciated product and the knowledge attained from the synergistic process. Working in a group, moreover, emphasizes "team learning," in which participation, friendship, and cooperation are nurtured. Students find such experiences immensely rewarding, both intellectually and emotionally.

Through empathy, educators bridge the gap between themselves and their students. Connecting themselves to their students assists students along their way and brings energy and insight to renew the educators' own lives. Parker Palmer notes that "Good teaching is an act of hospitality toward the young, and hospitality is always an act that benefits the host more than the guest."[8]

Like students, educators question their values and entertain the possibility of changing themselves, if they perceive the change will enable them to grow and be more effective in facilitating the learning of others.

Universities and colleges, consequently, have become sacred places of dialogue—places where everyone is included: students, faculty, staff, administrators, and the community at large. No one interested in learning is excluded from the intellectual, emotional, and spiritual exchange!

Telepresence

Using the robotic technology of telepresence, students enjoy face-to-face communication in present time, whether in the same space physically or whether connected through the Internet. Robots work in tandem with those in other locations; therefore participants such as students and faculty can be anywhere on the planet and yet be face-to-face in the learning environment.

Telepresence gives students and faculty actual presence in the classroom or conference hall. The robot, with video and audio capabilities, can be moved from classroom to classroom, even stopping at the coffee bar between classes for a latte and a chat with other participants.

The robots also have scanners and printers so that everyone everywhere can receive what the professor is handing out in a class or at an assembly. Zoom lenses enable everyone to see what is being written on the flip chart or chalkboard. Users can also manipulate the robot so as to see and talk to another student or colleague at the gathering. Students find the experience more intriguing than video games. Moreover, the robots are user-friendly. Most laypersons are able to competently manage the robot/computer technology within thirty minutes.[9]

Benefits

Business leaders are grateful to see universities desert the corporate organizational model. The need for critical-thinking competencies, along with emotional maturity, has become increasingly valued and evident among student graduates.

The business profession benefits from students who have learned to care, to be of service without being subservient, and to have empathy, who know how to co-create and cooperate, all the while truly valuing the whole community. For example, students have learned to become servant-leaders who use power not to oppress others, but to serve the common good, while respecting the rights of the individual, including themselves. They have developed the self-esteem, self-confidence, integrity, initiative, and mutual trust needed to rehumanize the corporate world, empowered to act beyond the rules and able to be particularly effective in unpredictable crisis situations.

CONCLUSION

In the New Millennium Emerging Worldview Story, educators, students, and the rest of the learning community share and engage in each other's thoughts, feelings, and values through openness and dialogue. Trusting one another, together we go on a lifelong journey. It is education for the long haul, a marathon, not a short sprint. On this journey, we are free to question everything and discover new insights, new methods, and new ways of thinking every day, with and through one another. No one ever claims to have the one right answer. We do not seek or find solutions. Instead, we discover new approaches that appear to work better, until we discover an even more effective approach.

While Modern Worldview education tends to start and end at training, New Millennium education uses training as a stepping stone to facilitate a learning culture in which students, by asking questions, discover how to learn, grasp new opportunities and possibilities, and live out their dreams.

In honoring questions, the Emerging Worldview is accessing the part of our mind that creates meaning and coherence, the foundation of wisdom.

CHAPTER ELEVEN

The Story of Effective Justice for Lawbreakers

The reformative effect of punishment is a belief that dies hard, I think, because it is so satisfying to our sadistic impulses.
Bertrand Russell
British Philosopher and Social Reformer

The degree of civilization in a society can be judged by entering into its prisons.
Fyodor Dostoyevsky
Russian Novelist

It is right not to harm anyone and wrong to do harm.
It is right to see good in others and wrong to see bad in anyone.
It is right to love people and wrong to hate them.
It is right to admire men for the good in them and wrong to rebuke them for their shortcomings and bad behavior.
Maharishi Mahesh Yogi
Founder of Transcendental Meditation

Everyone will experience the consequences of his own acts. If his acts are right, he'll get good consequences; if they're not, he'll suffer for it.
Harry Browne
American Libertarian Writer and Politician

Justice Understood

In the New Millennium Emerging Worldview Story, effective justice for lawbreakers is maintained by the Four R's: Restoration, Rehabilitation, Restitution, and Reconciliation. This approach replaces Retribution, which is the predominant notion of justice for lawbreakers in Pre-Modern and Modern Worldview assumptions.

Restorative Justice

Restorative justice promotes individual and community responsibility in creating justice for all. Toward this end, restorative justice changes the environment that leads to lawbreaking behaviors. It develops strategies for changing:

- Structural injustices which sow the seeds for individual lawbreaking, such as poverty, unemployment, lack of educational opportunities, and class and racial discrimination.
- Individual wrongdoing, both legal and illegal.

The goal of restorative justice in the New Millennium Story is to make life as fair as possible for everyone. Unjust laws are changed so that both the poor and the rich have equal opportunities to live meaningfully.

Restorative justice enables lawbreakers to understand the consequences of their lawbreaking behaviors. They then take responsibility for their actions. They do not blame others for what happens to them. Restorative justice empowers lawbreakers to become self-aware, to recover personally and socially from debilitating lifestyles, and to grow in empathy toward others. Their hope is restored. They no longer "have to" be lawbreakers; they *can* change. Not redeemed or saved by an *external* lifesaver, lawbreakers become empowered to create a meaningful life for themselves and others as they save themselves.

Rehabilitative Justice

Rehabilitative justice is concerned with the values, attitudes, and inclinations of individual lawbreakers and consists of a change of heart, with the determination to think of others, not simply of oneself.

Under rehabilitative justice, the larger community recognizes that structural injustice creates undesirable consequences. The community is motivated to create a more just society, a society in which poverty and oppression have been minimized or overcome.

Society itself also becomes rehabilitated, through a change of heart, with the intention of seeking the well-being of everyone and treating everyone equally. Policies and procedures are then established, enabling everyone to get an effective education, meaningful employment, and universal healthcare.

Restitution Justice

Under restitution justice, lawbreakers, as much as they are able, atone for the harm they have done to others. If they have stolen a sum of money, they return the whole amount, with interest, to the individual from whom they stole. If they have injured others, they make every effort to pay for each victim's healthcare, until those who were harmed have completely recovered. Lawbreakers also compensate individuals for continuing incapacity, including salary loss, until their victims are capable of working and supporting themselves once again.

We can never make restitution for the loss of a life. Still, lawbreakers, once motivated by empathy, do whatever they can to make amends to the family and others for such a terrible tragedy. In doing so, they experience the positive feelings of making amends. They learn to view restitution as, not a distasteful task, but a positive experience. To do so is truly in their own self-interest.

Reconciliation Justice

Reconciliation justice in the New Millennium Story builds on restitution justice by establishing harmony and friendship between the victims and the lawbreakers. The latter express genuine sorrow for the harm they have done. They do everything possible to make amends, to the best of their ability. The intent is for victims and their families to benefit by letting go of anger, hatred, and attitudes of vengeance toward those who hurt them.

Thus released from the stressful pain that comes from seeking revenge, those who have been harmed are able to find peace within themselves, over time, with the recognition that feelings of hatred and vengeance destroy one's own sense of well-being.

In forgiving, victims find peace and change their former way of thinking. Peace brings on feelings of cheerfulness and kind behavior. Each person learns that it is in her/his own self-interest to be reconciled with those who have hurt them.

Retributive Justice

In the Pre-Modern and Modern Worldview, retributive justice is assumed to be not only practical, but appropriate; it demands proper punishment for breaking the law. Punishment means inflicting harm on lawbreakers, often violently, in retaliation for the harm they have done and suffering they have caused. Punishment, however, generally does not transform the life of the victim.

Punishment is motivated by personal attitudes of revenge, and looks backward to blame and/or condemn those who break the law. Looking forward, punishment is based on the belief that the threat of punishment will deter future lawbreaking. Yet accumulated data indicates that the threat of punishment in fact does *not* curtail lawbreaking. It simply teaches people to discover new ways to avoid getting caught.

The Pre-Modern and Modern Worldview Stories of Justice

For Pre-Moderns and Moderns today, retribution or punishment is believed to be the most effective way to deal with criminals. To question punishment as a means of achieving justice and peace is to be soft on crime. People believe that justice has been served when criminals are hurt in the way they have hurt others, or to an even greater degree. And they believe that cruel treatment of others is a fair price to pay for being safe from "evil" people.

These models of punishment are based on the following assumptions:

- The way we see law and order is the way it is.
- Justice is a problem that needs to be solved.
- Humans are separate from each other.
- There are evil people in this world who wake up every morning intent upon doing evil.

Looking for defects in the behavior of others puts the faultfinder above others in the hierarchy of goodness, in the belief that if one can discover reasons to look down on others, one can feel better about oneself. "I might not be perfect, but I would never do what those 'perverts' did," is almost an unconscious assertion in the attempt to achieve personal satisfaction and superiority. Pre-Moderns and Moderns do not see empathy, or placing ourselves in the shoes of lawbreakers, in order to understand their upbringing and feel what they are feeling, as an appropriate response to lawbreaking behaviors.

For Pre-Moderns and Moderns, there is no distinction between a person and that person's behavior. If lawbreakers do evil things, they are automatically considered evil human beings and therefore deserve to be punished. Clearly, despite the Bible and the Qu'ran's teaching of forgiveness, in the Pre-Modern and Modern Worldview stories, lawbreakers deserve the punishment they receive and are undeserving of kind and humane treatment.

Punishment is considered part of the divine ordering of the world. People take biblical statements literally, as in the old law requiring that adulterous women be stoned to death.[1] Jesus's statement, "A man who does not live in me, is like a withered, rejected branch, picked up and thrown in the fire and burned,"[2] also has been often used to justify punishing lawbreakers.

Implications of the Pre-Modern and Modern Story of Justice

Contrary to the assumption that punishment decreases crime, modern criminal justice is largely ineffective, expensive, grossly inhumane, and filled with discrimination. Poor people and minorities compose the vast majority of people occupying jails and prisons all over the world. The United States, with five percent of the world's population, has twenty-five percent of the world's prisoners.[3] On February 29, 2008, *Washington Post* staff writer N. C. Aizenman wrote:

> More than one in 100 adults in the United States is in jail or prison, an all-time high that is costing state governments nearly $50 billion a year and the federal government $5 billion more, according to a report released yesterday. With more than 2.3 million people behind bars, the United States leads the world in both the number and percentage of residents it incarcerates, leaving far-more-populous China a distant second, according to a study by the nonpartisan Pew Center on the States.
>
> The growth in prison population is largely because of tougher state and federal sentencing imposed since the mid-1980s. Minorities have been particularly affected: One in nine black men ages 20 to 34 is behind bars. For black women ages 35 to 39, the figure is one in 100, compared with one in 355 for white women in the same age group. The report compiled and analyzed data from several sources, including the federal Bureau of Justice Statistics and Bureau of Prisons and each state's department of corrections. [The statistics] did not include individuals detained for noncriminal immigration violations.[4]

In the United States, it costs more to send a person to prison for one year than to a public college. The cost per year of keeping a person in prison in the United States is equivalent to the amount a lower-middle-class family earns in a year.[5]

More than 600 new prisons have been constructed in the U.S. since 1980 at a cost of tens of billions of dollars to the taxpayer. It costs taxpayers $100,000 to build each new prison cell. Every $100 million spent on prison construction commits taxpayers to spending $1.6 billion over the next three decades to operate such facilities.[6]

Recidivism Rate of Retributive Justice

The recidivism, or rearrest, rate of individuals who have served prison terms rose dramatically in the United Stated from 1985 to 1995. Similarly, around the world the recidivism rate, based on Modern Worldview assumptions, is between 80 and 90 percent.[7]

Prisons are greatly overcrowded. Basketball courts have been converted into dormitories offering little or no privacy. Education, rehabilitation programs, and job training have been limited, leaving inmates with few or no activities to prepare them for a meaningful life once released.

Women prisoners and their children find it particularly painful to be separated from one another. Moreover, prisons are often located at great distances from the homes of family members, making it exceedingly difficult for children, family, and friends to visit.

Upon release, it is nearly impossible for lawbreakers to find meaningful jobs, since many job applications ask whether the applicant has ever been arrested. Few ex-convicts are entrusted with important and valued work, no matter how competent they are.

The Mentally Ill

A 2007 study by the U.S. Department of Justice discovered that more than half the persons incarcerated in the United States are mentally ill. Many mental hospitals have been replaced by the building of more and more prisons. Nearly 73 percent of women prisoners and 55 percent of male prisoners were found to be suffering from symptoms of depression, mania, or psychotic disorders. Three out of four are dependent on drugs and alcohol, with 37 percent admitting they were using drugs at the time they committed their crimes. The study also found that mentally ill prisoners were likely to have been abused as children, as well as homeless in the year before their arrest. The mentally disabled moreover, tend to have a much higher recidivism rate and, when in prison, tend to break the rules, causing great difficulties for prison staff.

Further, as the number of mentally ill prisoners continues to grow, funds for mental-health care and drug rehabilitation are being drastically cut. Photographer and videographer Jenn Ackerman says:

> The continuous withdrawal of mental health funding has turned jails and prisons across the U.S. into default mental health facilities. A report in 2006 by the U.S. Department of Justice showed that the number of Americans with mental illnesses who are incarcerated in the nation's prisons and jails is disproportionately high. Almost 555,000 people with mental illness are incarcerated, while fewer than 55,000 persons are being treated in designated mental health hospitals.[8]

The New Millennium Story of Justice

Since people have changed and accepted the Four Fundamental Assumptions in the Emerging Worldview, a transformation has taken place all over the world with regard to how lawbreakers are treated. Punishment has been replaced by efforts to restore and rehabilitate, as well as provide opportunities for lawbreakers to make restitution for the harm they have caused and thus experience reconciliation with their victims.

We Are Forever in the Process of Discovering

The New Millennium Story assumes that no one knows "the truth" objectively and completely. People think and feel differently about justice and the treatment of people who break the law. Clearly, retribution or punishment makes matters worse for the community, the victims, and the lawbreakers. The operating mode of Emerging Worldview justice systems throughout the world includes restoration, rehabilitation, restitution, and reconciliation as the approach for relating to lawbreakers.

This approach to achieving justice, however, is not the last word. New Millennium Thinkers continue to be open to new and better ideas for creating effective justice, equality, and kindness throughout the justice system.

The Importance of Law

Although we assume no one knows absolutely what is right and what is wrong, we agree to laws—so that we can live together in an orderly and respectful manner. New Millennium justice seekers strive to establish *just* laws and equal opportunities, which are intended to encourage people to do what is good for themselves and others. The focus is not on laws with threats of punishment, but rather on establishing laws as guideposts for living a meaningful life.

Laws are made to protect everyone and to enhance the lives of everyone, not just certain "special" people. Hence, we have traffic lights to remind us when we need to stop and when we need to go. We have a speed limit within which we can safely proceed and laws to inform us of where we can and cannot park. These laws are established for the common good and apply to all persons, no matter how much money they make or what their role is in the community. At the same time, we make exceptions for ambulances and fire trucks as the common good takes precedence over the individual good. When we carry out the spirit of just laws, everyone benefits. Should anyone fail to benefit, the unjust law is democratically changed to achieve equal benefits for all. Protests against laws perceived to be unjust are welcomed and taken seriously.

In the New Millennium Story moreover, laws do not exist simply to keep people from hurting themselves and others. Laws are initiated to structure community activities that provide for the common good and encourage us all to help one another. For instance, laws are made to encourage individuals and institutions to help those who suffer from physical disabilities and mental illnesses. Similar laws for the poor provide education, training, and meaningful employment, which is in the community's self-interest, because people with fulfilling work can support their families and contribute to the common good.

For New Millennium Worldview Thinkers and Feelers, laws are not chiseled in stone and unchangeable, as is often the case in Pre-Modern and Modern Worldviews. In the New Millennium Story, by having an open mind and heart, we assume we can change our values and behaviors to better achieve justice. What was considered lawful and just in the past may no longer be considered so today. Two obvious examples are laws forbidding women to vote and laws that promote slavery.

The spirit of the law, rather than the letter of the law, takes precedence in the New Millennium Story. Instead of treating one another as children who must obey the letter of the law simply because it is the law, we are trusted and encouraged to find exceptions in following the spirit of the law.

We Create Our Own Reality

Among Pre-Moderns and Moderns, the assumption is: We'll believe it when we see it. In the Emerging Worldview Story, we assume that when we change our beliefs, we change our reality. In other words, when we believe it, we *will* see it. Genuine believing and seeing, however, are not so simple; both demand significant faith and discipline. We begin by appreciating what is positive about the existing justice system. Then, we imagine and create an even more favorable reality, envisioning a justice system which protects the public from harm while benefiting both victims and lawbreakers, as well as the community at large.

In an effort to build on their strengths, the community also seeks to focus on the virtues to be found in the individual lawbreakers. Their defects and negative behaviors, while not ignored, are not the major consideration. We do not seek to "fix" lawbreakers, or for them to fix themselves. Rather, we provide opportunities to educate and encourage them to envision meaningful and fulfilling lives. We provide an environment that empowers them to achieve their vision. The lawbreakers do the work of rehabilitation. We don't do it for them. By restoring themselves, they build their own self-esteem.

We Are All One

Since we believe we are all one, we identify with lawbreakers and seek to enable them to experience restoration, rehabilitation, restitution, and reconciliation. We recognize and admit we continually make mistakes as well. Hence, we constantly refrain from blaming and condemning, and we seek to reform our own lives, while seeking to empathize with them.

We Do What We Perceive Is Best

We assume that, when individuals break the law, they have done so thinking their behavior was in their own self-interest, not realizing the harmful effects on others. In their ignorance they largely do not think of anybody else but themselves. New Millennium Thinkers and Feelers assume lawbreakers live in their own world unaware, and therefore make mistakes or rationalize the harm their actions cause. Once lawbreakers are arrested, the community seeks to educate them about what is healthy, with no intention of punishing them for their unhealthy behavior.

Implications of the New Millennium Story

Prisons, in the New Millennium Story, no longer exist anywhere in the world. If lawbreakers need to be incarcerated to prevent them from harming others and themselves, small community restoration facilities, called "education camps," exist for this purpose. Never overcrowded (approximately 200 beds), these facilities are designed to provide restoration, rehabilitation, restitution, and reconciliation justice.

Assuming we are all one, New Millennium Thinkers and Feelers make sure lawbreakers receive excellent care in these facilities designed to enable them to learn more effective and satisfactory behaviors. Negative behaviors, including suicide attempts, self-mutilation, rule-breaking, and even violent incidents, are met with an extraordinarily kind response.

To the lawbreakers, nevertheless these "education camps" seem like punishment. After all, they have lost their freedom. In the eyes of the education-camp staff, however, lawbreakers are human beings who deserve to be treated with dignity and respect, no matter what they have done.

In education camps, lawbreakers are referred to as "interns" and prison guards are now called "caregivers." Interns wear civilian clothes rather than traditional prison garb and are addressed by their first names in a respectful manner.

Equipped with counseling skills, caregivers take pride in their work of restoring and rehabilitating individuals. They seek to counsel and educate rather than criticize and punish the interns. Well-trained in group process, caregivers offer group counseling programs, such as anger management groups, which enable interns to learn to get along with others and to pursue constructive activities.

Interns often come to realize the caregivers are there for them; in fact, the caregivers are not only respected, but actually become friends as well. Their influence on the interns tends to be positive, and a refreshing atmosphere of trust prevails. Experiencing attention, respect, and friendship from "the establishment," many interns begin to believe in themselves and their meaningful future on the outside.

Emphasis is placed on enabling the interns to function in the day-to-day world by teaching them the basics—the common language of the country, how to count money/make change/ open a checking account. Caregivers make every effort to give interns the tools necessary for success on the outside; classes provide techniques in leadership, communication, computer training, and operation of various machines. The education camp also conducts health fairs to educate interns on proper nutrition and on how to decrease the risk of diabetes and other diseases.

Interns also learn the value of exercise and are encouraged to develop a regular routine to care for their bodies.

Libraries

Education-camp libraries are filled with old and new books of every kind, including religious books. Interns are encouraged to study and read. If a certain book is not available, on request an intern can obtain it from another library. No books are off-limits to interns.

In 1991 Robert Waxler, a professor of English at the University of Massachusetts, founded "Changing Lives Through Literature" with Superior Court Judge Robert Kane and Wayne Saint Pierre, a probation officer. By 2009 this reading program for convicted criminals had expanded to eight other states. Changing Lives Through Literature is:

> ... an alternative sentencing program that allows felons and other offenders to choose between going to jail or joining a book club. At each two-hour meeting, students discuss fiction, memoirs and the occasional poem: authors range from Frederick Douglass to John Steinbeck to Toni Morrison, topics from self-mutilation and family quarrels to the Holocaust and the Montgomery bus boycott ...
>
> Reading has always provided a lifeline for prisoners, whether for utilitarian purposes or for spiritual searching ... In alternative sentencing programs ... books provide a more literal alternative to incarceration; and the authorities' job is not to censor books, but to supply them. [The program's] economic logic is unassailable: running it cost roughly $500 a head ...as opposed to about $30,000 for a year of incarceration ... The most conclusive study [of the program] shows participants achieving half the recidivism rate of a control group involving about 100 people."[9]

On a quest for learning, New Millennium caregivers and the entire justice system are constantly discovering new interventions, becoming ever more successful in addressing and overcoming violent attitudes and behaviors. No chance for education is off-limits, as in existing Modern Worldview legislation such as the withdrawal of Pell grants from U.S. prisoners, who in 1994 were ruled ineligible for federal college financing.

Genuine Benefits

Rehabilitated interns are often hired to be caregivers, following the Alcoholic Anonymous (AA) model. AA is an organization in which recovered alcoholics are the most effective in facilitating the recovery of other alcoholics. Similarly, recovered interns are the most effective in coaching their fellow lawbreakers in the direction of rehabilitation.

The restorative and rehabilitative system teaches lawbreakers not simply the negative implications of their actions, but the genuine benefits resulting from living authentic lives. The education camp provides them with a quiet and nurturing environment, which in turn gives them the opportunity to reemerge into society, gain significant employment, and contribute to the common good.

To achieve these results, education camps involve interns in meaningful work provided by local businesses and offer counseling sessions, school classes, vocational training, and opportunities for recreation and exercise (women's and men's football and similar sports, jogging, yoga, etc.). Group therapy and/or psychological education provide interns with alternatives for dealing with separation from their families and friends. Every effort is made to give the interns opportunities to acquire skills needed to attain, after release, the highest quality of life and productivity they are capable of achieving.

The interns give back even while in prison. One way is in training dogs both for disabled persons such as the blind or deaf, and for average folks like myself who are eager to receive one of these wonderfully trained dogs. Once released, many ex-interns support themselves through operating small businesses dedicated to training dogs.

The Mentally Vulnerable

Mentally vulnerable lawbreakers are treated in facilities created specifically for their care and are never placed with interns who have used violence in breaking the law. Rather, the mentally vulnerable receive treatment in outpatient clinics, inpatient psychiatric wards, or day treatment programs with options to live in supportive communities.

Addicted Lawbreakers

Individuals suffering from addictions are not arrested and incarcerated. They receive the respectful and competent treatment needed to overcome their illness. Addiction is understood as a dysfunction needing competent treatment and not as moral depravity.

Drug-rehabilitation centers consequently, have replaced jails and prisons in the New Millennium Story. These facilities are adequately financed so that chemically dependent individuals can begin recovery, stay as long as needed, and return to a drug-free life. The mission of drug-rehab centers is restoration, helping the addicts heal and once again contribute to society. Drug-rehabilitation programs, with a 70 percent patient success rate, are demonstrating that rehabilitation, not punishment, is largely successful.

Community Re-Entry Programs

Community Re-Entry programs have a mission to help former interns find their place in society after release from the education camp. Released interns are offered transition plans providing a variety of programs to assist them in finding meaningful jobs and finding places to live at a reasonable cost in a community of accepting people.

Released interns have case managers who, with small caseloads, take a personal interest in them. These case managers keep track of their ex-interns with the goal of helping them maintain emotional stability and avoid harm. By making home visits, they strive to be available to talk with former interns and their families. This is not surveillance intervention, nor are the ex-interns treated as children; having a case manager is an opportunity to continue to learn and grow through education and counseling. This approach provides smooth integration back into society. Ex-interns come to feel good about themselves—something they often have not felt for years—overcome their addictions, and proudly contribute to society's well-being. And they gladly volunteer to support others who are struggling with similar challenges.

The vast majority of former interns are never arrested again. They lead productive lives, contributing to the community. The education-camp experience is not considered a negative by any employers. Rather, employers perceive education camps as a positive experience, because the former interns have received a quality education plus occupational training.

The Pain of Lawbreaking

New Millennium justice seekers identify with the pain experienced by both victim and lawbreaker. We realize from our own sad experiences that when we are involved in behaviors that have dire consequences, we often punish ourselves. Punishment from others is neither necessary nor helpful. What is needed and beneficial is a counseling intervention, which enables each of us to understand how we've hurt ourselves. We need support from others who have successfully overcome a mistake. We further need to discover a vision of what we want from life, then believe in that vision and get involved with others to help them do the same. Similar to Alcoholics Anonymous sponsors, former lawbreakers see assisting others as an opportunity to make up somewhat for the harm and pain their past behaviors have caused.

Hospice Services

Hospice services exist in every education camp, designed to provide high-quality end-of-life care in the New Millennium for those who are incarcerated. An interdisciplinary team makes every effort to reduce or abate an intern's physical, psychological, and spiritual suffering. This team consists of a physician, a registered nurse, a social worker, a chaplain, security personnel, and trained intern volunteers. The latter may be murderers, armed robbers, and sex offenders, yet they reach out to their fellow interns with empathy and compassion. These volunteers are in turn touched by the opportunity to assist a dying person. It is a chance for the interns to explore and reevaluate their compassionate nature, atone for their misbehaviors, and discover inner peace.

Intern volunteers serve the dying interns by enabling them to eat, dress, and move about. They read, chat, watch television, hold a hand. As surrogate family members, they mostly listen, assuring that a fellow human being does not die alone. In the process, intern volunteers discover that serving others is the most powerful thing one can do to help oneself.

Brazil Story

An example of the effectiveness of the New Millennium Story assumptions can be found at a correctional facility in the Republic of Brazil. In 1993, Judge Nagahi Farukawa gathered together community leaders from the small town of Bragança Paulista in the State of São Paulo. He invited them to put their heads together and brainstorm to reconceive a correction facility which would successfully return lawbreakers to the community as "contributors" to, rather than "destroyers" of, community life. With the help of the business community and funds from the State of São Paulo, they renovated an old prison building.

I had the privilege of visiting the facility twice, in 2001 and 2003. On interviewing Mr. Ariel, the gentleman primarily responsible for its operation, I learned that recidivism (the number of lawbreakers who return to prison after release) at this facility was 13.7 percent. The average recidivism rate throughout the world is about 85 percent, so I asked Mr. Ariel to explain their amazing results. "Two reasons," he responded in English with obvious pleasure. "Respect and no overcrowding."

"No overcrowding" I understood. The facility was built for 200 occupants and the State of São Paulo had agreed never to assign more than that number to it.

"What do you mean by 'respect'?" I inquired. "How does that play out?"

"Many ways," he responded, and began to list a number of them. "To begin with, when lawbreakers are sentenced, if there is room in this facility, they can request to be sent here. Usually men ask to come here after serving time in a regular prison and then becoming repeaters! Second-timers believe they will have a better chance of 'going straight' if they come here.

"The inmates here are not called prisoners," Mr. Ariel continued, "but interns, and are addressed by their first names. They are not clothed in prison garb, but wear civilian clothes."

Later, when I toured the facility, I was unable to distinguish between interns and guards. The latter didn't wear uniforms or carry weapons. Only two were on duty at any given time, attending to 200 occupants. Mr. Ariel explained that group pressure curtailed violent behavior among the interns, and this accounted for the small number of guards.

"Thanks to the businessmen in town," he further explained, "the interns have regular jobs, if they want. The facility also hires some of the interns to do maintenance work and cleaning, although each man is responsible for keeping his own living space clean."

When I observed the men working, the tasks seemed comparable to assembly-line procedures in the United States, albeit with less modern technology. I wished I had had the opportunity to redesign the work, to provide greater opportunities for the interns to learn and grow on the job and develop skills for possible employment once they were ready to leave.

"The men work six days a week," said Mr. Ariel, "ten hours a day, from 7 a.m. to 6 p.m. with an hour for lunch. They earn a minimum wage, three-quarters of what the average Brazilian makes on the outside. They learn responsibility by giving a quarter of their earnings to the facility to pay for their room and board. The rest is used any way they wish. Many make restitution for

240

money they've stolen; some send money home to their families. Others apply the money to medical or dental bills, or pay for the assistance of social workers and lawyers. And of course they can purchase treats from the facility store."

Later Mr. Ariel confided with pleasure, "The facility has become nearly self-supporting. Every effort is made to prepare the interns to return and participate in community life. That is our clear number-one objective. We have the expectation that the interns here will reform themselves and never get in trouble again."

Social workers visit interns' families and help them make arrangements to visit their relatives in the camps; they also counsel the families on readjustment to normal life. Conjugal visits to the interns, complete with privacy, are encouraged every Thursday and Sunday afternoon. Mr. Ariel showed me the area set aside for these conjugal visits, where tents were constructed to provide privacy.

Townspeople volunteer to visit in the evenings after the supper hour. Some teach interns to read and write; due to illiteracy, many of the men had theretofore been unable to find jobs. This joblessness had been a major contributor to crimes such as theft or selling drugs, which enabled them to support themselves and their families.

In the evening, Christian Evangelicals minister and sing songs with the men. The interns are grateful for this personal attention and sing along gustily. The songs reminded me of those we sang as children around the fire at summer camp. Both Protestant and Catholic groups hold religious services. Periodically, musicians, actors, and poets perform for the interns. Entertainment is specifically designed to develop aesthetic appreciation.

Group counseling, anger-management groups, Alcoholics Anonymous groups, and other psychological help are available. Members of the wider community seem to accept responsibility for the failures of their neighbors and are determined to do whatever they can to restore and heal their hurting colleagues.

I asked Mr. Ariel if they were "coddling" these lawbreakers and making life so wonderful for them that they would never want to leave. Suddenly, he became very serious, speaking deliberately: "We can see in their eyes that there is no substitute for being free. No one wants to stay. They are all eager to leave as soon as they can. The men gradually understand they need this place in order to stay out of trouble in the future. Only two didn't get it and tried to escape."

As I walked through the facility, I noticed that many interns looked me in the eye. They responded to my greetings with smiles. The few who did not, I assumed, were relatively new and had not yet "gotten with the program." I also noted the presence of cats and kittens, and saw some interns cultivating gardens. I looked for a dog but failed to see one.

I asked one fairly clean-cut young man, "What are you here for?" I suspected he was probably caught stealing a woman's purse for the second time. The smile disappeared from his face, his expression sad, as he said, "I lost my temper, got into a fight, and killed a man."

Even though the facility contained some offenders who had violently broken the law, still, the recidivism rate was less than 14 percent. Restorative justice, rather than retribution and punishment of lawbreakers, is already making a positive difference.

Finland Story

Another group of New Millennium Thinkers and Feelers are the people responsible for administering justice in Finland. The Finnish justice system is based on "gentle justice." No prison hierarchy exists. Inmates live in clean, unlocked dormitory rooms, supervised by unarmed guards. According to Tapio Appi Seppala, Director of the National Research Institute of Legal Policy in Finland,[10] Finns think of their justice system as a creator of morals and a shaper of values, both of which lead to restoration, rehabilitation, and reconciliation, instead of punishment as retribution.

Denmark Story

In Denmark, the correctional-facility staff, besides being responsible for security, serve as vocational instructors, teachers, and social workers. They are responsible for supervising the interns as well as training them in skills they lacked at the time they got into trouble. The lawbreakers are, in turn, expected to work or attend school. Idleness is discouraged. Learning is rewarded with extra privileges.

In addition, the Danish facility staff provide emotional support to the families of inmates. Family visits are encouraged. Furloughs are permitted as a reward for good behavior. Low-security inmates are sent into the community to work during the day, returning to the facility to sleep at night. The correctional system is optimistic, in the belief that the majority of wrongdoers will straighten out their own lives when given another chance.

Danish facilities are limited in capacity to approximately 200 inmates. The smaller size, Danes believe, enables inmates and facility staff to get to know one another, develop trust, and figure out constructive ways to live in the community.

The Danes believe inmates need privacy and a place to escape from the noise often present in modern prisons, as well as time to evaluate their lives and reform themselves. Meditation rooms are set aside for such purposes.[11] Inmates are also encouraged to decorate their living quarters, so as to overcome the typical drabness of modern institutions.

Africa Story

Psychologist and wisdom teacher Wayne Dyer has described, in his programs for Public Broadcasting, what happens in a specific southern African community when one of its members behaves in a way that irritates and disappoints others. Regarding his approach to disciplining his teenage daughter, Dyer says he regrets not having known about this following African approach. The story goes back to other sources and is presented here as it appears on the website *Friends of Peace Pilgrim.*

The Babemba tribe of southern Africa has a social structure with an elementary criminal code.

Their close community living makes harshness unnecessary. A visitor was deeply impressed by the tribe's handling of antisocial, delinquent behaviors, which are exceedingly infrequent. When a person acts irresponsibly or unjustly, he/she is placed in the center of the village, alone, unfettered. All work ceases. All gather around the accused individual. Then each person of every age begins to talk out loud to the accused. One at a time, each person tells all the good things the one in the center ever did in his/her lifetime. Every incident, every experience that can be recalled with any detail and accuracy, is recounted. All positive attributes, good deeds, strengths, and kindnesses are recited carefully and at length. No one is permitted to fabricate, exaggerate, or be facetious about accomplishments or positive aspects of the accused person. The tribal ceremony often lasts several days, not ceasing until everyone is drained of every positive comment that can be mustered. At the end, the tribal circle is broken, a joyous celebration takes place, and the person is symbolically and literally welcomed back into the tribe. Necessity for such ceremonies is rare![12]

Imagine this happening in every household in the world when someone has misbehaved. Each family member states what behaviors he or she appreciates in the person who has apparently misbehaved. No one fabricates or exaggerates the accomplishments or the positive aspects of the troublesome member. The activity continues until all have expressed every positive point they can think of about the person in question, enabling the person to feel good about himself/herself, as well as toward all involved. This positive reinforcement motivates the person to repeat the behaviors appreciated by the family and eliminate the negative behaviors.

United States Story

In the United States, model programs display a remarkable level of sensitivity to the needs of interns. For instance, prisoner/author Kathy Boudin created a program called "Parenting from a Distance" for mothers interned at Bedford Hills State Prison in New York.

> Boudin leads groups for prisoners who are mothers, modeled on women's consciousness-raising groups that evolved in the late 1960s, where women talk about their sense of powerlessness, their shame, and their guilt about not being available to their children. They tell stories of abuse and disempowerment. They empower themselves by listening to each other's stories and accepting each other in spite of what each of them might have suffered and done in the past. And they talk about their feelings as mothers and how they can be better parents, even from inside prison walls.[13]

The women visualize themselves being loving mothers to their children. Their vision suggests actions, both inside the facility and on the outside once they're released. With confidence they begin to implement their visions.

More and more of these changes are happening throughout the world as people realize they can change their own behavior, create their own reality, forgive and be forgiven. New Millennium Thinkers and Feelers believe there are always opportunities for changing what we've been doing. As we work together, we continue to imagine and create. We invite you, the reader, to join us.

CONCLUSION

New Millennium Thinkers and Feelers have changed their beliefs and attitudes toward lawbreakers. Seeking justice and safety in the community through punishment has been replaced by achieving justice through the four R's: Restoration,

Rehabilitation, Restitution, and Reconciliation—all flowing from the Four Fundamental Assumptions of the Emerging Worldview Story.

In the New Millennium Story, we assume no one is absolutely certain about anything, so we have an open mind toward discovering *just* ways to make our communities safe. We assume that if we visualize a world where justice reigns, we will discover and implement ways to make justice a genuine reality. We are one with everyone, including interns, so we use empathy to better understand their behavior. We also assume we all intend to do what we perceive is good. Sometimes we make mistakes and evil consequences follow; we then seek to learn from our mistakes and learn to ask for help in doing so. Acting on these Four Fundamental Assumptions has had amazing, positive results in securing justice and public safety. Most former lawbreakers change their lawbreaking behaviors and act in a way that benefits both themselves and the community.

In the New Millennium Story, everyone is equal before the law. Justice is seen as an opportunity to enable lawbreakers to experience restoration and to be responsible for themselves. This is true equality.

Lawbreakers, their victims, and the victims' families are realizing that they are all one, capable of achieving restoration and reconciliation by rehabilitating themselves and, where possible, making restitution. What had appeared to be an unrealized dream has become, for most, a meaningful experience in the New Millennium.

CHAPTER TWELVE

The Story of the Environment

When we heal the earth, we heal ourselves.
David Orr
Founder of The Meadowcreek Project

[T]he environment should be put in the category of our national security. Defense of our resources is just as important as defense abroad. Otherwise what is there to defend?
Robert Redford
Actor, Director, Filmmaker, Environmentalist

When we try to pick up anything by itself we find it is attached to everything in the universe.
John Muir
Naturalist, Writer, Conservationist
Founder, Sierra Club

Shall I not have intelligence with the earth? Am I not partly leaves and vegetable mould myself?
Henry David Thoreau
American Transcendentalist Author and Naturalist

We must realize [that] when basic needs have been met, human development is primarily about being more, not having more.
The Earth Charter
International Earth Charter Initiative

What Are Environment and Ecology?

The *Oxford English Dictionary* defines *environment* as the conditions under which any person or thing lives or is developed; the sum-total of influences which modify and determine the development of life or character.

The environment includes all chemical releases by: air, gravity, soil, sun, water; as well as biological components such as living matter, including its emotional and spiritual features.

Cellular biologist Barry Commoner[1] cites the example of a worm: the worm is eating leaves, a bird snatches the worm, an eagle captures the bird, and then the eagle dies, rots, and becomes nourishment for new plant producing leaves for another worm to eat. This cycle exemplifies Mother Nature's ongoing activity: incalculable myriad transformations of atoms and molecules and energy conversions, into other forms—a night crawler, a robin, a peregrine falcon—all are works in progress. Any element or elements in the environment may alter Mother Nature's cycles—events such as droughts or floods, for example—and then nothing is the same again.

The formalized discipline that studies these environmental phenomena is called *ecology*. The term was coined by the German biologist Ernst Heinrich Haeckel in 1866 from two Greek words: *oikos*, meaning "house" or "place to live," and *logos*, meaning "word" or "study." The combination means the study of the place in which we live. *Ecology* also shares the same linguistic root as the word *economics*, indicating that the theory is concerned with the economy of nature. Hence, the New Millennium Story defines ecology as "the study of the relationships of organisms *with* their physical environment and *to* one another." The key word here is *relationships*.[1]

Barry Commoner states these four assumptions:
1. You can't throw anything away.
2. You can't do just one thing; everything is connected to everything else.
3. Nature knows best.
4. There is no such thing as a free lunch.[2]

We will see illustrations of these assumptions throughout this chapter.

Pre-Modern Worldview Story of the Environment

Most Pre-Modern Worldview thinkers believe that all natural phenomena were created by God. Forests, lakes, streams, plants, animals, and especially the Earth are sacred and need to be treated with respect. To treat with respect means to preserve and conserve what God has created.

Calamities such as hurricanes, tsunamis, and tornadoes are thought to be acts of God, punishment for human misbehavior.

American Indigenous Peoples

The indigenous peoples who inhabited North America before the European visitation followed four basic rules in their daily life:

1. Respect for Mother Earth
2. Respect for the Great Spirit
3. Respect for our fellow man and woman
4. Respect for individual freedom.

These rules generated the indigenous hierarchical value system environmentalist, Michael Cohen, tells us. In this prioritized order, respect for Mother Earth comes first, and individual freedom comes last. Good reasons exist for Pre-Moderns to act positively in accordance with Mother Earth's values.[3]

Implications of the Pre-Modern Worldview Story of the Environment

In the earliest period of history, our ancestors had relatively little impact on the environment. They relied on resources available in their immediate vicinity, hunting wild animals and harvesting wild plants for food, but taking only enough for survival. The human population was small, and the food supply generally was adequate to meet people's needs.

As populations increased, the hunting way of life became more difficult to maintain. Sources of food became scarce.

A significant transformation took place: the domestication of plants and animals, as hunter-gatherers became farmers and began to live together in agricultural communities and cultivate the land. Over time, however, with no understanding of how to protect the land from overuse, civilizations ceased to exist because they literally ran out of food.

The Commons

The commons refers to the realm of life which is the shared heritage of us all. Historically, this term referred mainly to land and water. For centuries in England, ordinary people, known as *commoners,* had the right to farm, fish, hunt, and forage on certain lands they did not own. Land was a source of sustenance for all, and everyone sought access to it. Similarly, today in the United States, people are free to catch a given number of fish in most of the lakes and streams throughout the country, provided they obtain a license.

The Modern Worldview Story of the Environment

In the sixteenth and seventeenth centuries, the Industrial Revolution began in England; it continued through the mid-twentieth century. With the rise of commerce and industry, private property escalated in value. The English government evicted commoners and declared the commons private property. Many commoners were forced off the land or forced to pay rent to absent landlords.

In time, privatization of the commons occurred virtually everywhere. Recently in Bolivia, privatization extended even to rainwater. Beaches, and even entire lakes, are being made private as the wealthy purchase the land surrounding the lakes and then prevent access. Countless ocean beaches have also been privatized, forcing most people to travel miles and miles to swim in the ocean.

In poor countries, squatters seek out unused land to build their shantytowns. But once the government or private owners see potential in the land, the squatters are sent packing, usually with no place to go.

In addition, significant advancements in science have radically changed the way people look at themselves and their relationship to the world. The older views of the world as an organic, living, and spiritual universe have been replaced with the notion of the world as a machine.

The Industrial Revolutionists believed the following:

- It's us against the environment.
- It's the individual (community or nation) that matters.
- It's us against other men; so competition is the road to happiness and prosperity.
- We can have unilateral control over the environment and we have an obligation, therefore, to control it.
- We live within an infinitely expanding frontier.
- Economic determinism is common sense.
- Technology will do it all for us.[4]

Moderns came to assume that human beings are distinct from, and far superior to, all other "things" in our universe. Secularists and even Christian Moderns, using the Bible as their source, assume that all of nature is here to be exploited by humans—from inorganic resources, such as water and rocks, to plants and animals. Referring to the Book of Genesis, Jewish and Christian Moderns believe that humans were created to rule over everything else in existence. Nature needs to be preserved, not because it is a sacred gift from God, but because it is a means of survival. Instead of faith in God, Moderns place their faith in technology, believing all will be well forever because of future developments and advancements.

Implications of the Modern Worldview Story of the Environment

Modern Worldview thinking marked a pivotal turning point in history. It led to inventions such as the heat pump, the steam engine, the internal-combustion engine, electricity distribution, railroads, automobiles, airplanes, and so forth.

Modern Worldview assumptions have also led to the emergence of a "throwaway economy" motivated by convenience. Instead of washing diapers and dishes, consumers welcome disposable plastic and paper versions. Not only are cities running out of landfills for this garbage, but the world is also fast running out of the depleted oil and forest resources used to manufacture and transport throwaway products.

Because we have lost our connection to Mother Earth, some worry that we face a tremendous threat and challenge to our very existence. According to author Marjorie Kelly, global temperatures have risen, water tables have fallen, wetlands have disappeared, rivers and lakes have run dry, and fisheries have collapsed. Forests have shrunk, and countless plant and animal species have disappeared completely.[5]

Global Climate Change

The gradual nature of global climate change has allowed some people to engage in denial, or a failure to take increased heat seriously. Although some still debate the issue, many reputable scientists believe global climate change is real—and the greatest threat to our planet. They suspect that it is currently causing dramatic water changes and threatening the health of every living thing on earth.

Strong evidence indicates that most of the warming over the last fifty years can be attributed in large part to the burning of fossil fuels to generate electricity and to transport goods and people.[6] Some scientists suggest that these human activities have drastically altered the chemical makeup of the atmosphere by contributing to the buildup of greenhouse gases, primarily carbon dioxide, methane, and nitrous oxide. These gases trap heat in the Earth's atmosphere, and this warms the planet. Some scientists recently expressed the fear that "If nothing is done, in about ten years the planet may reach a *tipping point* and begin a slide toward the destruction of civilization; after that point it would be too late for any action."[7]

According to former U.S. Vice President Al Gore, we are taking energy stored over hundreds of millions of years in the form of coal, natural gas, and oil, and releasing it suddenly. As a consequence, he believes, we humans are responsible for global climate change.[8] "The world won't end in ten years," says Gore, "but a point will have been passed, and there will be an irreversible slide into destruction." Gore further states, in his film *An Inconvenient Truth:* "We can turn this around if politicians in every nation have the courage to do what is necessary. It is not a political issue, it is a *moral* issue."[9]

The Biofuels Industry

The high price of oil has stimulated vast investments in fuel-crop production. With the absence of government restraints, the rising price of oil is therefore threatening biodiversity, ensuring a wave of plant and animal extinction while privatizers clear away rain forests to plant only high-fuel monocultures. The earth presently is capable of supplying enough food to satisfy human needs. But because nearly everything we eat can be converted into automotive fuel (in the form of biofuels, including ethanol, which can be produced from corn, sugar cane, sugar beets, wheat, or barley, and biodiesel, which can be produced from coconut oil, palm oil, soybeans, and rapeseed), food supplies are being threatened. In using food to supply fuel, we also deplete our reserves of drinkable water, crucial for survival.

As gasoline prices rise because of increasing demand, and as more potential food is used for fuel, the cost of food is also skyrocketing. The poor therefore find it difficult to survive, not because there is not enough food, but because the affluent continue to drive sport-utility vehicles (SUVs).[10] In 2004, the United States used 32 million tons of corn to produce 3.4 billion gallons of ethanol. At average world grain consumption levels, the corn could have fed 100 million people.[11]

Water Shortages

The demand for water has tripled over the last half-century. In his capacity as president of the Earth Policy Institute, Lester R. Brown has written:

Each year the gap widens between world water consumption and the sustainable water supply. Each year the drop in the water tables is greater than the year before. Both aquifer depletion and the diversion of water to the cities contribute to the growing irrigation water deficit and hence to a growing grain deficit in many water-short countries.[12]

In some places in India, underground water sources have dried up entirely. All agriculture is rain-fed, and drinking water is shipped in by truck. In the U.S. states of Texas, Kansas, and Oklahoma, the High Plains Aquifer, an underground water table has dropped by nearly 100 feet. Wells have gone completely dry on thousands of farms in the southern Great Plains. In Saudi Arabia, which has always been water-poor and oil-rich, irrigated agriculture has all but disappeared. Israel, a pioneer in raising irrigation-based crops, is running out of water. Part of the conflict with the Palestinians in Gaza and the West Bank has to do with the allocation of water. Because of the growing water shortage, Israel has forbidden farmers to grow wheat.[13]

Since the overpumping of aquifers is occurring in many countries at more or less the same time, the depletion of aquifers, coupled with the resulting harvest cutbacks, is leading to an extreme scarcity of food.

Polar Bears

Melting sea ice is destroying the habitat of polar bears and wreaking havoc in the arctic climates where they live and propagate. Polar bears are marine mammals. They rely on sea ice for all of their essential behaviors, including mating, maternity, and feeding. They eat mainly ringed seals and other ice-dwelling species.

For the first time, scientists have documented numerous deaths of polar bears in Alaska as the edge of the polar ice cap has continued to retreat to the north. The bears apparently drown after swimming long distances in the ocean while seeking solid ice floes from which to hunt and on which to raise their young. In the past, the drowning of polar bears was so rare it had never been documented; in recent years, researchers have discovered numerous dead polar bears floating in the water. "For anyone who has wondered how global warming and reduced ice will affect polar bears, the answer is simple—they die!" wrote Richard Steiner, a marine biology professor at the University of Alaska. According to the Center for Biological Diversity, the bear population has declined 14 percent since 1996.[14]

Deforestation

More than eighty percent of the world's ancient forests have been destroyed. Destruction of the Amazon rain forest, home to tropical birds, jaguars, tree frogs, the howler monkey, and millions of other species of wild life, jumped forty percent in 2005. According to recent satellite photo imagery, more than six million acres of this precious, irreplaceable habitat were clear-cut, slashed, and burned in just twelve months, to provide land for grazing cows and raising crops. This means more than ten acres were destroyed every minute! Over half of the tropical rain forests on Earth have already been destroyed, their complex ecosystems ripped apart. The tragedy is that once a rain forest is destroyed, it cannot be restored.[15]

The New Millennium Story of the Environment

During the late twentieth century and into the twenty-first century, the dominant Modern Worldview Story has undergone a profound reappraisal as Emerging Worldview thinking and feeling, with its adaptation of four fundamental assumptions, has begun to permeate a greater number of people's worldviews and begun to save us from destroying the Earth, our source of life.

Thinking and feeling differently about the environment has enabled New Millennium environmentalists to become a positive force for sustaining the earth, rather than destroying it. In our story, we have committed ourselves to creating a sustainable social and cultural environment in which people's present wants and desires are satisfied, with no diminishment for our grandchildren and their grandchildren. As a consequence, hope has been restored and fear eliminated.

Awareness and Reassessment

The global environmental crisis is one variable which has, among others, served as a catalyst for far-reaching reexaminations of basic values and assumptions in every area of human knowledge and life. This reassessment offers both a challenge and an opportunity for leaders in all the disciplines to reformulate fundamental questions and significant issues in their fields. Theologian and eco-philosopher Thomas Berry says that the time has come to "reinvent the human at the species level." He suggests that existing Pre-Modern and Modern worldviews are not dealing adequately with the issues facing us today. Following Thomas Berry's lead, Emerging Worldview environmentalists continue to draw on the evolutionary wisdom of the human species in its interrelationships with all other species and ecosystems, for our very survival.

New Millennium Thinkers and Feelers of all ages are more and more aware of changes in our environment. This awareness is being demonstrated across all walks of life. One example of this is the 2009 Academy Award–winning *Wall-E,*[16] a heartwarming and heartrending animated feature film that projects a future world of garbage, unfit to inhabit. Another example is found in the dedication of people like humanist and ecologist Edward O. Wilson, a Pulitzer Prize–winning Harvard biologist, who at the age of eighty is an active, tireless environmentalist. *Encyclopedia of Life,* a biodiversity e-library, is a new project of Wilson's that contains an e-page for every known species with everything known about the species—reachable through a single portal, on command.[17]

In a 2008 interview with *New Yorker* staff writer Elizabeth Kolbert, Wilson said that each species is a masterpiece of evolution which is highly adaptive. That means that for every species we lose, for example one species of tree, it takes down with it, on average, at least twenty other species of animals, especially insects. So when we lose a given species, we don't really know what we are losing with it! And, finally, losing *any* species is, in Wilson's opinion, immoral.

We Are Forever in the Process of Discovering

Since in the New Millennium Story many assume that we cannot know anything for certain about our environment—for example, whether the planet is actually becoming warmer, or, if it is, whether the warming is absolutely being caused by us humans—leaders have determined that *it is best not to take chances with our precious Earth.* All our efforts are designed to do whatever it takes to preserve and sustain our Earth for generations to come. Preserving and sustaining our environment has become our highest value. Many people are actually eager to pay taxes to support ongoing research to find more productive ways to preserve Mother Earth.

We Create Our Own Reality

In the New Millennium Story, we begin with the end in view. We *visualize* what humans are doing all over the world to sustain our environment. Once we visualize the very best sustainable activities, we act to create the environment we envision. We picture our Earth being as satisfying and rich for our grandchildren as it is for us.

We do not waste our time and energy focusing on the environmental issues arising from the Pre-Modern and Modern assumptions described earlier in this chapter. We understand them—then we move on with courage, using our minds, intuition, and imagination, to place our emphasis on what we want to create in the present, so that we, and generations in the future, will enjoy the kind of livable planet we all yearn for.

Our assumption that "we create our own reality" is exemplified by Imagine Chicago, a nonprofit community group founded in 1992, which helps harness imagination for the public good, encouraging and equipping people to become engaged in envisioning and creating hopeful futures for their families and communities through both discourse and action. Working in collaboration with local organizations—schools, faith communities, cultural institutions, businesses, and community groups—Imagine Chicago has initiated and facilitated dozens of creative partnerships in which people have worked together to understand, imagine, and create the future they value. The Imagine Movement has spread to over seventy projects in more than twenty countries spanning six continents and continues to grow. In recent years, large-scale Imagine projects in cities including Calgary, Alberta, Canada, and Durban, South Africa, have focused on citizen engagement in defining a hundred-year vision for *sustainable* development that informs government decision-making in the present.

> There is no Imagine "blueprint" but Imagine projects tend to share certain common features: strength-based and vision-oriented communications which invite participants to name what matters and how things could be different; intergenerational collaboration as a preferred way of working; . . . and a commitment to place-based intercultural communities of practice within which people share ideas, resources and practical tools that make a tangible community difference.[18]

We Are All One

"When we heal the earth," writer David Orr states, "we heal ourselves." Because New Millennium Thinkers and Feelers assume that we are one with all other human beings and one with the environment, in concert with the Buddhists we live a form of nonviolent ecology. We have become eco-centric rather than anthropocentric, because we view humans *not above* nature, but *one with* nature. We believe the Book of Genesis in the Bible reveals that humans are **not** created to rule over the Earth, but to take care of Mother Earth and all living things.

According to author Stephanie Kaza, "An environmental ethic is not something we apply outside ourselves: there is no outside ourselves. We are the environment, and it is us."[19] As explained by Kaza, Buddhism focuses on the relationship of mind and nature through three practices: direct knowing, discriminating awareness, and a truly deep sense of compassion. She writes:

> By cultivating these three practices, one's actions in relation to the environment come to be based in relationship and interconnectedness, rather than in dualistic subject-object modes of separation. Through this approach one's orientation to the world is fundamentally altered from the dominant species to member of a community, from part to process.[20]

Also in conjunction with Buddhist thought, there is interconnectedness between nature and the human being. We see the benefits of identifying with the welfare of all beings, all living forms of life, and everything in existence. We will not survive over time unless we do something to restore or replace these organisms, together with their physical environment.

Therefore, New Millennium environmentalists encourage one another to limit our personal consumption of these resources to the four basic needs of food, clothing, shelter, and medicine (basic sustenance). Our behavior avoids the extremes of both denial and overindulgence.

We Always Do What We Perceive Is Best

In the New Millennium Story, we assume everyone is acting in the best interest of the planet. Whenever an action of another person does not appear to contribute to the benefit of Mother Earth, we assume they are unaware of the dangers their behavior may be inviting. We use dialogue, not confrontation, to reach an understanding through consensus on what we all come to agree is the appropriate behavior for protecting and sustaining our environment.

Implications of the New Millennium Story of the Environment

Picture what is happening now as a critical mass of the world's population internalizes the Four Fundamental Assumptions described in this book. The use of gas/electric hybrid automobiles has enabled us to reduce our dependence on oil. The advancement of solar and wind power has achieved the same result because these resources are cheap, abundant, limitless, widely distributed, clean, and climate-friendly. They are safe, secure, locally grown, and decentralized. No other energy sources have all of these attributes. Hence solar and wind have largely replaced oil as Mother Earth's major source of energy. All over the world, people are investing in conservation and clean energy resources, having gone beyond fossil fuels and the dangers of nuclear power.

Substituting the GPI for the GDP (see Chapter Nine) has greatly influenced our progress in achieving a sustainable environment and the development of an honest market and accounting system. Through this system, we have become informed about all of the ecological costs of providing products and services. Now the market respects the sustainable-yield thresholds and values nature's role. The market favors long-term benefits over the old Modernist thinking of placing value only on quarterly performance.

The indirect costs of goods and services are incorporated into market prices through levies on environmentally destructive activities, such as the burning of coal and oil, which causes pollution and acid rain and raises healthcare costs. The added tax has encouraged investment in alternative sources of energy: wind, solar, and geothermal.

The tax structure has changed. Taxes are levied on what we all purchase. The heaviest taxes are on luxuries and environmentally destructive items, rather than on what we earn. As a result, people have become far more conservative in their spending habits. Much of this shift relates to taxes on road transport, including a substantial rise in vehicle and fuel taxes.

Recently, the International Center for Technology did a study assessing the real cost of a gallon of gasoline. The Center determined that a gallon of gas costs $11.00 This includes the healthcare cost of treating respiratory illnesses related to auto exhaust, along with oil tax breaks that were initiated under Modernist assumptions.[21]

In the Modern Worldview, "the world's taxpayers provide an estimated $700 billion in subsidies for environmentally destructive activities such as fossil fuel-burning, over-pumping aquifers, clear-cutting forests, and over-fishing,"[22] according to Lester Brown. Modern Worldview assumptions have led to the spending of hundreds of billions of dollars annually to subsidize our own destruction.

Not discouraged, we see many opportunities, not simply to control costs and make money—which is secondary—but primarily to promote human well-being, today and, particularly, long into the future. For instance, we have shifted subsidies from road construction to railways. At the same time, we have increased mobility and reduced carbon emissions. We have reduced the taxes of the average citizen and encouraged investment in wind-generated electricity, solar power, and geothermal applications—all of which are contributing to the health and well-being of every citizen. Further, we have expanded our efforts to recycle. Old cars and household items (refrigerators, washing machines, and computers) are now being recycled, enabling ninety-five percent of the world's steel to be reused rather than produced from virgin ore. Electric-arc steel mills and minimills are efficiently converting scrap iron into finished steel, which is contributing to the closing of iron-ore mines.

Manufacturers continue to design products using new processes to lower and, in some cases, eliminate toxic emissions. Retail stores throughout the world have voluntarily banned nonbiodegradable plastic bags and limited themselves to biodegradable paper bags; people often bring their own canvas bags from home. Recycling both at home and in the workplace enables nearly everyone to participate in conserving our remaining resources. Farmers and landowners in rain forest areas are using sustainable methods of growing bananas, coffee, cocoa, hardwoods, and foodstuffs that are not demanded by the biofuel industry. Unlike the clear-cutting of forest lands for crop growth, these techniques retain rainwater and consequently reduce soil erosion, flooding, and the destruction of homes and villages. Additionally, the retention of water and fertile soils under a canopy of healthy rain forest trees minimizes the need for fertilizers, pesticides, and herbicides—again, providing economic, energy, and health benefits. These initiatives are leaders in the process toward sustainability.

At the time of this writing, the United States House of Representatives has passed a bill, resonating with the New Millennium Worldview, that is designed to provide homeowners with thousands of federal dollars for the purpose of renovating their homes with better insulation and with energy-saving doors and windows.

The Curitiba Story

Curitiba means "pine grove" in Portuguese. This city in the south of Brazil is living up to its name. Over thirty parks, lushly full of pine and other trees and plants of many kinds, have come into existence since 1972, making Curitiba the ecological capital of Brazil. The city has become a model of sustainable urban planning, attracting persons from other cities who want to replicate its innovations in their own localities.

Curitiba's former mayor, Jaime Lerner, a leader in urban planning, believes that cities need to be rediscovered as "instruments of change." A catalyst for change in his own right, Lerner invited the residents of the city to think and feel differently about their urban environment. Instead of focusing on what was wrong, he urged the citizens to envision a new Curitiba.

The residents jumped at the opportunity to make change and made the public transportation system of the city their highest priority. From the citizens' perspective, transportation was the key to the improvement of Curitiba's residents' quality of life.

A complete overhaul of transportation in the city has produced citywide express buses, microbuses, and lift-equipped buses to serve persons with special needs. A creative rapid-boarding system has cut boarding times by one-half.

The city buses are privately owned, with no direct government subsidy. Two-thirds of Curitibans now use public transportation; there is twenty-five percent less congestion than in many other cities of similar size; this has led to noticeably cleaner air, according to the city's website.

Retired buses are used either as mobile training centers or as free transportation to the city's many new parks. The mobile training centers serve as educational facilities for Curitibans, who pay one dollar to take courses in such subject areas as auto mechanics, electrical work, typing, hairdressing, and artisan work. At the end of these training courses, students are placed in jobs throughout the city; many start their own businesses.[23]

A twenty-four-hour street has been designated, which serves as a town center. At any time of the day or night, residents and visitors can be found having coffee, conversing, or looking for friends. I have sauntered down this interesting street many times, often finding opportunities to meet and discuss politics, religion, or the latest news with friendly Curitibans eager to practice their English.

As mentioned, parks and other open spaces, filled with pine trees, have been enlarged and beautifully improved, inviting residents to balance their lives between work and recreation. They see *recreation* as a time to *re-create* their lives, rather than a waste of time.

In 1972, only five square feet of open space (the Commons) per resident was available. Curitibans were given two alternatives: subdivide available land for a new housing development, thus allowing the city to profit from added property taxes, or: preserve the space as green areas. The people determined that parks with pine trees were in their long-term self-interest. Today in Curitiba, there is at least 559 square feet-per-resident, even though the city has grown from a half million residents to nearly two million.[24]

One thousand plazas have been established throughout the city. Free newspapers are made available in these plazas, inviting residents to come, sit, enjoy the weather, and visit with their neighbors, as well as keep up with what is happening locally and internationally. Daycare centers also have been placed strategically throughout the city to aid parents who are shopping or running errands.

One key aspect of the revitalization of Curitiba has been its participatory and voluntary approach to implementing these changes. For example, recycling was introduced in Curitiba's schools, and children quickly caught on and convinced their parents to sort their garbage at home and recycle what has value. Today, two-thirds of the city's daily waste stream (one hundred tons) is recycled. Recovering alcoholics and homeless people are actively employed in the recycling program, and proceeds from the recycling go back into social services provided to the city's residents. The recycling program is voluntary, not mandatory, but it awards participants with food and transportation vouchers.

The success of recycling has reduced environmental damage citywide; this has in turn reduced the infant mortality and disease rates, particularity in impoverished areas of Curitiba.

Environmental education has been introduced in most of the schools, and after-school classes in ecology are offered in poor sections of the city, where parents often work late into the day.[25]

The recycling program has been extended to include hospital and chemical waste. Major businesses are getting on board as they come to see protecting the environment as indeed good for business.

Curitibans play an integral part in the planning of the city's changes because they are the ones who make the changes work. At the core of Curitiba's continuing success is the people's vision of their city as a place where people work, play, and enjoy their lives together. Curitibans work to make this a reality. They experience their power, and each success drives them on to further embrace and enliven their environment.

A Venice, California, Story

Renovating a 1920's bungalow near the beach in Venice, California USA, architect Angie Brooks utilized attractive reflective solar panels, which, she claims, "supply 95 percent of the building's electricity needs." Rooftop panels preheat water for the swimming pool and increase the efficiency of the gas-fueled water heater. And the home needs no air conditioning because of cross ventilation and protection from the western sun. Electric lights are used only on very cloudy days and at night. As an architect, Angie Brooks believes: "If we design with the environment in mind, we will have a better house which actually costs less."[26]

The American Institute of Architects singled out Angie's house as a residence to be imitated, based on sustainable design concepts. The Institute recognized that her home is energy-efficient, employs natural light, conserves water, and deeply embodies the values of sustainable development.

The Seattle Library Story

In Seattle, Washington USA, the city put four inches of topsoil on the 18,000-square-foot roof of the Ballard Library "with native grasses and succulent ground cover, designed to absorb and filter rainwater, remove carbon dioxide, and insulate the building in both summer and winter." The city also financed the application of a novel photovoltaic film over the library's windows. This resulted in a reduction of glare and heat from the sun while producing significant kilowatt power.

Residents see the library as a place where they can study and access all the usual services in comfort. They are also proud of the building's aesthetics and sustainability. The Ballard Library received the 2006 Award for Sustainable Design Concepts from the American Institute of Architects. [27]

The Herman Miller Story

Herman Miller is a furniture company with corporate offices in the state of Michigan in the United States. Sustainability managing, the art of integrating socially responsible business practices in order for companies to be profitable in the long term, is an important part of this company's practices.

Pursuant to this goal, the Herman Miller Company buys wind power from the state of Wyoming to provide twenty-seven percent of its electricity. The company is seeking other sources of wind power closer to Michigan, with the intention of boosting its use of renewable energy to sixty percent. According to the

Herman Miller management, "Herman Miller's use of 27 percent renewable energy eliminates the same amount of carbon dioxide emissions that would be created by 14,700 automobile trips from New York to Los Angeles."[28] At Herman Miller, recycling generates $1.5 million in revenue each year. In addition to saving over $1 million in energy and landfill costs, the company's emphasis on sustainability has resulted in a doubling of its size since 1994 and has increased annual sales to about $2 billion. In addition, in order to reduce landfill waste, the company has encouraged suppliers to use returnable packaging, such as plastic crates instead of cardboard boxes, while shipping out its own finished products wrapped in blankets.[29]

The Eco-Baron Story

Journalist Harry Hurt, writing in the *New York Times* in 2009, states:

> Scientists and environmentalists have reached a growing consensus that time is running out for Planet Earth. The polar ice caps are melting. Three-quarters of the world's flowering plant species are at risk of extinction. One in eight bird species is vanishing. Ninety percent of big fish like cod, tuna and swordfish that once swam the oceans have already disappeared. Air, water and ground pollutants from fossil-fuel sources are poisoning major population centers.

CONCLUSION

The world's economy is no longer dependent on carbon-producing forms of energy, automobiles, and a throw-away approach to living a meaningful life. The New Millennium Emerging Worldview economy is powered by abundant sources of renewable energy: wind, solar, geothermal, and hydropower. Gas-electric hybrid cars, advanced-design wind turbines, highly efficient refrigerators, and water-efficient irrigation systems are widespread in every community on our planet. Everywhere one looks, wind farms, solar panels, recycling facilities, bicycle paths, and reforestation projects are present.

A comprehensive reuse/recycle economy is in place. Single-use beverage containers are things of the past. Consumer products, from autos to computers, are designed to be disassembled into their component parts for complete recycling.

The change in our fundamental assumptions, reinforced by economic incentives, accounts for this transformation of Mother Earth. Investment capital comes from private capital markets, from companies in the energy business, as well as from federal and local governments.

From the restructuring of global energy subsidies to the development of wind and other renewable sources of energy, the Earth has a life again. Wind-energy and hybrid-vehicle industries have become partners in an effort to reduce gasoline consumption. Gas-electric hybrid engines along with advanced-design wind turbines have drastically reduced the use of oil throughout the world.

The reduction of oil use has been further facilitated by fees levied on cars entering commercial areas of cities. (Electric sensors identify each car, then charge the owner's credit card.) And a progressive carbon tax has further contributed to a reduction in the use of automobiles.

Large cities are no longer congested, noisy, or polluted. Urban transit systems are heavily used: a combination of light-rail trains, frequent, dependable buses, bicycle pathways, and pedestrian walkways.

People are literally slowing down. They enjoy walking for health and pleasure. They relish having time to visit with friends and with strangers in city parks and other recreational areas.

City police departments now make routine patrols with bicycles. Not only are bikes more mobile; they're less costly than patrol cars, enabling the city to hire more officers with the money saved.

Bicycles have also been found to be more effective for delivering packages in urban areas. With designated lanes in the streets, people can use bicycles both for commuting and and for recreation—contributing to the health of the population.

Some cities offer free use of bicycles for light-rail and bus patrons. At the entrance/exit of each station, bicycles with baskets are available to those with a ticket as evidence that they used the train or bus that day. Patrons cycle to work or to the mall for shopping, returning their bike to the station before boarding to return home. To accommodate this change, many companies have installed showers in the workplace so that employees can shower after their bicycle journey to work.

A redesign of planning and development laws has helped to advance the massive investment in rebuilding cities and the infrastructure of nations. This has led to an improved quality of life for all citizens and has reinforced the belief that Mother Earth is no longer choking to death, but has begun to breathe again.

CHAPTER THIRTEEN

The Story of Politics

Blessed are the peacemakers: for they shall be called the children of God.
Jesus Christ, Sermon on the Mount

When will our consciences grow so tender that we will act to prevent human misery rather than avenge it?
Eleanor Roosevelt
U.S. First Lady and Author

There is no solution for civilization or even the human race, other than the creation of a world government.
Albert Einstein
Renowned Physicist

We need first and foremost a world democracy, a government of this planet for the people and by the people.
Robert Muller
Former UN Assistant Secretary General

Love of country is a wonderful thing, but why should love stop at the border?
Pablo Casals
Renowned Cellist

What Is Politics?

In the New Millennium we define *politics* as: the art of the possible in creating the common good with others, through mutual governance.

It is both fundamental and paramount that all world citizens appreciate their power and ability to be agents on behalf of what matters to themselves and to others. We engage in politics based on the understanding that we cannot achieve the common good by ourselves. If we are to achieve our goal of successfully creating a world that works for all of us, we need and desire to work together with a substantial number of other people. Lone Rangers need not apply.

The Common Good

In the New Millennium, to work for the common good means to exclude **no one** from our concerns. It means promoting global social values: building a just and secure society, serving the poor and vulnerable, and empowering everyone in the world to become what we have the potential to be, that is, a unique individual with a singular and personal nature.

Politicians

Professional **p**oliticians are people who dedicate at least a portion of their lives to creating a world which works for everyone. They invite the rest of us to think and feel differently about what is happening in our lives and the lives of others. For example, Emerging Worldview politicians challenge pervasive injustice by creating in us an awareness of the social factors that generate the wide disparity between affluent people and poor people. When successful, they merit the title of statesman or stateswoman. In the New Millennium, parents encourage their children to consider politics as a career because being a politician is considered an honorable vocation.

All Called to Be Politicians

Although not all of us in the New Millennium become professional *politicians*, every one of us, by reason of being an individual and a member of a community, is called to be *political*. Each of us has the vocation of politician: dedicated to serve the universal common good and bring about peace with justice. Artists, for example—persons whose creative work shows sensitivity and imagination—are adept at this vocation. If awake, all of us know we are needed, because democracy cannot function without an informed and involved citizenry.

Hope

Hope is the engine that drives human endeavor, the force that propels us into action. Only with hope can we muster the courage to overcome thoughts and feelings of powerlessness. Because we hope without ambivalence, we are far from being discouraged by challenges and difficulties; politicians are able to instill in us the *hope* that says, "Together we can democratically create our own reality." Politicians make manifest our belief that we can each make a difference.

Empowerment

Politicians in the Emerging Worldview facilitate a process by which we, the people, experience the power to courageously enter into the political arena with the realization that we can promote justice and peace everywhere. As the thirty-fourth President of the United States, Dwight D. Eisenhower, said in 1959:

> I like to believe that people in the long run are going to do more to promote peace than are governments. Indeed, I think that people want peace so much that one of these days governments had better get out of the way and let them have it.[1]

Pre-Modern and Modern Worldview Stories of Politics

Pre-Modern and Modern Worldview stories are based on four assumptions, as follows.

First Assumption

A certain political and corporate elite group of men are enlightened to the point at which they know far better than anyone else what is good for the rest of us. Believing they are wise men, they assume they know "the truth." The rest of us are wise also, if we **do not question** the authority of the elite. The issue is one of being in control under the pretense of having "the truth."

According to the Pre-Modern Story, a hierarchical power arrangement exists in which God inspires holy men to pass on "the truth" to the king and his court, who rule by divine right. See Figure 13.1.

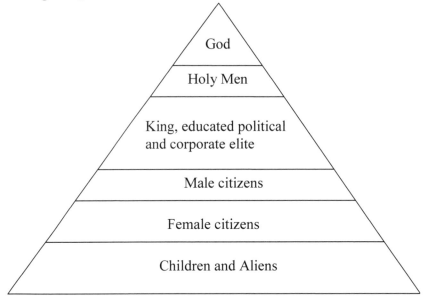

Figure 13.1

For the Moderns, God and holy men have been replaced by Science and Scientists, who are beholden to the corporate elite. In most nations, the king is now represented by politicians. The Modernists assume politicians and corporate leaders are the wise elite who alone know what is "good, true, and beautiful" and deserve to be in control. Therefore, they make the laws and direct the males, who instruct the females, who then tell the children and aliens what to do.

According to this assumption, the hierarchy furthers the formation and legitimization of vertical power structures based on the assumed superiority and inferiority of people in terms of such characteristics as gender, race, ethnic origin, education, wealth, class (status), and sexual orientation.

Second Assumption

Life on this earth is primarily a problem to be solved. If we could only search out all of the wrongs and make them right, justice and peace would follow. Based on this assumption, all problems can be found and solved, but only by the wise elite, with the help of technology. The rest of us need only to trust them and follow their direction. If we do so, all of our worries and problems will be resolved.

Third Assumption

We clearly are all separated from each other. We are told, therefore, from our earliest days, that we must compete to survive. Without competition, Moderns believe, we would still be in the Stone Age. This assumption is often bolstered by reference to Darwin's theme of the survival of the fittest. Males, particularly, are taught to compete successfully to be the best and to put down the adversary. Rewards are given for this aggressive behavior. The very top prize for winning is acceptance into the "club" of the wise elites.

Pre-Moderns and Moderns also assume that, based on our separation, education and especially wealth make us better and more deserving of the resources of this earth. A sign of wisdom is to be able to accumulate material wealth. "He who dies with the most toys wins," and winning is everything!

Fourth Assumption

The world is composed of both good and bad people. All the "we's" identify with the strong and virtuous. Those who disagree with "us," because they have other values, are "the bad guys," the enemy. When the "bad guys" threaten the strong and virtuous, the "bad guys," or enemies, become evil (names often used are: "thugs," "terrorists," "perverts," and "scumbags"—to name only a few) and must be defeated, captured, punished, even tortured by any means available, including, and, certainly, war.

In the end, "might makes right," the ends justify the means, and any doubts about fairness, justice, and other "niceties" tend to be lost because the winners write the history books.

The wise elite believe they have the wisdom and capability to achieve justice and peace by destroying the enemy. All they need, they believe, is the power and the freedom to make the world a safe place for the "good people," defined as docile and compliant citizens. All the "good people" need to do is simply be patient and trust that the wise elite, in due time, will be successful and provide justice and peace for the rest of us by conquering the enemy, whoever the elite determine the enemy to be.

Nationalism

An outgrowth of these assumptions, structures, and approaches is extreme nationalism, commonly referred to as *patriotism*. Extreme nationalism is the belief that one's country is better than all of the others in the world; and in the United States and many other countries, it is symptomatic of a knee-jerk, pro-war reaction—replete with flag waving and shouting "We are number one!" Further, under the guise of patriotism's "in the national interest," nations have historically used force and cunning to carve up the earth into sections, with little or no concern for ethnic, linguistic, or natural boundaries. Pre-Moderns and Moderns hardly conceive of political activities as being designed for the mutual interest of all the nations of the planet.

Implications of the Pre-Modern and Modern Stories

The history of the world under Pre-Modern and Modern assumptions is filled with oppression, atrocities, and wars. Try to imagine history books written without mention of wars!

Ideologues

Adolf Hitler, Josef Stalin, and Pol Pot, along with their followers, are obvious examples of ideologues ostensibly helping their country through acts of genocide. War lords in Africa and the Middle East, along with their associates, are more recent perpetrators of genocide under the pretense of love for country and, sometimes, love of God. Yet, many of these ideologues were and are educated men. They act out of a belief that they are correct and have "the truth" in creating their idea of a better tomorrow for their people (in the exclusive sense of people who share their values).

Most of these ideologues live an "enviable present" while creating a living hell for many, most, or even all of the citizens. Thus these ideologues live far better and more secure lives than those subservient to their commands. The world works for only the few.

Almost all German Nazi leaders, for example, were educated men who appeared quite normal. They loved their families, were kind to animals, and saw themselves as cultured and civilized. They enjoyed Richard Wagner's music and could quote Goethe's poetry. Many enjoyed sophisticated luxuries. Yet, right up to the end, these "gentlemen" were completely lacking in remorse for exterminating Jews, gypsies, homosexuals, the disabled, and political opponents of the fascist party—particularly, social democrats and communists whose only crimes were thinking, feeling, and acting differently from what the Nazis prescribed.[2]

Creating Separateness

This effort of the Nazis to "purify" what they defined as the Aryan race did not result in regret. Afterward, regret was practically nonexistent; although denial, self-pity, and false accusations against others were commonplace during the Nuremberg Trials.

I was told by a death camp survivor that the Nazi guards were cautioned not to look into the eyes of their Jewish victims lest they recognize their humanity. Nazi leaders feared that, if the guards had empathy, they would not be able to carry out their orders to eliminate the Jewish people and other "undesirables."

While in Gaza in 2005, I asked some Palestinians if the Israeli soldiers ever change their minds and hearts. Mohammed responded, "Yes, the soldiers who remain here for a considerable time do change their hearts. Knowing this, the military rotates the soldiers out of here every two or three days."

When people begin with a conviction that they have "the truth," others who disagree with them are automatically wrong and therefore inferior, even despicable. Torturing and killing them then becomes an act of patriotism.

Even the International Court of Nuremberg could not influence Pre-Moderns and Moderns to see the need for empathy, which brings compassion. Believing we know what "the truth" is and "what is right" eliminates further thinking and clouds self-awareness—Indifference and lack of feeling in the face of human suffering are the results.

Redemptive Violence

Pre-Modern and Modern ideologues continue to believe in their truth of redemptive violence as the key to peace. Both are convinced that those with the biggest, most devastating bombs, the latest in technology, and the most determination, are the ones who will eventually achieve victory over the evil enemy. Hence, killing is justified as an effort to bring about a greater good. The end justifies the means and those in charge make every effort to validate and defend the just-war theory.

As a consequence, suicide bombings, for example, continue despite or because of retaliation. Calls for tough responses raise and escalate the violence among all parties, resulting in a vicious killing cycle with the highest number of causalities being innocent men, women, and children.

Deterrence

Deterrence (specifically, nuclear deterrence) seemed effective during the Cold War. Western Pre-Modern and Modern thinkers continue to see deterrence as a reasonable strategy for bringing about world peace. They rely on deterrence in spite of myriad evidence that Pre-Modern suicide bombers in the Middle

East are willing to give their lives for their idea of "the truth." The willingness of a small group of hijackers to kill themselves in order to destroy the Twin Towers of the New York World Trade Center in 2001 is a striking example of the failure of deterrence against ideological determination. Continued suicide bombings in Iraq and Afghanistan are daily reminders that not even one's own death is a deterrent to acting in accordance with one's knowledge of "the truth."

Military Armaments

Although enough nuclear bombs exist to destroy life on earth, the United States has spent billons of dollars on developing more and more deadly weapons of mass destruction. In 2010, the U.S. Obama Administration officially revealed to the world that the United States has 5,113 nuclear weapons in its arsenal. "The bulk of nuclear weapons is concentrated in the United States and the Soviet Union," according to Mikhail Gorbachev, a recent past leader of the former Soviet Union. "Meanwhile, ten percent or even one percent of their potential," he states, "is enough to inflict irreparable damage on the planet and all human civilization."[3]

There are over 50,000 nuclear devices on earth with an explosive capacity of 20,000 tons of TNT. Given that the world population is estimated at 6.7 billon people, this works out to be an average of at least three tons of TNT waiting to kill each man, woman, and child on Earth, as Dr. Helen Caldicott, an Australian physician and anti-nuclear advocate, made clear in an interview with me.

Dr. Caldicott said that the reason for this "nuclear madness" is what some political scientists call the "Iron Triangle"—the military, the politicians, and the industrialists who profit by millions of dollars. She stated strongly that we live on a terminally ill planet and insisted that only grassroots democracy can save our world.[4]

Dr. Yevgeny Chazov, Nobel Peace Prize laureate and a co-founder of International Physicians for the Prevention of Nuclear War, pleads with us, "You come to us [doctors] to save your children. Why, when we ask you to help us save mankind, are you indifferent?"[5]

Eight nations now acknowledge that they have nuclear weapons: the United States, England, France, China, North Korea, Pakistan, India, and Russia. At least fifty-two nations, Dr. Caldicott indicated, have nuclear research facilities. Many of these nations' leaders believe that if they are to be treated as equals by other world governments, they, too, must possess nuclear capability to destroy the world. And nations that do possess nuclear weapons are doing everything possible, except getting rid of their own, to prevent these others from becoming members of the "Nuclear Club."[6]

The United States has developed a fifty-eight-pound backpack nuclear bomb.[7] It can be carried by one person and is a perfect tool for suicide bombers, who can now kill more people than whole armies could in the past.

Preparations for war in the United State, just since 1981, have cost eight trillion dollars. This amounts to $23,000 for each American household. Yet people throughout the world are now *less* secure. Moreover, they have even less freedom, education, healthcare, shelter, and food.

Wealth and Wisdom

Believing wealth makes us wiser and better than others, Pre-Moderns and Moderns continue to accumulate as much wealth as possible. Wealth, however, is not being spread with equity. The social and economic gap between the world's richest billion people and the poorest billion is increasing. The latter, under Modern assumptions are trapped at a subsistence level, and the rich are becoming wealthier by the minute. In the last decade, the wealthiest one percent have doubled their share of national household wealth in the United States—from twenty percent to close to forty percent.[8] The economic gap can be seen in nutrition, education, disease patterns, family size, and life expectancy.

The Emerging Worldview Story of Politics

Imagine if you will that peace and justice prevail throughout the world. After centuries of oppression and wars, the change of four fundamental assumptions about life has altered dramatically how nations around the world relate to one another.

Assumption: We Are Always in the Process of Discovering

We now assume that no nation's view of any situation is absolutely correct or completely right; this opens the door to discovery of better approaches. Consequently, nation-states or individuals do not attempt to force their viewpoint or values on others. Trained in, and given the tools for, consensus-based decision-making, both leaders of nation-states and individuals make every effort to understand one another. Empathy reigns supreme. Through dialogue, we reach agreements on issues based on the best information available. At the same time, nation-states, and each of us, remain open to changing our position when new information suggests that greater benefits will result from thinking and feeling differently.

Assumption: We Create Our Own Reality

We assume we have power to change what is going on and create a reality which benefits everyone. As people dialogue together to determine what is good for all of us on our planet, *the focus is on appreciating what is working,* not on fixing what we perceive as "problems." While not ignoring obstacles and difficulties—which we choose to see as challenges and opportunities—we place major emphasis on *what we are doing well* and *how our activity can be further developed or improved.*

Together, we imagine how we can better cooperate to make life more fulfilling for all citizens of the Earth. We then work together to implement our vision and create a reality that works for everyone.

Assumption: We Are All One

We assume that we individuals are all one. Since the world has become a single community through this assumption, people act to contribute to the well-being of one another, not to compete with one another, no matter one's national heritage, skin color, or religious affiliation.

As we learned from Mahatma Gandhi in India and Nelson Mandela in South Africa, nonviolence is far more effective in moving toward peace-with-justice than is war. From the New Millennium perspective, war makes no sense. To go to war against another nation means fighting with ourselves—to kill another, a neighbor, is to kill oneself! Through dialogue, people realize how interdependent and interconnected we are in terms of trade, protection of the environment, resisting terrorists, and on and on. It has become evident to a critical mass of people throughout our planet that an interdependent world cannot function effectively without international cooperation and a willingness to understand one another's beliefs and values while retaining each individual's autonomy.

Assumption: We Always Do What We Perceive Is Best

Whenever nation-states and individuals act in a way that brings harm to others, we assume that these individuals and nations have made a mistake. We assume their well-intentioned actions went awry. Although restitution may well be in order and is carried out, no blame or condemnation follows.

We make every effort to understand how the mistake could have happened. Together we imagine how the damage can be repaired. Finally, we take action to avoid similar harm in the future.

Implications of the Emerging Worldview Story of Politics

One-World Government

Finally, the world is at peace. Based on our assumption that we are all one, we have achieved peace through voting into existence a World Democratic Union, *viz., a nation in which supreme power rests in all the citizens entitled to vote; this power is exercised by representatives elected, directly or indirectly, by them and responsible to them.* The new world governing neighborhood has an international constitution and an international court modeled on the United Nations' nonviolence charter and its International Court of Justice.[9] Internationally renowned professor of philosophy (Temple University, Philadelphia) Dr. Sidney Axinn says this:

> To live in a single economic world and refuse even to consider a single political world is to be guilty of cultural lag! I hope that at least those professionally involved in law and social philosophy will not continue to ignore the demands of a unified world law.
>
> As Hobbes has explained, when the weakest can kill the strongest . . . it is time for an international legal system . . . a single world government. Following Kant, we may hope for it. Following common sense, we must talk about it, plan it, and produce it.[10]

We have come to realize, listening to Albert Einstein, that in the twenty-first century no better alternative exists. Einstein said:

> [T]he United Nations is an extremely important and useful institution, *provided* the peoples and governments of the world realize that it is merely a transitional system toward the final goal, which is the establishment of a supranational authority vested with sufficient legislative and executive powers to keep the peace.[11]

Four layers of government exist in each nation: national, state/province, county, and city. In addition, a fifth supranational layer of government has come into existence; it signals the willingness of people throughout the world to live in peace, through transferring certain of their national sovereign rights to a supranational organization, similar to what colonists did in 1789 to form the United States of America and what the European nations did in 1993 to form the European Union.

Former nations accept some restrictions for the security of the whole. Local affairs are now handled by local governments, national affairs by national (state/province) governments; and regulation of international affairs and maintenance of peace are handled by the government of the World Democratic Union. The people have accepted the sovereignty of the World Democratic Union—to acquire law and order and the protection of the lives and liberties of *all* people on Earth.

A democratically elected President, similar to the Secretary General of the United Nations, heads the executive branch of the one-world government. In addition, duly elected representatives from each country come together, forming a World Parliament to enact laws which pertain to the interaction between and among former nations. Individual nation-states continue to determine their own form of government. Thus, Saudi Arabia has a king, and some countries have titular-only royalty such as Thailand's king and England's queen or king. Some countries have federal republics similar to the United States.

Each nation-state has retained its freedoms—political, social, and economic—as long as these freedoms do not work to the disadvantage of other nation-states as determined by the World Court. All freedoms are retained—that is, except the freedom to make war. Article IX of the 1947 Japanese Constitution states, "Japan . . . forever renounces war as a sovereign right . . . and [renounces]the threat or use of force as a means of settling international disputes." Likewise, all nations on the one-world planet have committed themselves to this goal. The hierarchy of nations has been dethroned. All nations are joined together in a circle of peace. They acknowledge that our diverse world is interlinked and interdependent. **All are equal before the law.**

Deliverance from Debt

Michael Rowbotham, in his book, *The Grip of Death*, points out that the world's richest nations in 1998 were the ones carrying the heaviest debt. In 2011, according to the Global Edition of the *New York Times*, the United States' national debt is in excess of $14trillion, Germany has now exceeded $1.7 trillion dollars, Canada's debt has reached $814 billion, and Britain has a national debt fast approaching $1 trillion dollars. Again, a Google search indicates the interest on the United States' debt in 2009 was 383 billion dollars or more than a billion dollars a day. If all the nations of the world are in debt, to whom do they owe the money? It is owed to the international bankers, who transcend national boundaries.[12] Consequently, under the Modern Worldview, an inordinate amount of individuals' tax money goes to pay the interest on those debts, instead of being used to improve the infrastructures of the nations of the world.

In the New Millennium, the central world government not only prints one currency, (no more Federal Reserve Bank) but also controls the amount of money in existence. Governments no longer borrow and pay interest to international bankers. Rather, the central world government increases or decreases the money supply, saving billions in interest while preventing inflation and deflation. As a result, local governments of the world are no longer drowning in red ink.

Funding and Taxes

Campaign-financing laws are in effect; they enable rich and poor alike to have an equal chance at the presidency or parliament. In campaigns for political office, campaign funds come equally to each candidate from the government. Personal or private funds from lobbyists or anyone else are no longer legal.

Disarmament

Within the central government a Department of Peace—similar to that suggested by USA Congressman Dennis Kucinich for the United States government—has been instituted. It has resulted in general and complete disarmament of all nuclear, chemical, and conventional arms—motivated by the realization that removal of tools for killing people is in everybody's self-interest. All national armed forces also have been dismantled.

We are beyond the point where military power is protective. Nothing we aspire to is worth a nuclear war. As a consequence, all military armaments have been removed from the control of individual nation states. People are finding security, not in instruments of death, but through a world government with laws, courts, and effective enforcement.

A world peace force is ensuring, without violence, the peace and safety Pre-Moderns and Moderns had hoped to achieve with national armed troops. Our peace force operates without weapons, because guns and similar instruments designed to harm others are unlawful and no longer being manufactured. At long last, we are out of the arms race and enjoying a higher quality of life, using money previously spent on armaments for healthcare and a quality education with a personal touch for everyone.

People who worked to design and build instruments for the military are now designing and contributing to instruments for promoting wellness and the growth of wisdom.

The hopeful prediction of the eighteenth President of the United States, Ulysses S. Grant (1869-1877), has finally come true:

> I am convinced that the Great Framer of the World will so develop it that it becomes one nation, so that armies and navies are no longer necessary . . . I believe at some future day, the nations of the earth will agree upon some sort of congress which will take cognizance of international questions of difficulty and whose decisions will be as binding as the decisions of our Supreme Court are upon us.[13]

International Court

An International Court, along with a world peace force, monitors laws throughout the world. The words of Pope John Paul II have come to fruition: "The international community should support a system of laws to regularize international relations and maintain the peace in the same manner that law governs national order." A World Court now resolves disputes between nation-states. It settles thousands of commercial disputes which, in the past, frequently led to military conflicts. The **"law of force"** has been replaced by the **"force of law."**

The World Democratic Union has been designed to be fair and impartial; therefore, both minorities and majorities realize that they are better off when relying on laws and courts than when relying on violence, even though they do not always receive what they want.

Social Justice

The objective of the World Democratic Union is social justice for the entire world community through international unity. The dream of the noted English historian and futurist, H. G. Wells, has materialized:

> A federation of all humanity, together with a sufficient means of social justice to ensure health, education, and a rough equality of opportunity, would mean such a release and increase of human energy as to open a new phase in human history.[14]

Government programs of the World Democratic Republic feed the hungry and provide shelter until people are able to take responsibility for satisfying their own wants and desires. Education and training are universally available, so everyone can actively participate in contributing to the common good.

Sustainable Development

The new government of the World Democratic Union is focusing on world-wide sustainable development with the appropriate use of natural resources. The quality of the air we breathe and the water we drink has improved dramatically. The positive results of these efforts are outlined in Chapter Twelve.

Languages

As in the United Nations, French and English are the official languages in the new international political arena. At the same time, at international meetings, simultaneous translation of others languages is always available. The many and varied languages of all world cultures are now protected from extinction and *encouraged.*

Wellness

Diseases such as AIDS, malaria, small pox, and many others have been completely eradicated from the face of the Earth. High-quality universal healthcare is available everywhere. (See Chapter Eight.)

Freedom of Religion, Language, and Customs

No matter the nation-state, every person practices the religion they prefer, speaks their native language, and follows customs of their ethnic heritage. Since we are all one, people in every nation-state appreciate and support one another as national groups. We recognize that it is in our self-interest to facilitate the intellectual, emotional, and spiritual growth of other ethnic groups everywhere.

No more identity-politics, which holds that ethnics, women, and homosexuals are subcultures—a position which discriminates by making them "other." As diverse ethnic and religious groups become more mature and more able to experience their human potential, further engagement between them brings extraordinary benefits to everyone involved.

CONCLUSION

In the New Millennium Emerging Worldview Story, the world has become a single community—a one-world participatory democratic government. All the nations of the Earth are states or provinces under global unity. Consisting of a world parliament, an international court, a debt-arbitration mechanism, and a global tax procedure, this global entity *ensures equality* among all nations. No more rich and poor countries.

People are confident that we can rule ourselves. We don't need elite leaders to determine what is best for us. Through free-speech, everyone has equal access to information and decision-making. Particular care is taken, through institutionalized processes, to prevent accumulation of power and wealth in the hands of a few individuals or groups. One-world citizens respect each other as free and intelligent neighbors capable of developing and creating something new. This bottom-tier-up world democratic process brings security and tranquility to the global/local community.

Flag-waving nationalism has disappeared as interdependence and interrelatedness have taken center stage. Patriotism is "doing what is *for the good of all*," understood to mean the freedom, welfare, and survival of everyone in the world. No patriotic duty is more immediate than the abolition of war. The "might makes right" mentality has lost all meaning or practice. War has become illegal. Money used for making instruments of destruction is now given to universal healthcare, quality education, and the development of meaningful work—extreme poverty is obsolete.

Recent advances in internet technology and travel make Mother Earth easier to navigate. Far from being reluctant, people are eager to travel to remote areas of the world, devoting their lives to promoting the common good.

Everyone feels closer to, and more intimate with, people from other cultures and religions. We relish diversity as we perceive its creative and innovative benefits. In our political story, we celebrate our unity, we relish our differences. Peace is not simply a word; it is an actuality.

CHAPTER FOURTEEN

The Story of Spirituality

The real revolution to come is the spiritual awakening of humankind and out of that awakening will be born a civilization of love, a universal society with an engaged heart.
Wayne Teasdale
A Monk in the World

The spiritual quest begins for most people as a search for meaning.
Marilyn Ferguson
American Psychologist

For some, spirituality lies in the awareness of God in nature, for some in the experience of God in service. For still others, spirituality lies in the development of meditative states. For all, spirituality is the way we come in contact with God.
Sister Joan Chittister, OSB
Spiritual Writer and Activist

The most beautiful thing we can experience is the mysterious. It is the source of all true art and science. He to whom this emotion is a stranger, who can no longer pause to wonder and stand rapt in awe, is as good as dead, his eyes are closed.
Albert Einstein
Renowned Physicist

Science is not only compatible with spirituality; it is a profound source of spirituality.
Carl Sagan
American Scientist

What Is Spirituality?

Spirituality, in the New Millennium Story, I assume to be: a story or a journey seeking and experiencing deeper meaning in our lives. It is a journey, not a wandering, a story containing within itself an appreciation for life as deeply meaningful.

Spiritual writer Timothy Freke describes spirituality as
. . . a journey of awakening to who we really are; a journey of opening the heart to the love that permeates the universe; a journey from confusion to meaning; a journey from fear to faith; a journey from ennui to a life filled with magic and wonder; a journey from feeling alone in a hostile world to *being at one with everyone and everything.*[1]

Unfortunately, some people never set out on such a spiritual journey. Perhaps it never occurs to them to seek an encounter with mystery in their daily lives. Possibly they've tried it and found it fruitless or too time-consuming. Others call it "poppycock" and belittle those who indulge in such insanity or superstition. Some, on the other hand, *are* motivated to search for transcendent values in life, which, as Marilyn Ferguson suggests, is the beginning of the spiritual quest.

The Pre-Modern Story of Spirituality

Most Pre-Moderns assume that their personal faith and spiritual approach to God is the correct approach. Anyone who does not agree with them is decidedly wrong and undeserving of eternal salvation, which they describe as everlasting union and happiness with God in the next life.

Many Western Pre-Moderns conceive of the world as three hierarchical echelons. God is on top with his angels and the *good* people who have died, in a place called *heaven.* This echelon is just above the sun, moon, and stars. Far below is the third and lowest echelon, a place of fire and suffering, named *hell,* occupied by Satan, by other fallen angels called demons, and by all the evil people who died unrepentant.

And in the middle is Earth, the center of the universe. Pre-Moderns believe the earth was not created all at once along with the sun, moon, and the stars in a sort of "big bang," but almost piecemeal with inorganic and organic matter such as plants, fish, animals, and humans being created a day at a time. Evolution is an incorrect assumption in their eyes. On Earth we are separated from God.

Life is described as a valley of tears, not meant for happy existence. Attention is on problems. We find solace in sharing our pain as we repeat the adage, "Misery loves company!" Only in the next life can humans truly be at peace and enjoy happiness with God.

Most Pre-Moderns also tend to believe that one can be truly or genuinely spiritual only by adopting and practicing formal, official religious dictates and rituals. Salvation can be found only in the teachings of people such as Muhammad, Buddha, Moses, or Jesus, and only in an absolute sense. For Christians, this means that there is no authentic spirituality apart from faith in Jesus Christ as found in sacred scripture and interpreted by the church. Various other religions also claim this fullness of revelation, in light of which all other religions are not only inferior, but wrong. Exclusiveness tends to be more important than the uniqueness and meaningfulness of one's religion.

Moral Laws

Because religions claim a higher wisdom through exclusive revelation, they therefore claim the right to legislate and dictate what is morally acceptable in society, particularly in terms of individual behavior—be it the Mosaic Law, the Code of Hammurabi, Christianity, or the laws that accompany the Qur'an. Once beliefs are written down in the "Holy Book," they become absolute in the minds of Pre-Moderns.

Moral teachings are designed to dominate and control people's lives for their own good. The possibility of religious laws being designed to protect and liberate people so that they might assume greater responsibility for their own happiness and fulfillment is threatening to Pre-Moderns. Requisites to a relationship with God include performing ascetic exercises, accepting correct doctrines, and saying the right prayers. In doing so, many Pre-Modern spiritual seekers are in a perpetual state of fear and unworthiness. Instead of believing in a loving God, they believe in a threatening God who is demanding and exacts punishment on those who do not do what is "right." The similarity among all the various religions of Pre-Modernism is each one's belief that it alone owns the single set of universal truths; certainty is on its side. Therefore, all others must believe as its members do, else they'll not find happiness in the next life. Hence, each religion tends to be an exclusive "club"—inviting conflict.

Implications of the Pre-Modern Story of Spirituality

Priority of God's Transcendence

For Pre-Modern spiritual seekers, the transcendent God above and outside the universe takes priority over the God who is immanent in the world of our experiences. Worship is emphasized—praise, adoration, and thanksgiving—whereas the presence of God in one another and in the rest of creation is minimized, if not ignored. What takes place in a church or temple is far more important than what takes place outside in nature, or in personal relationships, or in empathy toward each and all regardless of origin or status. Believers perceive themselves as religious, but only and because they believe and worship an *elsewhere* God.

Patriarchal

Though perhaps not consciously intentional, Pre-Modern and Modern religion is patriarchal (male-dominated), endocentric (having a one-sided approach to all relationships, in which males are assumed to be more authentic, stronger, better, holier), and sexist (ordering life exclusively by way of gender). Images of God are largely likenesses of *male* human beings (homocentric).

Emotionality

In terms of spirituality, Pre-Moderns tend to view emotions from a narrow perspective. Placing emphasis on the rational, many religions repress the emotional and passionate sides of humanity. Religions that worship in a highly emotional manner are looked upon as "flaky," lacking in depth. They are sometimes regarded as too feminine. Indeed, because women are stereotyped as being rich in feelings and innately passionate, they are often considered sources of temptation for men, resulting in cautions to shun and avoid them. In turn, women seeking the spiritual life are encouraged to be celibate and have little to do with men.

For the most part, Pre-Moderns consider marriage the doorway to paradise and a requisite to sexual intimacy. Monogamy reigns for many, although some religions, such as Islam, allow for up to four wives if the man can afford them all at the same time.

While it is not intended, religion devoid of emotions tends to be heartless and incapable of empathy. It blames the millions across our planet who are impoverished and destitute as somehow being so through their own fault—or simply considers them too huge a problem to manage. Many seek to separate themselves from such poor persons lest they become "contaminated" by being near them or even just seeing them. Affluent Pre-Moderns are willing to pay just enough taxes to keep "them" out of sight. Hence, in poor countries, beggers are the norm. In affluent nations they are hardly ever seen.

Disengagement from Worldly Affairs

Pre-Modern spiritual seekers see their task in terms of disengaging from this world—putting up with it, as it were, while anticipating the joys of the next life. Instead of empowering individuals to engage with the world, Pre-Modern spiritual thinking often encourages seekers to detach themselves from worldly affairs. Their belief holds that our final destination is the achievement of salvation/nirvana/enlightenment, a sacred place where the elsewhere God resides, far removed from this physical, imperfect, spiritually deficient world.

The Modern Approach to Spirituality

Denying or ignoring the existence of a Mystery/God that cannot be humanly understood now or in the future, science has replaced God in the hierarchy of being. According to spiritual writer Diarmuid O'Murchu,

> The so-called educated are locked into the closed-system thinking of the West. It is linear thinking worshipping rationality and starved of the capacity for imaginative and creative reflection.[2]

Thus spirituality is not even an afterthought. The Modern approach also involves "a stoic view of life," writes O'Murchu, "which considers the passions to be diseases of the mind that are unnatural and intrinsically evil." Usually described as Secularists, many do what they can to remove religious symbols such as the cross and even the very idea of God or the mention of the word "God" from the common lexicon. It is a worldview that Marc Luyckx described as the period of Disenchantment (see Chapter Two).

The New Millennium Story of Spirituality

With the coming of the New Millennium Emerging Worldview Story, a shift in our understanding of the universe has occurred. It has brought about an entirely different perspective, a new framework within which we seek to make sense of what we see, hear, taste, smell, and touch.

In our hunger for deeper meaning, many in the New Millennium Story ask questions such as:

- What is the purpose of life, and, in particular, of my life?
- Is there meaning to suffering?
- What does it mean to be holy?
- Is there life after death?
- Does God exist?

Responses to these questions transcend the material world. By definition, they are spiritual. Deep within, some spiritual seekers come to realize, despite all indications to the contrary, that there is a sacredness which goes beyond logic and rational wisdom. Something more sacred exists, something more than the materialistic gratifications passing for happiness, something capable of making sense out of the shortcomings and disappointments in our lives. This sense of the sacred motivates many to keep an open mind and heart, to keep searching. A sense of wonder and mystery enables us to finally find deeper meaning in our lives.

God

New Millennium Thinkers and Feelers assume that it is impossible for finite human beings to define, or even describe, God, who is an unfathomable mystery beyond our words and images. A God who can be defined or described cannot possibly be God.[3] (That does not mean that we cannot encounter God, as we shall see later in this chapter.) The best we can do is to assume what God is *not*. God is neither feminine nor masculine; not human, not corporeal; has no beginning or ending.

In the New Millennium, knowledge of God is forever *limited* and questionable because God is *unlimited*. Our limited minds and hearts cannot, we assume, comprehend the limitless essence of God.

Limited as we are, we tend to ascribe all human attributes to God. We assume that God created our human attributes and that God necessarily possesses them to perfection. We therefore speak of God as *omnipotent* (all-powerful), *omnipresent* (existing everywhere, holding everything in existence), all-knowing (*omniscient*), and *all-loving*; yet we realize that these descriptions fall short because they are finite. God is beyond words or symbols.

We do, however, continue to search for ways to refer to God. We speak of God as Eternal Oneness, Creative Energy, Ultimate Life Force, The Source of All Being, and Mystery. These names and others uphold a sense of reverence, awe, and respect for divinity. In this book I will tend to refer to God as Eternal Oneness.

Personal God

Many in the New Millennium Story have come to believe that everything was created by a personal God who did so out of an ever-flowing abundance of love. Again, the word "personal" contains all the attributes of a human person and far beyond. Without empirical evidence, we encounter God knowing and loving us. A New Millennium thinker and Feeler, spiritual writer Michael Morwood, indicates:

> The best way we can know what God is like is when we love one another and care for one another because we believe that's when we can see the influence of God's presence among us.[4]

Faith

Faith for New Millennium spiritual seekers is a particular kind of consciousness, the consciousness of God loving each of us and caring about each of us—a personal-relationship response through the gift of God's love and goodness, freely given and unencumbered by achievement. Being so blessed, we do not think ourselves better than others, nor do we find fault with those who haven't received this precious gift of spiritual faith. Through the gift of faith, we assume that God creates us and sustains us. Believing this, we presume that we are safe and secure—our faith includes trust.

Religion

What follows from faith is the practice of faith, namely, what we do with this experience of being at one with God. This activeness in the Emerging Story is called "*doing* religion". It comprises our efforts to be faithful. When we are faithful, we are spiritual.

At its etymological root, religion means reconnecting with God. Believing that God both is within us and transcends us, we seek to find meaningful practices to reconnect our minds and hearts with our creator. Some people are spiritual without formal religious practice. Others practice religion without being spiritual. A person can be religious without being transformed—by identifying with formal institutionalized structures, rituals, and beliefs which belong to one of the official religious traditions, including Islam, Sikhism, Christianity, Judaism, Hinduism, Buddhism, Baha'ism, and many others.

No *single* religious tradition, in the New Millennium Story, leads to ultimate meaning exclusively. There is no *single* way any of us can be absolutely certain; such a thing would be knowledge, not faith. Consequently, human beings on their journey continue to discover many different ways to find meaning. Some embrace Shamanism, Hinduism, and ancient paganism, and worship many gods and goddesses. Others worship one personal God, as in Judaism, Christianity, Islam, and Baha'ism. Still others, such as Taoists and Buddhists, relate to an impersonal Oneness.

Franciscan priest and author Richard Rohr states, "In the West, religion became preoccupied with telling people what to know more than how to know, telling people what to see more than how to see." Rohr points out that particularly "Western Christianity has tended to objectify paradoxes in dogmatic statements that demand mental agreement instead of any inner experience of the mystery revealed."[5]

O'Murchu seems to agree, and adds, when speaking of religious organizations, that they appear to have created a set of formal structures with definitive and even dogmatic boundaries. These boundaries translate laws and regulations by which certain peoples and behaviors are included and others excluded. Without these boundaries, it is feared there would be widespread anarchy, chaos, and disintegration.[6]

While all these religions perceive reality differently and have their own conceptual language and cultural biases, they share much in common. All perceive the oneness of the Divine. Even those believing in many gods appear to recognize a hierarchy with one God at the top.[7] All that exists appears in aspects of this one Supreme Being.

Sacred and Holy

Everything in the universe is holy because God created everything. This is affirmed by many mystical writers, including the medieval theologian Thomas Aquinas: "[T]he whole universe together participates in the divine goodness and represents it better than any single being whatsoever."

God and creation are not identical or merged. God transcends, is more than, all in existence. Transcendence does not mean being *outside* of the universe; it means being *more than* the universe by reason of being its creator. At the same time, God is not separate from creation. Spiritual writer Cletus Wessels tells us: "[E]very being and every activity flows from the inner presence of God and there is no way to separate the natural from the supernatural."[8]

Every existing thing, from the Emerging Story perspective, is therefore holy and sacred and calls out to us to treat every person and thing as holy and sacred, including those persons whom Pre-Modern and Modern thinkers label as enemies. Once we assume that everything is all us and sacred, as Einstein said, the rest is detail.

Experiencing God

At some stage in the New Millennium spiritual journey we experience God in ourselves. This experience is the created effect of God's love. Trappist monk Thomas Merton writes: "This gift of God's own self is given to us to be shared."

Many spiritual seekers believe God reveals Herself/Himself in nature, including human nature, and in word—sacred books such as the Qur'an for Islam, the Bible for Christians, the Torah for Jews, the Guru Granth Sahib for Sikhs, and the Vedas, Upanishads; or Epics for Hindus—and so forth.

Other spiritual seekers believe God reveals Herself/Himself through romantic love, affection in family life, a stranger's kind word, a beautiful sunset, and myriad other human experiences.

Even people who claim not to be religious often experience God through nature and art. They experience what Michelangelo, the Italian Renaissance artist, described: "Every beauty which is seen here below . . . resembles, more than anything else, that celestial source from which we all come."

Science, too, can be for many a source of spiritual experiences. Albert Einstein, the great theoretical physicist, wrote: [T]he most beautiful thing we can experience is the mysterious, it is the source of all true art and all science. He to whom this emotion is a stranger, who can no longer pause to wonder and stand rapt in awe, is as good as dead, his eyes are closed.

Christians believe that Jesus of Nazareth, who lived two thousand years ago, is both divine and human. Likewise, others believe that Sai Baba, living presently in India, is divinity in human form. Sai Baba himself claims that all of us are divine. Jesus, too, affirmed that since we are all united with Him, all of us have divinity within us. Others believe that because we were created by God, we share in God's existence and therefore share in God's divinity. Richard Rohr believes that creation is God's Body. Thus, in getting "in touch" with any part of all that is, we experience God.

None of these beliefs are empirical. They belong to the realm of the spiritual, the verdant meadow of pure faith beyond reason. Truth about God in the New Millennium Story is achieved, if at all, only by a spiritual experience deriving from God's gift of faith.

Prayer

Prayer in the Emerging Worldview Story is much more then reciting memorized words. While such words have merit, effective prayer is a genuine conversation with God, in which we sit quietly and listen to what God has to say to us. We may speak as well, depending on what is going on in our lives. Prayer's purpose is to change our minds and hearts into thinking and loving like God, which means being able to love and be kind to those who hurt us, to strangers, to our friends, to our families, all God's creation. Hence, prayer is not for God's sake. Prayer is in our own self-interest.

Peace and quiet in our environment greatly help most of us to avoid distractions during our prayerful encounter with God. To quiet our mind and heart, we need silence and solitude. Without them, intimacy with God is extremely difficult.

Moreover, since we assume that we are all one, we are aware that we are not simply individuals when we pray. When each of us prays, all of us are praying. The mind and heart praying in one of us is praying in all of us. In this sense, we are praying even when we are sleeping.

In the New Millennium Story, we pray specific prayers of gratitude for our health and for the gift of our very existence, together with thanking the Eternal Oneness for our parents, relatives, and friends. The mystic Meister Eckhart said, "If the only prayer I ever say is thank you . . . that is enough."

Michael Morwood adds: "God has no need of our prayers . . . Prayer needs to change us. It needs to develop a profound sense of awe and respect about the dignity of human life—all human life. Prayer should be more about who and what we are and lead us to accepting the responsibility for who and what we are."[9]

Meditation

Meditating is another form of praying, but it is not a mental activity like talking and listening to God. According to Albert Nolan, It is a way of emptying our minds of all thoughts and feelings . . . Linked sometimes to the rhythm of one's breathing, the aim of this practice is the calming of the heart and the mind.[10]

Spiritual writer Beatrice Bruteau adds: Meditation is not a duty to be performed; it is not just a learning device whereby we get ideas; it is not a soothing routine whereby we put ourselves into an eternal state of consciousness, or a way of eliciting material from the subconscious so that we can know our empirical personality better. Meditation is a way of meeting God.[11] Meditation usually requires gentle and enlightened tutoring. It is accompanied by the desire and capacity for quiet. Some find it meaningful to meditate with a group at regular intervals, perhaps once or twice a week.

New Millennium spiritual seekers who practice meditation in silence and solitude find peace within themselves, with the Eternal Oneness, and with the world. They appear then to be fortified with courage to be peacemakers in the world.

Contemplation

Contemplation, in the Emerging Story, is the highest form of prayer. It leads to and provides for intimacy with the Eternal Oneness. In contemplating, we pay attention to God. Contemplation is not passive attention, but an active involvement empowering us to be aware of God enveloping everything.

While contemplating, we subjectively experience the oneness of mind and body, inside to outside, action to consequence, past to present—in other words, the absence of dualities, or polarity-based thinking. We come to identify ourselves not as separate or isolated, but as connected with Eternal Oneness and all creation. Hence, contemplation, according to Richard Rohr, is a radical shift away from judging others. Nor is contemplation simply a God-and-me dynamic. Appreciating that we are one with others, we find in contemplation that our hearts are filled with empathy, compassion, and understanding—free from looking for sin, error, or mistakes in ourselves or others. At the same time, Rohr writes, "This 'little ol me' stops being the significant reference point of anything."[12]

Mysticism

Mysticism is an encounter with the Eternal Oneness that takes place without words, names, ideas, or any knowledge at all. We abandon all our images of God and all we thought we knew about God. We are absorbed into God's Oneness.

New Millennium spiritual seekers believe the mystical is the deepest level of spirituality. We assume we are *all* called by God to be mystics, to love God more than anything else, and to experience, through transformation, our immortal and eternal selves as one with the Eternal Oneness.

Experiencing oneness with God, similar to the intimacy described in Chapter Seven, is an evolutionary process that rarely happens in an instant. Falling in love with God tends to be a slow, growing experience. We come to be so *at one* with God that, in a sense, we have become God and God has become us. Hence, separation from God, which we call "sin," no longer exists.

A sign that we have made a major stride towards mysticism is *immediacy*. According to "monk in the world" Wayne Teasdale, "Mystical awareness is, for me, primarily being conscious of God's Presence most of the time."

We Are Forever in the Process of Discovering the Truth

A sense of the Ultimate enables New Millennium spiritual seekers in their spiritual journey to remain open to a multitude of possibilities. Free from the constraints of absolute thinking, we are able to question what we automatically took for granted as true spiritually, and to be open to spiritual experiences. Faith governs the intellect and emotions, and through faith we assume we are one with the Eternal Oneness, here and now, who is orchestrating a symphony of life in an evolving and expanding universe.

In the New Millennium Story, mature adults have a fresh perspective, refusing to accept previous programming. In giving new attention to what we are experiencing, it is as if we are seeing events, behaviors, and ideas for the first time. By giving attention to the present moment, we experience being touched, vulnerable, and renewed. Waking up and keeping our eyes wide open enables us to *see!* Waking up and keeping our hearts wide open enables us to *love!*

Our desire is to stay open to the unexpected, to relish life's surprises. Since we no longer fool ourselves into believing we know what absolute truth is, we are able to be open, to question, to risk, to spiritually *be!*

We Continually Create Our Own Reality

To be spiritual, in the New Millennium Story, is to remind one another that being "alive" is something special. Life is not a valley of tears, it is a gift from God, a wonderful experience for which we are grateful and joyful. We look forward with pleasure to every day of our lives.

In our spiritual journey, we do not see ourselves as "fixers," "helpers," or "advisers," but as "servants." When one "fixes" a person or an organization such as a church, one begins with the assumption that something, or someone, is broken. In fixing and advising, there is an inequality of expertise which can easily create moral distance. New Millennium spiritual seekers assume that we cannot serve from a distance. We can only serve those to whom we are profoundly connected, those whom we are willing to thank, touch, appreciate, even hug and kiss.

Helping is based on inequality. As author Rachel Naomi Remen points out, "It isn't a relationship among equals." When we are aware of what is going on within ourselves, when we are helping another, we find that we are always helping someone who is not as strong as we are, who is needier than we are. When we *help*, we see others as weak; when we fix and give advice, we see others as broken.[13] When we *serve*, we see others as whole and sacred. In Calcutta I observed Mother Teresa serving others, not because they were broken, but because she saw them as sacred.

Many New Millennium spiritual seekers believe that we have been created by God out of love and are sustained by God through love. Such spiritual faith, unlike that in previous worldviews, results in a recognition of being sacred, which in turn brings cheerfulness and gratitude. This faith also results in our picturing and treating everything in existence as truly sacred.

Visualizations

In our spiritual story, we picture ourselves as sent to Earth by God to carry out a mission. A divine purpose encompasses our lives. In waking up and becoming aware, we intuitively grasp, in moments of deep spiritual insight, our mission to be co-creators with God in facilitating a wonderful life for ourselves and everyone else. People who "get it," who understand our mission, experience life as holy, wholesome, and incredibly joyful.

Every Monday is a "Happy Monday!" Every Tuesday is a "Happy Tuesday!" To live life to the fullest is a precious opportunity, a *gift* to be seized and relished, and for which to be grateful.

Hence, New Millennium spiritual thinkers no longer place a major emphasis on problems. Our focus is *not* on defects, imperfections, sins, or what is wrong. While we are keenly aware of these conditions, we simply accept them as part of being human. Thus we are free to look for what is good and effective in our spiritual lives, grateful for these benefits as we seek to improve and increase them.

Visualization is not magical. Picturing ourselves as sent to Earth by God to carry out a mission is a sincere belief that gives us hope and motivates us to *take action*, to do whatever is necessary to achieve our mission which we perceive as what God wants us to do. Our belief further empowers us to see which actions we *can* take and which situations and events will contribute to achieving our vision. It's obvious to us that, had we not persistently visualized the ends we desire, we would not have noticed and taken advantage of the means to achieve these ends.

The visualization process gives us energy, motivation, and courage to transform ourselves. We realize and appreciate that only God's presence in our lives enables us to visualize our very transformation.

Life's Challenges

In the New Millennium Story, people understand that all the challenges in life's daily existence, painful though they may be, are opportunities to grow in enlightenment toward greater levels of spiritual understanding and intimacy with God.

In experiencing pain, we get to question: "What can I learn from this experience?" In the face of suffering and apparent obstacles, we ask ourselves, "Am I being the person I really want to be?" Pain and suffering wake us up and challenge us to imagine living a different life, a meaningful life in which we are the loving persons we are determined to be.

We Are All One

As New Millennium spiritual seekers wake up spiritually, we experience our innate oneness with God and all creation. The sense of being a separate-self vanishes as Eternal Oneness consumes all things within it. God is everywhere, holding everything together. There is only Eternal Oneness!

Connections, not divisions, engage our hearts and imaginations. We've discovered that life is "both/and" oneness rather than "either/or" dualism. We assume dualisms are constructs of the human mind. Through faith we transcend the mind and believe in the oneness of all in God's creation.

Author Joseph Campbell tells us that "Eternal Oneness is both transcendent and immanent. God Reality is both beyond us and within us and within all creation. God is everywhere."

Delightfully, we, together with God, are conscious of the universe, witnessing the evolving and unfolding of life through our particular bodies. Christian mystic Meister Eckhardt affirms: "Our truest 'I' is God."

To serve one's own self separate from the rest of humanity is self-defeating. Being self-centered or self-absorbed cuts us off from our true identity (See Chapter Seven on Intimacy). It is unhealthy for us and unhealthy for all those with whom we come into contact. Not least, it brings us only isolation and suffering. Self-serving behavior is clearly not in our self-interest. Our oneness with God includes everyone. Benefiting others benefits oneself. Harming others harms oneself.

Nor is self-centeredness prized in the Emerging Worldview—no "I" or "we," but only Eternal Oneness acting in and through all things. Being truly spiritual, we love ourselves and see beyond ourselves by opening our hearts in order to love all others. We experience ourselves, both individually and united with God and all others, in the mystical experience of the *whole* of reality.

The essence of love is to seek unity. "To truly love," Freke says, "is to enter a holy communion in which we transcend our individual existence and partake in a greater identity . . . God is love and those who live in love live in God and God lives in them."[14]

"Love is how oneness feels; it is how we experience the paradox of being an individual part of an *indivisible* whole."[15] To repeat what I have been saying here: once we assume that everything is all us and sacred, the rest is detail.

We Always Do What We Perceive Is Best

New Millennium spiritual seekers, acting in our own perceived self-interest, find fulfillment in loving God, ourselves, and all other human beings—no matter how offensive we perceive certain human beings' actions to be.

Freedom means that we are free to determine what is best for us. Freedom is not the same as choice. Once we freely determine what seems best for us (is in our self-interest) and what seems best for others (is in their self-interest), both of which we believe God wants—then we are not free to act differently. We are free, we assume, to look at various alternatives leading up to what we perceive is best (given our particular situation and obvious constraints). We cannot assume, however, that we are free to intend to do evil or to indulge in what previous religious worldviews describe as "sin."

This old thinking regarding sin requires three conditions:

1. The action has to be wrong in itself, such as committing murder.

2. We know the action to be wrong, truly an offense against God and our neighbor, such as committing murder.

3. We desire to do it anyway. With our will we give full consent to the action of murder.

O'Murchu states clearly, "The person who robs and murders is doing an evil act—not for the sake of evil—but for a perceived good. In a world of so much outrageous suffering and injustice, this statement can feel like banality that enrages and disgusts the hearer, but it is a conviction of spirituality that we must retain and continually strive to appreciate."[16]

In the New Millennium Story, there is no way that anyone can do evil for its own sake. However, all of us are capable of *making mistakes.* Unlike flowers that always lean toward the sun, or the deer who eats the flowers when hungry, we make unhealthy determinations sometimes, in spite of the existence of alternatives. (See Chapter Six.) In the Emerging Worldview Story, these unhealthy behaviors are called *mistakes,* not "sins." One of the etymological meanings of *sin* is "missing the mark," or, in other words, a "miss-take." Without knowing better, we do things that are harmful to ourselves and to others. At the same time, we are and take responsibility for not knowing better. Such behavior is an opportunity to learn and to change our minds and attitudes.

Intending always to do what is best as we understand it, we assume that to act otherwise indicates a mental disability. We sometimes do act otherwise, as evidenced by the pain and unhappiness caused by the deliberate killing of innocent people. Given that we are not mentally ill, we rationalize the harm we do as good, such as invading another country, murdering, and destroying hospitals, schools, and people's homes. We argue we are simply seeking justice and the deaths of innocent people are merely collateral damage. In other words, we perceive our doing a good thing.

Despite the enormous harm which often follows our flawed behaviors, the strong faith of New Millennium spiritual seekers results in perceiving God not as a prosecuting attorney (as Pre-Moderns perceive Him), but rather as a defense attorney.[17]

When we resist God's love for us and fail to love others, instead of creating an environment in which we all experience peace and joy, New Millennium spiritual seekers realize that we actually cause misery and suffering. And yet we experience God coming to our defense.

God—because He/She created us—loves and does not cease to love us, even when we deliberately hurt ourselves and others. Nor does God stop loving us when we fail to come to our senses and recognize the painful effects of our actions. Even if we remain unrepentant because we believe what we are doing is for the good of ourselves and others, God continues to be our defense attorney and our intimate friend.

In seeking intimacy with God, we become ever more aware of our mistakes. Continuing to question old beliefs creates opportunities to comprehend reality differently. Forever being open to the possibility that we can be mistaken and thus engage in unhealthy behaviors protects us from arrogance and from inflicting vengeful punishment on other spiritual seekers who disagree with us or behave differently. We take no joy in their mistakes, much less condemn them. Thus, when we slip and fall, we, too, are met with empathy and compassion. God acts through others to bring us restoration and reconciliation with the very people we've hurt. As for God, we become aware that, no matter what we do, God never leaves us—and never rejects us, even if we may reject God.

Implications of the New Millennium Story of Spirituality

Contemplation in Action

Contemplation and action, the heart and the head, are not opposites. Both coexist, complementing one another in oneness. Thus, we move from hopelessness, fear, and unbelief to a life filled with joy, courage, and confidence—a complete, authentic, and mystical transformation involving a fundamental shift in perspective. Oneness with an ever-present God. Oneness with others. Oneness with all of God's creation. Oneness with the common good. Albert Nolan explains: As we grow in our experience of togetherness and inseparability, we begin to direct all we do and say toward what we call the common good. What that means in practice is that we come to see that what is best for everyone is best for us too. There is no possible conflict between our good and the common good. Sharing follows quite naturally from this.[18]

For the contemplative, sharing means more than giving to the poor out of our abundance. Contemplative oneness, in the New Millennium Story, means that we identify with others and they identify with us. We need one another to heal, to learn from one another, to love and to share. For the contemplatives, oneness with God, with ourselves, with others, and with the universe forms what Nolan calls a seamless whole: "Any attempt at union with God while remaining alienated from other people and from nature would be pure fantasy. Likewise, an experience of closeness to nature that excludes human beings and one's own wholeness would be incomplete and ineffective. A genuine experience of oneness with everybody and everything, however, would include oneness with God even if one is not fully aware of God's presence."[19]

Sins Are Learning Opportunities

Spiritual seekers in the New Millennium Story understand that our "sins" are mistakes and are meant to be learning opportunities. We do not punish ourselves or others when we make errors and do evil; rather, we intend to learn. We seek to enable ourselves and educate others to recognize and admit misdeeds, to appreciate that we are responsible for our ignorance, to hold and be held accountable for the hurt and harm we've created. Our intent is to learn which patterns of behavior are not self-defeating and harmful but are instead in our own self-interest and the interest of others. We then integrate those behaviors into lives of genuine equality.

In waking up, we have learned that respectful, nonpunishing actions toward others who have made mistakes cause us to recognize our own mistakes (See Chapter Eleven on Justice). We respect and love others who have hurt us. In this way, we get to enjoy the marvelous experience of healing, loving relationships.

If we die without coming to our senses and changing our evil behaviors, or even perhaps commit suicide, New Millennium spiritual seekers find consolation in our faith that *God still does not abandon us*. We assume that God directly enables us to see the light. Even after death, our assumption is that we are able to discover what is truly in our own best interest. Despite having regrets for not having understood sooner, we find joy in finally realizing our intimate oneness with God and one another.

Pluralism and Ecumenism

Assuming that we are all one and that no one knows the truth absolutely, spiritual seekers of the various religions in the New Millennium Story accept and love each other in spite of our differences.

Pre-Moderns and Moderns who believe they know the truth and are always right (all who disagree being wrong) often seek to persuade others, to get them to think and believe their way. Failing to convert others to their way of believing, some Pre-Moderns and Moderns use religion as a reason to kill. This kind of violence happened in Northern Ireland between Protestants and Catholics; it is now occurring in the Middle East between Muslims and Jews, and among themselves (Shiites and Sunnis), and in many other places in the world. These murders result from an exclusivistic mentality which believes there is only one way to God, "my" way.

Pluralism, in the New Millennium, does not mean that all religions are saying the same thing. But beneath the stories, rituals, and beliefs, a commonality does exist—namely, a reverence for the Mystery in which our lives are engaged, a seeking for personal integrity and decency, an ethic of empathy and compassion for others, and a motivation to leave the world a little better than we found it. Spiritual seekers not only tolerate, but appreciate, religious diversity.

In setting aside exclusion, New Millennium spiritual seekers make peace with one another and are agents of peace all around the world. We achieve this by coming together and accepting diversity as a cultural and existential constant.

We do not, however, come together to convert each other or debate who is right at the expense of others' being wrong. Instead, we come together to discover common ground. Through dialogue, we share the blessings of our own beliefs and seek to understand each other. In doing so, we come to appreciate, and are deeply inspired by, those who tell us how their religious practices create meaning and fulfillment in their lives. Genuine joy and gratitude fill our hearts as we listen to the spiritual insights and positive results that others experience in their personal religious faith and practices.

In a sermon given at Westminster Presbyterian Church in Wooster, Ohio, on June 11, 2006, the Reverend Richard G. Watts tells of an experience he had when he and a small group traveled to Chicago. They visited a community of Sikhs. He confessed that they taught him a powerful lesson in doing away with hierarchy:

> With the Sikhs, we shared a Friday evening service of scripture readings and hymn singing, followed by a community meal. During the meal, everyone sat on the floor, a symbolic way of expressing the Sikh creed, born in rejection of India's caste system, namely, that before God all are equal, none sitting higher than the others. As we ate together, I remembered all those meals Jesus had with his followers, likewise creating an inclusive new community in a culture marked by rigid social barriers. I recall that I could hardly wait to get back to my own church to lead Sunday worship—not because there we would at last "get it right," but because I suddenly knew myself to be a part of a far wider, deeper community of faith than I had ever before imagined. And so, I have become a Christian pluralist, confident that we have much to learn from one another in our shared journey from birth to death.

Far from being weakened, the religious faith and spiritual commitment of New Millennium Thinkers and Feelers are strengthened because we dialogue with people from other spiritual paths. In so doing, we are motivated to better understand our own religious tradition and to live it with greater devotion.

And as Reverend Watts emphasizes, we find that we hold far more spiritual concepts in common with spiritual seekers of other religious traditions than we had first imagined. In the same sermon, he tells a story about Murray Rogers, an Anglican priest who spent over forty years in Asia, and who summed up his experience in these words: "Being blessed with friends from these "other" spiritual paths (Hindu, Buddhist, Taoist), I have grown to know that there are no "other faiths," except in the most external and sociological terms . . . I gladly share, without fear of disloyalty to Christ, their treasures of experience, their perceptions of mystery, their ways of breathing the reality beyond all name and form. And "they" has almost disappeared and in its place is "we."

New Millennium spiritual seekers assume that God's intention—for all of us from every race, nationality, and religion—is for us to be happy here now on earth *and* hereafter. How to make this happen can be found in the holy books of all religions. From our Jewish brothers and sisters we receive, among other gifts, the Ten Commandments, which we interpret as guideposts to happiness. They tell us what we need to do to be happy. They explain how we are empowered through God's grace to effectively bring happiness to ourselves and others. Many New Millennium spiritual seekers are adopting the Jewish Jubilee Year, wherein all debts are forgiven and we start again to live our lives every fifty years.

In like manner, we borrow meditation and compassion techniques from our Buddhist brothers and sisters. They, in turn, receive insights into the blessings we ourselves experience from our faith in a personal God. Through New Millennium dialogue, Muslims become better Muslims, Buddhists more faithful Buddhists, Hindus more devout Hindus, and Christians more in tune with the life of Jesus the Christ.

Jesus scholar Marcus Borg has researched the similarities between the teachings of Buddha and Christ:

Do unto others as you would have them do unto you. *Luke 6:31*
Consider others as yourself. *Dhammapada 10:1*

If anyone strikes you on the cheek, offer the other also. *Luke 6:29*

If anyone should give you a blow with his hand, with a stick, or with a knife, you should abandon any desires and utter no evil word. *Majjhima Nikaya 21:6*

Put your sword back into its place; for all those who take the sword will perish by the sword. *Matthew 26:52*
Abandon the taking of life, the ascetic Gautama dwells refraining from taking life, without stick or sword. *Digha Nikaya 1:1:8*

This is my commandment, that you love one another as I have loved you. No one has greater love than this, to lay down one's life for one's friend. *John 15:12-13*
Just as a mother would protect her only child at the risk of her own life, even so, cultivate a boundless heart towards all beings. Let your thoughts of boundless love pervade the whole world. *Sutta Nipata 149-150*[20]

Grace and truth came through Jesus Christ. *John 1:17*
The body of Buddha is born of love, patience, gentleness and truth. *Vimalakirtinirdesha Sutra 2*[21]

Blessed are you who are poor, for yours is the kingdom of God. *Luke 6:20*
Let us live most happily, possessing nothing; let us feed on joy, like radiant gods. *Dhammapada 15:4*[22]

Those who want to save their life will lose it, and those who lose their life for my sake will save it. *Mark 8:35*
With the relinquishing of all thought and egotism, the enlightened one is liberated through not clinging. *Majjhima Nikaya 72:15*[23]

Through meditation on the contents of the holy books, Emerging Story seekers assume that we have always been united with God and cannot be estranged. Our union with God is something God makes happen, not something we do. Hence, we don't deserve it. Being united to God is a pure gift.

Our Sacred Earth

New Millennium spirituality, having disengaged from the Modern Worldview's dualistic stories, has rediscovered the sacred body of God in the created world. As the U.S. astronaut Edgar Mitchell stated, "On the return trip home, gazing through 240,000 miles of space toward the stars and the planet from which I had come, I suddenly experienced the universe as intelligent, loving, and harmonious. My view of the planet was a glimpse of divinity. Being one with us, I saw our Earth as our dear friend. It is not flawed."[24]

New Millennium spiritual seekers seek to treat the Earth, God's body, as our friend, with gentle care, dignity, and profound respect.

No More Social Comparisons

Dr. Beatrice Bruteau writes: Our sense of feeling good in being ourselves does not come from any kind of contrast or comparison with others. It comes directly and immediately out of our realization of being a creative act of God, simply unique and absolutely precious.[25]

What a relief it is not to compare ourselves with others! We rejoice in the goodness of others and are grateful for the precious blessings we have received. No one, in the New Millenniuum Story, is concerned with who is holier or better than anyone else. We all assume that our goodness is simply God's gift to each of us as God determines and acts.

God's Unconditional Love

In the New Millennium Story, having accepted the Four Fundamental Assumptions, we have come to believe that we are not loved *conditionally*. God does not love us only when we are being good and doing what is right. God continues to love us, even when we continue to do evil, even when we do not seek to be forgiven. We assume that God is never offended. Nor does God need to be appeased. God has always loved us and continues to love us even when we continue to make mistakes and mess up our own lives and the lives of others. Recognizing this, New Millennium spiritual seekers desire to love God and ourselves, even in our mistakes. We intend to love everyone else unconditionally, even those who are perceived as enemies.

Christians

Christians in the New Millennium Story assume that Jesus the Christ is God and that He became a human being for the purpose of revealing to human beings what God is like. Christian spiritual seekers believe that when Jesus spoke of God as "Abba," meaning "Father," "Papa," or "Daddy," he was using a metaphor to reveal to us a God who loves and protects us and will never hurt us.

New Millennium Christians assume that when Jesus said "Love your enemies," he was not speaking symbolically or metaphorically, but literally. Studying the life of Jesus in the four Gospels, Emerging Worldview Christians believe that Jesus lived a nonviolent life, choosing love over life. In the process, Jesus forgave the very people who were responsible for his death.

For New Millennium Christians today, and the values by which they live their lives, war must be rejected and love trumps survival. Christians believe that Jesus laid down his life out of love for all, even those who were putting him to death; and in order to be at peace and have peace, Christians are invited to courageously seek to do the same. Such a belief is in perfect agreement with our Third Assumption, that we are all one.

Amish Community Story

Loving someone who has hurt us and returning good for evil is exemplified in the forgiveness and love exhibited by the Amish community in Nickel Mines, Pennsylvania, in 2006. Charles

Carol Roberts IV, who lived in the community, shot and killed ten little Amish girls whom he had trapped in their schoolhouse.

The parents of the little girls, along with most of the Amish community, immediately went to the home of the killer, bringing food and comfort to his family. They returned good for hurt and pain. Then the whole Amish community came together to help one another through their grief.

Since the time of this painful incident, Amish teenagers have continued to befriend the son of the man who killed the ten little girls. They attend his Little League baseball games and support him in many other ways. The Amish women continue to offer friendship, kindness, and assistance to the wife of the murderer.

Immaculée Ilibagiza's Story

It was Easter Sunday, 1994. Rwanda's Hutu President had just been killed in a plane crash, and the minority Tutsis were being blamed. The majority Hutus were urged to seek revenge, intending genocide. In the course of three months, nearly one million Tutsis were slaughtered. Most Americans were unaware of what was happening in Rwanda. Immaculée tells her story:

I heard the killers call my name. They were on the other side of the wall and less that an inch of plaster and wood separated us. Their voices were cold, hard, and determined.

"She's here . . . we know she's here somewhere . . . Find her. Find Immaculée."

There were many voices, many killers. I could see them in my mind: my former friends and neighbors, who had always greeted me with love and kindness, moving through the house carrying spears and machetes and calling my name.

"I have killed 399 cockroaches," said one of the killers. "Immaculée will make 400. It's a good number to kill."

I cowered in the corner of a tiny secret bathroom without moving a muscle. Like the seven other women hiding for their lives with me, I held my breath so the killers would not hear me breathing . . .

The killers were just outside the door, and I knew that in any second they were going to find me. I wondered what it would feel like when the machete slashed through my skin and cut deep into my bones. I thought of my brothers and my dear parents, wondering if they were dead or alive and if we would soon be together in heaven.

I put my hands together, clasped my father's rosary, and silently began to pray: Oh, *please, God, please help me. Don't let me die like this, not like this. Don't let these killers find me. You tell us in the Bible that if we ask, we shall receive . . . Well, God, I am asking. Please make these killers go away. Please don't let me die in this bathroom. Please, God, please, please, please save me! Save me!*

The killers moved from the house, and we all began to breathe again. They were gone, but they would be back many times over the next three months. I believed that God had spared my life, but I've learned during the 91 days I spent trembling in fear with seven others in the closet-sized bathroom that being spared is much different from being saved . . . and this lesson forever changed me. It is a lesson that, in the midst of mass murder, taught me how to love those who hated and hunted me—and how to forgive those who slaughtered my family.[26]

God heard Immaculée's prayer. When she stepped out of that bathroom, reduced to skin and bones, she was protected by the French army as she met the very ones who brutally killed her family and hunted her like an animal. This twenty-two-year-old Tutsi woman looked into the eyes of the man who killed her dear family and forgave him from her heart. When the prison officers questioned how she had forgiven him instead of spitting on him in revenge, she responded, "Forgiveness is all I have to give."[27]

CONCLUSION

The essence of the spiritual life in the New Millennium Emerging Worldview Story is a journey—not to God, for God is within us—but one of developing an intimate relationship with God, the Eternal Oneness.

Appreciating the fundamental unity of everything within the world, we assume that our ultimate fulfillment is not to be found in escaping to a life beyond. It is found in fuller engagement with the world itself. In rediscovering our mutual interdependence with the world, we are able to reclaim our spiritual identity and reconnect ourselves with the Eternal Oneness ever-present in our lives. This enables us to be co-creators with God. Creation then continues to expand and evolve into a more loving and fulfilling existence, a one-world community characterized by love, justice, peace, and freedom.

Our intimacy with God on Earth is the love we have for ourselves, for others, and for all of God's creation. New Millennium spiritual seekers assume that the love with which God first loved us and sustains us is the same love with which we love ourselves and others. We continue to discover that the more we love ourselves, the more we are able to love others. And the more we love others, the more fulfilled and happy we are. Hence, our vocation is to make life wonderful for others as well as for ourselves. We assume, however, that we cannot do it alone. So God invites us to connect with one another and to do it in community—because we are interdependent and interconnected beings and therefore need to interact with each other in an inclusive, rather than an exclusive, manner.

Through the New Millennium assumptions, we have discovered the secret of loving our enemies with an unconditional love. This discovery comes from the wisdom of making a distinction between a person and that person's behavior. We may detest a person's behavior while loving the person, as all loving parents do in the case of their own children. While parents may become upset and hate their child's behavior, they never cease to love and forgive the child.

To forgive is to give completely, we assume. It means entering into the lives of others so that they, too, may live lives of meaning and fulfillment. We recognize our oneness with them in the present moment. We love them where they are. We believe God forgives and loves them and us in the same way, albeit with more understanding.

We have learned from our experience that loving unconditionally those who have hurt us is *the* most effective way to create friends out of enemies. In the New Millennium Story, enemies no longer exist. Love and peace exist.

Our intention is to reduce suffering in the world by challenging unjust and oppressive social structures and by promoting peace with justice, equality, and dignity for all. True love of ourselves and others is measured by the degree of effort we exert to achieve meaning and fulfillment for ourselves and others. Toward that end, we devote our very lives to contemplation and action, which are the essence of spirituality in the New Millennium Story.

About the Author

HARRY J. BURY is an American Roman Catholic priest and a Professor Emeritus of Organizational Behavior and Administration. He has taught and consulted not only in the United States, but also in Thailand, Vietnam, China, Cambodia, Malaysia, Brunei, Indonesia, Brazil, Canada, Costa Rica, and a number of other countries.

Professor Bury holds a Ph.D. from Case Western Reserve University and is known for his political activism. In 1971, along with three others, he chained himself to the US Embassy gate in Saigon to protest the Vietnam War. More recently, in 2005, Harry was abducted in Gaza while serving as a human shield between Israeli soldiers and Palestinian citizens.
www.homepages.bw.edu/~hbury

PERMISSIONS

1. Excerpt from pp. 190-1 ("Our deepest fear... automatically liberates others.") from A RETURN TO LOVE by Marianne Williamson (RETURN)

2. Copyright (c) 1992 by Marianne Williamson. Reprinted by permission of Harper Collins Publishers. Portions reprinted from A COURSE IN MIRACLES. Copyright (c) 1975 by Foundation for Inner Peace Inc.

3. Title: THE CULTURAL CREATIVES by Paul H. Ray, Ph.D. and Sherry Ruth Anderson, Ph.D.

4. Excerpts from pages XIV, 17-18, 17, 30 & 31-32. Copyright (c) 2000 used by permission of Harmony Books, a Division of Random House, Inc.

5. Excerpts pp. 33, 86, 255 from GLOBAL SHIFT, by Edmund J. Bourne, Noetic Books/New Harbinger (2008).

6. Excerpt from p. 6. NO CONTEST by Alfie Kohn, Houghton Mifflin Harcourt, (1986).

7. Excerpts from pp. 54, 68, RADICAL OPTIMISM: PRACTICAL SPIRITUALITY IN AN UNCERTAIN WORLD, by Beatrice Bruteau, Sentient Publications, (2004).

8. Excerpts from pp. 94, 165, 175-176, JESUS TODAY: A SPIRITUALITY OF RADICAL FREEDOM, by Alfred Nolan, Orbis Books, (2007).

9. Excerpt from Friends of Peace Pilgrim Newsletter, http://www.peacepilgrim.org, Wayne Dyer, PBS presentation (1998).

10. Excerpts from pp. 176 & 179 THE KNOWLEDGE SOCIETY by Marc luyckx Ghisi.

11. Excerpts pp. 44, 50, THE COURAGE TO TEACH: EXPLORING THE INNER LANDSCAPE OF A TEACHER'S LIFE, by Parker Jossey-Bass/John Wiley & Sons Inc. (1998)

12. Excerpt p. 252, PRISON MADNESS: THE MENTAL HEALTH CRISIS BEHIND BARS AND WHAT WE MUST DO ABOUT IT by Terry Kupers, Jossey Bass/John Wiley & Sons Inc. (1999)

13. Excerpt pp.1-2, MAVERICK: THE SUCCESSFUL BEHIND THE WORLD'S MOST UNUSUAL WORKPLACE by Richardo Semler, Hechette Book Club. (1993)

NOTES

Chapter 1

1. A popularization of this idea can be found in Rhonda Byrne's book *The Secret* (New York: Atria Books, 2006), and the film based on it, released by Prime Time Productions (2006).

Chapter 2

1. Willis Harman, *Global Mind Change: The Promise of the 21st Century* (Petaluma, Calif.: Institute of Noetic Sciences/ Knowledge Systems, Inc., 1988. For those who would like to investigate another worldview, I suggest Walter Wink's *Engaging the Powers: Discernment and Resistance in a World of Domination* (Minneapolis, Minn.: Fortress Press, 1992).
2. Marc Luyckx Ghisi, the Knowledge Society, A Breakthrough Toward Genuine Sustainability/Kerala, India, Arunachala Press, 2008)
3. Luyckx, 2008, ibid. p. 176.
4. Paul H. Ray and Sherry Ruth Anderson, *The Cultural Creatives: How 50 Million People Are Changing the World* (New York: Three Rivers Press, 2000), pp. 31–32.
5. Luyckx, 2008, ibid. p. 179.
6. Ibid Ray and Anderson, 2000, p. 27.
7. Ibid., pp. 27, 30.
8. See Sharif Abdullah, *Creating a World That Works for All* (San Francisco: Berrett-Koehler Publishers, 1999).
9. Ibid Ray and Anderson, 2000, p. xiv.
10. Ibid., pp. 17–18.
11. Sandra Duffy, "A Shift in Worldview," *The Oregonian*, Dec. 22, 2007.

12. In 1616, Cardinal Roberto Bellarmino personally handed Galileo an admonition enjoining him from either advocating or teaching Copernican astronomy.

Chapter 3

1. Press conference given June 6, 2002, at NATO headquarters, Brussels, Belgium.
2. Figure presented with explanation at a Landmark Education Forum in Cleveland, Ohio. 2000
3. Figure based on Landmark Forum presentation.
4. In Joyce S. Osland et al., *Organizational Behavior: An Experiential Approach*, Eighth Edition (Upper Saddle River, N.J.: Pearson Higher Education/Prentice Hall, 2007), pp. 218–219.
5. Laurie Pawlik-Kienlen, "7 Ways to Make People Like You," suite101.com, Feb. 4, 2009.

Chapter 4

1. Joseph Jaworski, *Synchronicity: The Inner Path of Leadership* (San Francisco: Berrett-Koehler Publishers, 1998), p. 178.
2. Anthony de Mello, S.J, *Awareness: A de Mello Spirituality Conference in His Own Words*, ed. J. Francis Stroud, S.J. (New York: Doubleday, 1990), p. 5.
3. This idea is captured in *Celebrate What's Right with the World*, a video by photographer DeWitt Jones (Star Thrower Distribution, 2001).
4. Jim Lord and Pam McAllister, *What Kind of World Do You Want? Here's How We Can Get It* (Seattle, Wash.: New Futures Press, 2006), p. 12.
5. Marianne Williamson, *A Return to Love: Reflections on the Principles of "A Course in Miracles,"* rev. ed. (New York: Harper Collins: 1996), pp. 190–191.
6. Frances Hodgson Burnett, *The Secret Garden* (New York: Harperfestival Publishing, 2007), p.71.

7. Recommended reading: Susan Scott Krabacher, *Angels of a Lower Flight* (New York: Touchstone/Simon & Schuster, 2007). Contact Mercy and Sharing at 201 North Mill Street, Suite 201, Aspen, Colo. 81611; 877-424-8454; www.haitichildren.org.

Chapter 5

1. Alfie Kohn, *No Contest: The Case Against Competition* (Boston: Houghton Mifflin, 1986), p. 6.
2. Bertrand Russell, *Why I Am Not a Christian and Other Essays on Religion and Related Subjects* (New York: Touchstone/Simon & Schuster, 1957), p. 82.

Chapter 6

1. The terms used in economics to describe this process are *optimizing* and *satisficing*.
2. Anthony de Mello, *Awareness*, pp. 24–25.
3. Peter P. Dawson, *Fundamentals of Organizational Behavior* (New York: Prentice Hall, 1985), p. 167.

Chapter 7

1. I am indebted to my dear friend and colleague for sharing these observations in a personal letter.
2. From a personal interview with Marshall Rosenberg, Ph.D., creator of the methodology of Nonviolent Communication; Founder and Director of Educational Services for the Center for Nonviolent Communication, an international nonprofit organization.
3. Edmund J. Bourne, *Global Shift: How a New Worldview Is Transforming Humanity* (Petaluma, Calif.: Noetic Books and New Harbinger Publications, Inc., 2008), p. 86.
4. Quoted at www.poetinthetrenches.com.
5. Based on the first portion of the original Serenity Prayer (1930s) composed by American theologian Reinhold Niebuhr.

Chapter 8

1. Council of Economic Advisers, *Economic Report of the President 2003* (Washington, D.C.: Government Printing Office, 2003), p. 145.

2. P. B. Beeson, "Changes in Medical Therapy," *Medicine* 59 (1980), 79–84. A 1975 study showed that 60 percent of treatments in a 1927 medical textbook were useless and many of them were actually harmful.

3. Jeffrey D. Sachs, *The End of Poverty: Economic Possibilities for Our Time* (New York: Penguin Press, 2005, pp. 188.

4. Ibid., p 82.

5. Dan Brown, *Earth Policy News*, Feb. 2006. http://www.earthpolicy.org/books/seg/

6. Sachs, pp. 233ff.

7. www.organizingforamerica.com

8. National Center for Complementary and Alternative Medicine, *NCCAM Publication No. D347*, February 2007, (Bethesda, Md.: National Institutes of Health, 2007). The list of what is considered CAM (Complementary Alternative Medicine) changes continually as those therapies that are proven to be safe and effective become adopted into conventional healthcare and as new approaches to healthcare emerge.

9. For further information, see helpful books and CDs such as Joe Vitale's *The Key: The Missing Secret for Attracting Anything You Want* (Hoboken, N.J.: John Wiley and Sons, Inc., 2007).

10. Edmund J. Bourne, *Global Shift*, p. 253.

11. Joseph A. Califano, Jr., *High Society: How Substance Abuse Ravages America and What to Do About It* (New York: Public Affairs/Perseus Book Group, 2007), p. 6.

12. Advances in preventive medicine have made great progress in eliminating transmissible and contagious illnesses, as well as the common illnesses caused by climate, foodstuffs, and working conditions. See *www.preventivemedicine2008.org*.

13. The process began in the 1960s and 1970s through the OEO Neighborhood Health Centers, the Children and Youth Projects, and the Maternity and Infant Care Projects funded by Title V of the Social Security Act. Now this approach has blossomed, not only in the United States but throughout the world.

Chapter 9

1. Gleitman, Henry. *Basic Psycology*, 5th Edition. Illustrations of Abraham H. Maslow's Hierarchy Norton Publishing (p.614).
2. See Batten's *Tough Minded Management* (San Jose, Calif.: Resource Publications, 2002).
3. Edmund J. Bourne, *Global Shift*, p. 33.
4. Cleveland *Plain Dealer*, November 3, 2006, p. A8.
5. Joel Bakan, *The Corporation: The Pathological Pursuit of Profit and Power* (New York: Free Press/Simon & Schuster, 2004), p. 66.
6. Ibid., p.37.
7. Quoted in Bakan, p. 69.
8. *Bangkok Post*, March 10, 2009.
9. IMF/International Monetary Fund, *World Economic Outlook* (Washington, October 2008), p. 1.
10. *Bangkok Post*, March 17, 2009.
11. *New York Times*, Global Edition, March 18, 2009.
12. Lowell L. Klessig, "An American Gold Medal in the Greed Olympics," http://ezinearticles.com/?An-American-Gold-Medal-in-the-Greed-Olympics8id=1398591.
13. Juan Somavia, "Dealing with the Global Jobs Crisis," *Bangkok Post*, February 2006.
14. Wayne Teasdale, *A Monk in the World: Cultivating a Spiritual Life* (Novato, Calif.: New World Library, 2002), p.113.
15. International Labor Organization, *ILO Global Employment Trends Report 2009*, p. 24.
16. See David L. Cooperrider and Diana Whitney, *Appreciative Inquiry: A Positive Revolution in Change* (San Francisco: Berrett-Koehler Publishers, Inc., 2005).

17. Robert K. Greenleaf, *The Servant as Leader* (Westfield, Ind.: Robert K. Greenleaf Center, 1982).

18. Robert Costanza, "Toward an Ecological Economy," *The Futurist*, July/August 2006, p.

19. *Bangkok Post*, August 10, 2010.

20. Dee Hock, "The Chaordic Organization: Out of Control and Into Order," 21st Century Learning Initiative, 1996, collaborativeleadership.com/docs/chaordic/pdf.

21. Ibid.

22. Ibid.

23. Ibid.

24. Ibid.

25. Ricardo Semler, *The Seven-Day Weekend: Changing the Way Work Works* (New York: Penguin Group, Inc., 2004), p. 7.

26. Ibid., p. 8.

27. http://semco.locaweb.com.br.

28. Cleveland *Plain Dealer* blog, cleveland.com, "Breaking News," Feb. 13, 2007.

29. Arnat Leemakeej, Thammasat University, Thailand. arnat@velocall.com.

30. News.bbc.co.uk/2/hi/technology/4718719.stm.

31. Arnat Leemakeej, Ibid

32. See Note in Chapter Four regarding Susie Krabacher.

33. From Emma Lazarus, "The New Colossus" (1883).

Chapter 10

1. Throughout the Occident and the Orient, Abdu'l-Baha was known as an ambassador of peace, a champion of justice, and the leading exponent of the new Baha'I faith. He was described by a Jewish leader as a "living example of self-sacrifice," by a Christian orator as "One who led humanity to the "Way of Truth," and by a prominent Muslim leader as a "pillar of peace" and the embodiment of "glory and greatness." Abdu'l-Baha died in November 1921 at the age of 77.

2. Jeffrey Williams, "Brave New University" (Symposium: English 1999), *College English* 61:6 (July 1999), pp. 742–751.
3. Lionel S. Lewis and Philip G. Altbach, "The Dilemma of Higher Education Reform in the United States," *International Higher Education*, No. 6, Nov. 1996. pp. 6-7.
4. Hubert H. Humphrey Institute of Public Affairs, University of Minnesota, Minneapolis, Minn., USA, December 5, 2008. See www.experiencecorps.org.
5. See Glenna Dirard and Linda Teurfs, "Dialogue and Organizational Transformation," in *Community Spirit: Renewing Spirit and Learning in Business*, Kazimierz Gozdz, ed. (San Francisco: New Leaders Press, 1995), pp. 143–53.
6. Parker J. Palmer, *The Courage to Teach: Exploring the Inner Landscape of a Teacher's Life* (San Francisco: Jossey-Bass, 1998), p. 44.
7. Williams, "Brave New University," p. 750.
8. Ibid. Palmer, p. 50.
9. For more information, consult the following websites: http://tinyurl.com/legd5; http://tinyurl.com/nqjtt; http://www.Pebblesproject.org.

Chapter 11

1. Deuteronomy 22:20.
2. Gospel of John 15:7.
3. Paige M. Harrison and Alan J. Beck, "Prisoners in 2004," *Bureau of Justice Statistics Bulletin*, October 2005.
4. N. C. Aizenmann, "New High In U.S. Prison Numbers," *Washington Post*, February 29, 2008.
5. Ibid.
6. Ibid.
7. Terry Kupers, *Prison Madness: The Mental Health Crisis Behind Bars and What We Must Do About It* (San Francisco: Jossey-Bass, 1999).
8. Copyright © 2008 Jenn Ackerman, www.jennackerman.com.

9. Leah Price, "Read a Book, Get Out of Jail," *New York Times*, March 1, 2009.

10. Warren Hoge, "Finnish Prisons: No Gates or Armed Guards," *New York Times*, January 2, 2003 (online), www.nytimes.com.

11. Kupers, *Prison Madness*, pp. 254–55.

12. See www.peacepilgrim.com/FoPP/newsletter/pdf/n148.pdf. On page 2 of Number 48 of Friends of Peace Pilgrim's newsletter it is noted that the story first appeared in the Fall 1998 issue. Further research discovered that "the original source of the story was a book, *Contact, The First Four Minutes,* by Leonard Sunin, now out of print."

13. Kupers, *Prison Madness*, p. 252.

Chapter 12

1. Michael Cohen, *Educating, Counseling and Healing with Nature* (Friday Harbor, Wash.: Institute of Global Education, 2008), p. 31.

2. Ibid., p.32.

3. Ibid, p.32.

4. Gregory Bateson, *Mind and Nature: A Necessary Unity,* Advances in Systems Theory, Complexity, and the Human Sciences (Cresskill, N.J.: Hampton Press, Inc, 2002, new edition).

5. Marjorie Kelly, *The Divine Right of Capital: Dethroning the Corporate Aristocracy* (San Francisco: Berrett-Koehler Publishers, 2001), p. 6.

6. http://yosemite.epa.gov/oar/globalwarming.nsf/content/climate.html.

7. Robert Ebert, "A Review: 'An Inconvenient Truth,'" *Chicago-Sun-Times*, June 2, 2006.

8. *An Inconvenient Truth,* film by former U.S. Vice President Al Gore (2006).

9. Ibid.

10. Lester Brown, *Plan B 2.0: Rescuing a Planet under Stress and a Civilization in Trouble* (N.Y.: W. W. Norton & Co., 2006), pp. 32–34.

11. Ibid., p. 35.
12. Ibid., p. 56.
13. Ibid., p. 48.
14. Center for Biological Diversity, Tucson, Arizona; www. biologicaldiversity.org.
15. According to Tensie Whalen, Exec. Dir., Rainforest Alliance; www.rainforest-alliance.org.
16. "Wall-E" is the acronym for "Waste Allocation Load Lifter Earth-Class."
17. www.eol.org.
18. www.imaginechicago.org
19. Stephanie Kaza, "Towards a Buddhist Environmental Ethic," *Buddhism at the Crossroads*, Fall 1990: 20–25; *www. buddhapia.com, Bangkok, Thailand.*
20. *Ibid., p. 22.*
21. Brown, *Plan B 2.0*, p. 231.
22. Ibid., p. 233.
23. See http://www.sustainable.org/casestudies/international/INTL_af_Curitiba.html, 1995.
24. Ibid.
25. Ibid.
26. Jerry Adler, "How to Design a Healthier Planet," *Newsweek*, March 5, 2007, p. 68.
27. Ibid., p. 67.
28. Peter Krouse, "Furniture Maker Calls Sustainability Profitable," Cleveland *Plain Dealer*, May 16, 2007.
29. Ibid.

Chapter 13

1. Quoted in Benjamin B. Ferencz and Ken Keyes, Jr., *PlanetHood: The Key to Your Future* (Coos Bay, Ore.: Vision Books, 1988), p. 190.
2. *PlanetHood*, Ibid. p. 18.
3. Quoted in *PlanetHood*, p. 27.
4. From personal interview, 1999.
5. Quoted in *PlanetHood*, p. 27.
6. From 1999 interview with Dr. Caldicott.

7. *PlanetHood*, Ibid. p. 27.
8. Marjorie Kelly, *The Divine Right of Capital: Dethroning the Corporate Aristocracy* (San Francisco: Berrett-Koehler Publishers, 2001), p. xi.
9. The International Court of Justice (ICJ) is the principal judicial organ of the United Nations (UN). The Court's role is to settle, in accordance with international law, legal disputes submitted to it by nation-states and to give advisory opinions on legal questions referred to it by authorized United Nations organs and specialized agencies. The Court is composed of 15 judges, who are elected for terms of office of nine years by the United Nations General Assembly and the Security Council. It is assisted by a Registry, its administrative organ.
10. Sidney Axinn, "World Community and Its Government," in *Autonomy and Community: Readings in Contemporary Kantian Social Philosophy,* ed. Jane Kneller and Sidney Axinn (Albany: SUNY Press, 1998), p. 126.
11. Albert Einstein, *Open Letter to the General Assembly of the United Nations*, October 1947.
12. Emily Kaiser, "Bernanke dives into political fray on debt," New York Times, Global Edition, Feb. 7, 2011.
13. Michael Rowbotham, *The Grip of Death: A Study of Modern Money, Debt Slavery, and Destructive Economics* (Charlbury, Oxfordshire: John Carpenter Publishing, 1998), p. 431.
14. Quoted in *PlanetHood*, p. 50.
15. Quoted in *PlanetHood*, p. 108.

Chapter 14

1. Timothy Freke, *Encyclopedia of Spirituality: Essential Teachings to Transform Your Life* (New York: Sterling Publishing Co., 2000), p. 152.
2. Diarmuid O'Murchu, *Reclaiming Spirituality* (New York: Crossroad Publishing Co., 1999), p. viii.
3. See Joan Chittister, OSB, *Called to Question: A Spiritual Memoir* (Lanham, Md.: Sheed and Ward, 2004), p. 172.

4. Michael Morwood, *Children Praying a New Story: A Resource for Parents, Grandparents and Teachers* (South Bend, Ind.: Kelmor Publications, 2099), p. 22.

5. Richard Rohr, *The Naked Now: Learning to See as the Mystics See* (New York: Crossroad Publishing Co., 2009), p. 33.

6. O'Murchu, Ibid *Reclaiming Spirituality*, p. 33.

7. See Karen Armstrong, *The Great Transformation: The Beginning of Our Religious Traditions* (New York: Alfred A. Knopf, 2006). Armstrong points out that the Vedic tradition in its later period, about 1000 BC, held Brahman as the High God and inexpressible. Earlier there were many gods, but once the belief in Brahman evolved, the sense of God, for Hindus, changed to one personal God—who is not the same as one among many.

8. Cletus Wessels, *Jesus in the New Universe Story* (Maryknoll, N.Y.: Orbis Books, 2003), p. 37.

9. Michael Morwood, *From Sand to Solid Ground* (Victoria, Australia: Spectrum Publications Pty Ltd, 2007), p. 25.

10. Albert Nolan, *Jesus Today: A Spirituality of Radical Freedom* (Maryknoll, N.Y.: Orbis Books, 2007), pp. 94, 95.

11. Beatrice Bruteau, *Radical Optimism: Practical Spirituality in an Uncertain World* (Boulder, Colo.: Sentient Publications, 2004), p.54.

12. Rohr, Ibid. *Naked Now*, p. 136.

13. Rachel Naomi Remen, *Noetic Sciences Review*, Spring 1996.

14. Freke, Ibid. *Encyclopedia*, p. 170 (quoting I John 4:16, KJV).

15. Ibid.

16. O'Murchu, *Reclaiming Spirituality*, p. 174.

17. Dennis Linn, Sheila Fabricant Linn, and Matthew Linn, *Good Goats: Healing Our Image of God* (Mahwah, N.J.: Paulist Press, 1994), p.58.

18. Nolan, Ibid. *Jesus Today*, p. 165.

19. Ibid., pp. 175–76.

20. Marcus Borg, *Jesus and Buddha: The Parallel Sayings* (Berkeley, Calif.: Ulysses Press, 1997), pp. 15–17.
21. Ibid., pp. 22–27.
22. Ibid., pp. 56–57.
23. Ibid., pp. 78–79.
24. In O'Murchu, Ibid *Reclaiming Spirituality*, p. 45.
25. Bruteau, Ibid *Radical Optimism*, p. 68.
26. Immaculée Ilibagiza, *Left to Tell: Discovering God Amidst the Rwandan Holocaust* (Carlsbad, Calif.: Hay House, Inc., 2006), pp. xix-xx.
27. Ibid., p. 204.